THE TEXAS GOLF
Guide

Second Edition

by

ART STRICKLIN

foreword by LEE TREVINO

Republic of Texas Press, Inc.
Plano, Texas

Library of Congress Cataloging-in-Publication Data

Stricklin, Art.
The Texas golf guide second edition / by Art Stricklin ; foreword by Lee Trevino.
   p.   cm.
Includes indexes.
ISBN 1-55622-682-9
1. Golf--Texas--Directories.   2. Golf--Texas--History.   I. Title.
GV982.T4S87   1997
796.352'06'8764--dc21   97-37339
                                                         CIP

ISBN 1-55622-682-9
10 9 8 7 6 5 4 3 2 1
9903

All inquiries for volume purchases of this book should be addressed to
Wordware Publishing, Inc., at 2320 Los Rios Boulevard, Plano, Texas
75074. Telephone inquiries may be made by calling:

(972) 423-0090

Contents

Foreword

by Lee Trevino

The greatest shotmakers that have ever played the game of golf are from Texas. This is because of the great variety of courses (public, semiprivate, private) we play here, the different grasses, fluctuating weather, and the varying conditions of courses.

These conditions force golfers from Texas to improvise and to learn lots of different kinds of shots for all the different situations he or she will face.

That's why Texas is such a great place to live and learn the game, and why I was fortunate to have grown up here and learned to play golf in Texas like I did.

This book, which covers every course in the state, should be an invaluable guide to those who love to play golf in the Lone Star State.

Preface

Dear Golfer:

Welcome to *The Texas Golf Guide*, your most complete source of great golfing information in the Lone Star State.

No matter if you're a longtime Texas resident, or one of the thousands of newcomers who arrive each week, you doubtlessly noted the great number and variety of golf courses in our state, along with the year-round golf weather which prevails in most of the regions.

The idea behind this book was simple. To give golfers, along with those who know and love one, the basic information about every public and private course in Texas, nearly 800 in all. Of course, every course isn't for every player. Some are very hard, some are easy, some are very expensive, while others are a real bargain. There are courses which are exclusively private, open only to a privileged few, while others welcome all golfers. But the plan is to present every course in the state and let you, the golfing public, decide which you would like to play.

Along with the course listings, you'll also read about the rich golf history in this state. You'll learn about the many legends in Texas, from Byron Nelson and Jackie Burke to Ben Crenshaw and Lee Trevino, who wrote the foreword for this book. There is also a listing of the major championships in Texas, great golfing moments, and a Texas-tough trivia quiz. The hope is that you'll enjoy this book and use it as a handy resource tool for your Lone Star golfing experiences.

On a personal note, I want to thank my wife, Belinda, who has been so helpful and supportive in this project, along with the good folks at Republic of Texas Press in Plano, with whom I've worked closely for several months. Most importantly, I want to give all glory, praise, and honor to my Lord and savior Jesus Christ, who has given me this writing ability. Happy golfing!

See you on the tee box,

Art Stricklin

Texas Golf Courses: Hallowed Ground

Texans have long had an appreciation for the wide-open spaces which make up the Lone Star State. But Texas golfers also have a special feeling for dozens of special layouts where much of the state's golf history has been created.

With nearly 800 courses in this great golfing state, players from Texarkana to El Paso, Borger to Brownsville have more than enough chances to play their favorite sport on the many varied and challenging layouts.

But the true Texas native or golf historian knows there are nearly two dozen courses in the state which hold a special significance. They have been walked by legends, touched by greatness, or hold a very unique place in Texas golf lore.

The following is a brief roundup of some very special Lone Star golf courses. Every golfer has his or her favorite layout, but these Texas courses are truly hallowed ground.

Galveston Country Club: Texas' First Chartered Course

This club's moment in the golf limelight was brief but significant. The scenic seaside layout, lying next to the Gulf of Mexico, was the first private club officially chartered in the state in 1898. The club quickly drew members interested in the sport newly introduced to Texas with several scenic holes overlooking the usually calm Gulf of Mexico.

But it was the seaside site which proved to be its undoing. The great Galveston Hurricane of 1900, which killed 6,000 people in one of the largest natural disasters in U.S. history, wiped the course from the map.

Club members rebuilt the course and reopened it in 1901 at a site several miles inland. The course moved again in 1945, still farther inland to its current location, after surviving another hard blow from Mother Nature.

Dallas Country Club: Golf in North Texas

Richard Potter and Henry Lee Edwards grew up playing golf in their native country of Wales. So when they came to America, and settled in Dallas to begin their business careers, they were determined to bring golf with them.

It was these two men who first opened a primitive six-hole course in Dallas in 1896, moving to a nine-hole layout near what is downtown Dallas today. The first members' call for Dallas Country Club brought out mainly friends of the two men or early North Texas businessmen who shared their passion for the sport.

Three years later, the members decided to sell stock, raising money for a full 18-hole layout. The course was officially incorporated in 1900 as Dallas Country Club and became an instant hit, athletically and socially, for the rapidly growing city.

The course moved to its current location in Highland Park in 1912 and is now surrounded by multimillion dollar homes—a far cry from the humble beginnings in a Dallas cow pasture, spurred on by two friends with a passion for golf.

Austin Country Club: Home of the Penicks

The first Austin Country Club, now known as Hancock Park Municipal, claims to be the oldest course in continuous operation at the same spot. The course was founded in 1898 by former Austin mayor Lewis Hancock, who led a committee of members in walking off the first nine-hole layout.

But its largest and most lasting claim to fame came 15 years later when young Harvey Penick, one of five Penick brothers, was hired as a caddie at the going rate of 20 cents a day.

Club officials may not have known it in 1913, but that one hiring would turn out to be pivotal. For the next 83 years, a Penick would be on the payroll at ACC. Harvey Penick was promoted to assistant pro in 1921, while in high school, and was named head pro in 1923. It was a position he held until his retirement in 1971. His son, Tinsley, took over for his dad and served as head pro until his retirement in 1996.

"I'm old enough to have worn out two courses and I'm working on the third," Harvey Penick, who died at age 90 in 1995, once said.

The original Hancock location, which featured the first green grass putting surfaces in Austin, was the home of ACC from its founding until 1949. The course moved to its Riverside location in 1950, where Penick taught future champions Ben Crenshaw and Tom Kite. In 1984 the course moved to its current location next to Lake Austin. It was here Penick wrote *Little Red Book*, the first of four books containing his golfing wisdom. His first effort became the best-selling sports hardback of all time, with nearly two million copies sold.

The courses have also attracted legendary architects. While Hancock and members designed the first course, the grass greens were installed by John Bredemus, known as

Texas' first golf architect. The Riverside course was designed by Perry Maxwell, who laid out dozens of highly rated courses nationwide in the 1950s and '60s.

The current ACC course was built by Pete Dye, who's known for his dramatic use of golf architecture worldwide.

The Penicks' presence turned Austin Country Club into hallowed ground in several Capital City locations.

Brackenridge Park: Texas' Most Historic

There has been enough history played out at San Antonio's Brackenridge Park Golf Course to have its own wing in any golf museum.

Start with architect A.W. Tillinghast, who has his name on some of the nation's most famous courses and who made Brackenridge one of his first in Texas in 1916. The location, the former estate of local businessman George W. Brackenridge, was the first 18-hole public layout in the state. It was also the first to feature real grass putting surfaces—a fact not lost on Austin's Harvey Penick.

"I remember the first time I saw grass greens," Penick said. "My parents drove me down to San Antonio, I paid my green fee at Brackenridge, and played on grass greens for the first time. I went home and said it wasn't right for a municipal course to have grass greens and our country club to have sand."

Brackenridge was the site of the first Texas Open in 1922, the PGA Tour event which is the fifth oldest on the professional golf schedule. It was also the site of Jug McSpaden's practice round score of 59 in 1939, in a foursome which included Sam Snead, Ben Hogan, and Paul Runyan. It was the place for Mike Souchak's record-setting 72-hole total of 257 in 1955, a PGA record which still stands more than 40 years later.

The high-beamed stone and wooden clubhouse looks like a castle from the outside. The building next to the clubhouse served as the studio for the architect who conceived and executed the carvings on Mount Rushmore.

Brackenridge Park, one of six public courses owned by the City of San Antonio, also served as the site of the Texas State Junior Championship for nearly 50 years, giving many of today's brightest professional players their first taste of elite competition. It's also unique for another reason—there is no alcohol sold on the premises, a condition of Brackenridge's original deed.

In recognition of its standing as Texas' most historic course, "Old Brack," as locals call it, was honored as the first course inducted in the Texas Golf Hall of Fame in 1996.

Cedar Crest: PGA Playground

In the early 1920s, Dallas banker Sol Dreyfuss was determined to bring golf's best players to North Texas to play the new Cedar Crest Country Club, which he helped found. Noted golf architect A.W. Tillinghast had designed the course which opened in 1919, just south of downtown.

Dreyfuss came up with enough money and political pull to convince the PGA of America to bring the 1927 PGA Championship to Dallas. It was the first major golf championship ever held in the Southwest and the winner was golf legend Walter Hagen, who captured his fourth straight PGA title. Among those in the gallery for the tournament was a young Byron Nelson, who followed Hagen in each of his final two matches.

Now a City of Dallas municipal course, golfers still come by the thousands to walk in the steps of Hagen and Nelson and challenge the graceful Tillinghast design.

Memorial Park: Houston's Public Playground

John Bredemus was known as the father of Texas golf for the many courses he helped design, build, or renovate. Among the courses to his credit are Brackenridge Park in San Antonio, Colonial in Fort Worth, and Scott Schreiner in Kerrville. But many think his best work was on Memorial Park Municipal in Houston.

Opened in 1936 in lush Memorial Park, just west of downtown, it served as Houston's favorite public golf playground for nearly 60 years. It was the one-time site of the Houston Open and hosted several PGA Tour events. Memorial was shut down in 1994 to help repair 60 years of wear, but architects Dave Marr and Jay Riviere stayed close to the original Bredemus design for the course which reopened in late 1995 to rave reviews.

Glen Garden: Caddie Kingdom

Unlike the top professional golfers of today, many of the great pros in the 1930s and 1940s began their golfing career as caddies, learning the game as they carried the clubs of others around the course.

Nowhere was that tradition stronger or the results more spectacular than at Fort Worth's Glen Garden Country Club. Opened in 1914, Glen Garden attracted two young Cowtown schoolboys, Ben Hogan and Byron Nelson. They were caddies there for several years, but the highlight was the 1927 caddie tournament where Nelson prevailed over Hogan by a single shot in a nine-hole playoff.

Undoubtedly the pair learned their golfing lessons at Glen Garden well as they went on to achieve two of the greatest playing records in professional golf. Nelson still lives within 30 miles of Glen Garden, and while he no longer visits regularly, his spirit along with the spirit of the late Ben Hogan is still very much alive.

Former U.S. Women's Open Champion Sandra Palmer also learned the game here with Jack Grout, a former Glen Garden pro. Grout later left Fort Worth and moved to Ohio where he taught another pretty fair junior golfer, Jack Nicklaus.

Colonial: Leonard's Legacy

Marvin Leonard made a name for himself with a highly successful department store in downtown Fort Worth. Then he decided to open a golf course for his friends to play, one which would be a championship test of golf.

The result was Colonial Country Club which opened in 1936 and became one of the most famous courses in the state. A trio of highly respected architects, Perry Maxwell, Ralph Plummer, and John Bredemus, helped design the course under Leonard's exacting standards.

Colonial was one of the first courses in Texas to have bentgrass greens and its classic, tree-lined design along the Trinity River has stood the test of time.

Leonard prevailed on the United States Golf Association to bring the 1941 U.S. Open to Colonial, the first (USGA) championship held in the South. The event proved so successful that Leonard helped start an annual PGA event, now known as the MasterCard Colonial, in 1946. Only the Masters has been held at the same site longer than the Colonial PGA tournament.

The Women's U.S. Open was played at Colonial in 1991 while the PGA Tour held two Players Championships at the course in the mid-1970s.

Tyrrell Park: Babe's Bastion

Babe Didriksen Zaharias is considered one of the true greats in women's professional golf. While she also earned stardom in Olympic competition, Didriksen won 55 amateur and professional golf titles, including three U.S. Open titles and one U.S. Amateur.

Didriksen learned her golf at Beaumont's Tyrrell Park golf course. The public layout attracted many top local golfers including Didriksen's Beaumont High classmate Harry Homberg.

While Didriksen went on to athletic fame worldwide and was named Athlete of the Half-Century in 1950, Homberg stayed close to home, working as a municipal golf professional for several decades. Today, Homberg Park, located on Babe Zaharias Drive, stands as a monument to the two Southeast Texas golf legends.

Horizon Hills: Future Pros Playoff

Horizon Hills is not famous for its particular style or architect. It hasn't hosted U.S. Opens or PGA Championships, but the former El Paso course did host one highly competitive amateur match which helped shape the careers of both participants.

A very young Lee Trevino was serving as assistant pro at Horizon Hills in 1966 when a young Air Force veteran named Raymond Floyd came through El Paso looking for a money game. The two future golf superstars played for two days with Floyd finally emerging with a one-stroke victory.

Floyd left to continue his travels and Trevino soon left his job as assistant pro, but both men would go on to dominate professional golf for the next 30 years.

McAlister Two-Hole Ranch: East Texas Wonder

East Texas is known for its scenic trees, deep forests, and some pretty deep ideas. So it's not totally surprising that Mike and Judy McAlister's Two-Hole Ranch and Country Club in the Hopkins County town of Yantis is a novel part of the East Texas scenery.

Like the name says, the McAlister course may never host a national 72-hole tournament, but the course is extremely flexible and expandable, capable of giving golfers of all skill levels a full afternoon's worth of enjoyment. The McAlister course actually has nine holes which play to two large greens. The course, which Mike McAlister built himself, is part of his family ranch south of Sulphur Springs which includes their home and nongolf acreage. But nothing tops the uniqueness of the Two-Hole Ranch and Country Club.

Champions: Major Championship Haven

Jack Burke Jr. and Jimmy Demaret had already achieved plenty in their professional golf careers when they decided to turn their attention to building courses in the late 1950s.

The two native Texans wanted to build a course which would attract national golf championships along with attracting the best players in the Houston area. They chose some deeply wooded acreage in northwest Harris County and personally walked off the holes, imagining how the layouts would look and what types of shots would be needed to reach the greens.

Since opening in 1958, Champions Golf Club has more than lived up to its name, hosting more national championship golf tournaments than any course in the state. Burke and Demaret brought the 1967 Ryder Cup matches, the only one ever held in the Southwest, the 1969 U.S. Open, and the 1993 U.S. Amateur and 1998 Women's Mid-Amateur to Champions.

Champions has hosted several Houston Opens and was the site of the last competitive round by Ben Hogan. The PGA held its Tour Championship at Champions in 1990 and returned in 1997 and 1999.

The club is also home to four former PGA Championship winners—Burke, Dave Marr, Jay Hebert, and 1995 winner Steve Elkington.

"All a golf course is, is a proving ground for your skills. That's what we have here," Burke said.

Consider it mission accomplished for Houston's championship test of golf.

Pecan Valley: PGA Proving Ground

Perry Maxwell has been credited with designing some of the greatest courses in America, but 10 years after his death, his son, Press, designed a course in San Antonio which would have made his dad proud.

Press came to the Alamo City in 1962 at the request of local businessman E.J. Burke, who was building a luxury housing development south of downtown and wanted a championship course to go along with it.

Maxwell certainly produced on his end of the deal, building a shot-maker's paradise which was dedicated by Texas Governor John Connally on Labor Day 1963. The course was so good that Burke was able to convince the PGA of America to bring the PGA Championship to Pecan Valley in 1968. It was the only major championship ever held in San Antonio and the course proved its championship caliber.

Pecan Valley is now a public course, but the clubhouse is decorated with photos and trophies, saluting Maxwell and Burke's achievement and Pecan Valley's glorious past.

Crown Colony: East Texas Jewel

The huge pines and lush forests of East Texas make it a natural spot for all kinds of recreation, including highly scenic golf courses. But it took a true visionary like Arthur Temple and top architects like Bruce Devlin and Robert Von Hagge to create an outstanding course called Crown Colony in Lufkin.

Due to its remote East Texas location, Crown Colony will likely never host a national golf championship or PGA Tour stop, but its East Texas beauty and Devlin-Von Hagge challenge has earned it a reputation as one of the top courses in the state. With its 100-foot pine trees, numerous bunkers, and target greens, Crown Colony has attracted a loyal following who make the trip into the woods regularly to play the course.

Temple, who grew up in nearby Diboll, made his fortune in forestry and paper products. His business empire took him to commercial centers all over America. After returning from another trip in the early 1970s, Temple decided he would build a world-caliber course in his own backyard much like the ones he played in his business travels. The result was Crown Colony, an East Texas vision of golf paradise.

Northridge Country Club: Texarkana Training Ground

Northridge Country Club in Texarkana is only in the state limits by a few miles, but that didn't stop the Northeast Texas course from producing a player Texans will always love and remember.

Bill Rogers grew up in Texarkana and played much of his early golf on the tree-lined fairways of Northridge CC. Rogers attended the University of Houston and went on to a memorable professional golf career. The highlight for him came in 1981 when he won five times on three continents.

He captured titles at the World Series of Golf and the Texas Open, but his most memorable win came at the British Open at Royal St. George's. To celebrate, Northridge CC members hoisted the British flag at the club entrance as a salute to Rogers when he returned.

In 1990 Rogers became director of golf at San Antonio Country Club. But his name and legacy live on at Northridge where his brother, Rick, is the head professional.

Horseshoe Bay: Hill Country Heaven

Cousins Norman and Wayne Hurd put down $55,000 in 1971 to purchase 2,100 acres to back a dream. They wanted to build a world-class golf resort on the scenic shores of Lake LBJ in Marble Falls, some 50 miles west of Austin.

The pair ignored the naysayers who told them no one would make the trip to play an out-of-the-way golf course with limited facilities. The Hurds contacted noted architect

Robert Trent Jones Sr. to design the first course, Slick Rock, which opened in 1974. In addition, they built some outstanding hotel and conference facilities, including their own airport.

Ram Rock, acknowledged as one of the toughest courses in the state, opened in 1979, followed by Apple Rock in 1986 with Jones doing all three layouts.

While the Hill Country area is now crowded with top golf resorts, Horseshoe Bay was the first and is still one of the best, thanks to the Hurds' vision.

Onion Creek: Senior Launching Pad

Sometimes a course is hallowed for its designers or founders, sometimes for a particular historic event which took place within its boundaries. For Onion Creek Country Club in Austin, it's both.

The course itself was designed by golf legend Jimmy Demaret and noted architect George Fazio and opened in 1974. But it will forever be known as the birthplace of the Senior PGA Tour.

The Tour, which brought back former pros over 50 for another chance in the golf spotlight, started with the Legends of Golf at Onion Creek in 1978 and was won by Sam Snead and Gardner Dickinson. It was a five-hole playoff in '79, captured by Julius Boros and Roberto De Vincenzo, which riveted the sports-watching public. The television ratings convinced sports executives there was a future for the over-50 set.

Today, seniors play in more than 40 tournaments for tens of millions dollars worth of prize money, thanks to the boost received at Onion Creek.

Reeves County: 11-Hole Surprise

West Texas is known for its wide-open spaces and wide-open ideas. So perhaps it's only natural the 11-hole Reeves County Golf Course in Pecos fits into the scenery. This is a region, after all, which boasts Stanley Marsh's Cadillac Ranch and Amarillo Slim's backyard golf course.

A few hundred miles to the southwest is the Reeves County layout. The 11 holes on the site of the former Pecos Air Corps base came about because of the irrigation problems and frequent droughts in this arid region. Course officials will often flood two holes at a time during the winter months.

During the floods, course members still have nine dry holes to play. When the holes are not being flooded, golfers can play the first nine, then mix in the two new holes on the back nine to find some new challenges.

The course is owned by the county government but is open to anyone looking for a game and a unique challenge in the area.

Tour 18: Texas Fantasy Land

Many great golf visionaries have produced some of the outstanding courses in the state as a tribute to their passion and drive. But a pair of true forward thinkers in Houston produced a unique layout which has become a golf fantasy land for thousands of golfers.

Dennis Wilkerson and Barron Jacobson developed Tour 18 Golf Course, which first opened in the Houston suburb of Humble, then added a second course outside of Dallas in Flower Mound.

Tour 18 is made up of exacting replicas of the most famous golf holes in America. Each course has the three-hole layout of

Amen Corner from Augusta National along with the par-3 island green from TPC-Sawgrass and the church pews from the famed Oakmont CC layout. Each teebox contains a sign which lets the golfer know what makes that hole so famous and unique.

The concept has turned out to be wildly popular with the general public, who might never get a chance to step on the real courses. While Tour 18 owners had to fight off a lawsuit from some courses not as pleased with the concept, they intend to take the unique layout to cities across the nation, perhaps making it the most successful Texas export since chili.

Texas Golf Legends

John Bredemus, San Antonio. Former New York native who moved to San Antonio to teach school. He was a regular at Brackenridge Park Golf Course and later became an assistant pro. Started the Texas PGA and helped found the PGA Tour's Texas Open. Helped design dozens of courses including layouts in Del Rio and Kerrville Memorial Park in Houston, and Colonial Country Club in Fort Worth.

Jackie Burke, Houston. Co-founder of Champions Golf Club, site of U.S. Open, U.S. Amateur, Ryder Cup matches, and Tour Championship. Won four straight PGA events in 1952, the second-longest streak in PGA history. Won the Masters and PGA Championship in 1956 and was named '56 PGA Player of the Year.

Charles Coody, Abilene. One of the best players ever out of West Texas. Won the 1971 Masters along with the '71 World Series of Golf and has excelled on the Senior PGA Tour.

Ben Crenshaw and **Tom Kite**, Austin. University of Texas teammates who have enjoyed hugely successful pro careers. Kite has won more than $10 million in prize money, second only to Greg Norman, and captured the 1993 U.S. Open title at Pebble Beach. Crenshaw captured Masters titles in 1984 and 1995, with the '95 victory coming one week after the death of longtime teacher Harvey Penick.

Jimmy Demaret, Houston. Co-founder of Champions Golf Club along with Jackie Burke. Three-time Masters champion, who also helped design Onion Creek Golf Course in Austin, birthplace of the Senior PGA Tour. Hosted Shell's "Wonderful World of Golf" in the 1960s.

Ralph Guldahl, Dallas. Winner of two consecutive U.S. Opens, including the first by a Texan in 1937. He captured a Masters victory in 1939 and was hailed as the best golfer in the 1930s.

Dick and **Butch Harmon**, Houston. Two of four brothers who became head golf pros in Houston. Dick Harmon is head pro at River Oaks CC, following Jack Burke Sr. Butch Harmon is the former head pro at the exclusive Lochinvar CC, and the personal teacher to 1997 Masters champion Tiger Woods.

Sandra Haynie, Southlake. Two-time LPGA Championship winner and U.S. Women's Open Champion, among 42 professional titles. Was taught by her father, Jim, a Texas golf pro. Director of golf at Timarron GC in Southlake.

Ben Hogan and **Byron Nelson**, Fort Worth and Dallas. Caddie mates at Glen Garden Country Club in Fort Worth who grew up to be two of the greatest pro golfers ever. Hogan won four U.S. Open titles and captured three Grand Slam Tournaments (Masters, U.S. Open, British Open) in 1953, after recovering from a near-fatal car accident. Nelson won a record eleven straight PGA tournaments in 1945 and eighteen total that same year. First Texan to win a major title, the 1937 Masters.

Dick Jackson, Houston. Local doctor and inventor who designed first motorized golf cart in 1948, used at Houston Country Club. Now commonplace all over the world.

Don January and **Miller Barber**. Dallas and Sherman. First stars on Senior PGA Tour, dominating play in the early 1980s. PGA Tour veterans with dozens of victories. January captured 1967 PGA Championship.

Marvin Leonard, Fort Worth. Retail merchant who founded Colonial Country Club in Fort Worth and helped bring 1941 U.S. Open to Colonial. Helped start PGA's Colonial Tournament in Fort Worth in 1946. Also founded Starr Hollow Golf Course in Tolar, outside of Granbury, one of the state's most unique layouts. Daughter Marty now runs Starr Hollow and Leonard Practice Links in Fort Worth.

Lloyd Mangrum, Trenton. One of the first Texas superstars on the PGA Tour. Won the U.S. Open in 1946 in a three-person playoff along with 36 other PGA victories. Made six Ryder Cup teams and was captain twice. Recently inducted into World Golf Hall of Fame.

Billy Maxwell, Abilene. First Texan to win U.S. Amateur title in 1951. Teamed with Don January and coach Fred Cobb to lead North Texas to three NCAA titles in the 1950s.

Orville Moody, Sulphur Springs. Former Army sergeant who captured 1968 U.S. Open title at Champions Golf Club in Houston, his only major title, along with '69 World Series of Golf victory. Currently a Senior PGA star.

Harvey Penick, Austin. Hired as a caddie at Austin Country Club in 1913. Served as head pro from 1923-1971. Teacher for dozens of PGA pros including Ben Crenshaw, Tom Kite, Kathy Whitworth, Betsy Rawls, and many others. Served as head golf coach at the University of Texas from 1931-63, and co-wrote the best-selling sports hardback of all time, *Little Red Book*.

Bill Rogers, Texarkana and San Antonio. Captured 1981 British Open title along with three PGA Tour events in the same year and was named 1981 PGA Player of the Year. Won tournaments on three continents. Now director of golf at San Antonio Country Club.

Lee Trevino, Dallas. Former caddie who learned the game at Tenison Park Golf Course and Hardy's Driving Range in Dallas. Won the 1969 and 1971 U.S. Open and 1972 British Open along with 1984 PGA Championship. Known worldwide as the "Merry Mex." Has enjoyed very successful Senior PGA career.

Kathy Whitworth, Monahans and Trophy Club. All-time leading winner on the LPGA Tour with 88 victories, including six major titles, three of which are LPGA Championships. Leading LPGA money winner eight times and Player of the Year seven times. Student of Austin's Harvey Penick.

Dave Williams, Houston. Founded University of Houston golf dynasty. Led the Cougars to sixteen national titles and college golf into a new, modern era. Taught PGA pros Fred Couples, Blaine McCallister, Bruce Lietzke, Phil Rogers, among others.

Babe Didrikson Zaharias, Beaumont. Perhaps the greatest female athlete and golfer ever. Won nine major golf titles including three U.S. Women's Opens and one U.S. Women's Amateur in her 55 professional and amateur golf victories. Named Athlete of the Half-Century in 1950.

Great Texas Golf Moments

1. John Bredemus arrives in San Antonio, 1919.

2. Harvey Penick hired at Austin Country Club, 1913; becomes head pro, 1923.

3. U.S. Open comes to Colonial, 1941.

4. Byron Nelson wins eleven straight tournaments, 1945.

5. Jackie Burke wins four straight PGA events, 1952.

6. Ben Hogan captures three major championships, 1953.

7. Mike Souchak fires all-time PGA 72-hole record at Texas Open-Brackenridge Park, 1955.

8. Lee Trevino wins 1971 U.S. Open, 1972 British Open.

9. Legends of Golf Senior PGA event founded at Onion Creek, 1978.

10. Ben Crenshaw captures 1995 Masters one week after Harvey Penick's death.

Texas Major Championships From 1927-1999

Year	Event	Site	City	Winner
1927	PGA Championship	Cedar Crest GC	Dallas	Walter Hagen
1941	U.S. Open	Colonial CC	Fort Worth	Craig Wood
1952	U.S. Open	Northwood Club	Dallas	Julius Boros
1954	U.S. Public Links	Cedar Crest GC	Dallas	Gene Andrews
1963	PGA Championship	Dallas Athletic Club	Dallas	Jack Nicklaus
1967	Ryder Cup	Champions GC	Houston	United States
1968	PGA Championship	Pecan Valley GC	San Antonio	Julius Boros
1968	U.S. Public Links	Tenison Park GC	Dallas	Gene Towry
1969	U.S. Open	Champions GC	Houston	Orville Moody
1969	U.S. Girls Junior	Brookhaven CC	Dallas	Hollis Stacy
1969	U.S. Women's Amateur	Las Colinas CC	Irving	Catherine Lacoste
1969	U.S. Sr. Women's Amateur	Ridglea CC	Fort Worth	Carolyn Cudone
1972	U.S. Jr. Amateur	Brookhaven GC	Dallas	Robert Byman
1981	U.S. Public Links	Bear Creek GC	Houston	Jodie Mudd
1984	NCAA Championship	Bear Creek GC	Houston	Houston
1987	Tour Championship	Oak Hills CC	San Antonio	Tom Watson
1987	U.S. Mid-Amateur	Brookhollow CC	Dallas	Jay Sigel
1989	U.S. Sr. Amateur	Lochinvar GC	Houston	R.S. Williams
1989	U.S. Women's Mid-Amateur	Hills of Lakeway	Austin	Robin Weiss
1989	U.S. Sr. Women's Amateur	Woodlands TPC	Woodlands	Anne Sander
1990	Tour Championship	Champions GC	Houston	Jodie Mudd
1991	U.S. Women's Open	Colonial CC	Fort Worth	Meg Mallon
1993	U.S. Amateur	Champions GC	Houston	John Harris
1994	NCAA Championship	Stonebridge CC	McKinney	Stanford
1997	U.S. Mid-Amateur	Dallas Athletic Club	Dallas	Ken Bakse
1997	Tour Championship	Champions GC	Houston	David Duval
1998	U.S. Women's Mid-Amateur	Champions GC	Houston	Virginia Darby Grimes
1999	Tour Championship	Champions GC	Houston	

Tremendously Tough Texas Golf Trivia

1. What year did Harvey Penick begin his employment at Austin Country Club?

2. What Texas course has hosted more of golf's major championships than any other?

3. What two major golf championships has Cedar Crest Municipal in Dallas hosted?

4. Who was the first Texan to win the U.S. Amateur? Who was the second, 30 years later?

5. Which Dallas driving range did Lee Trevino work at while growing up in the city?

6. What course in what city did Ben Hogan and Byron Nelson caddie at while they were growing up?

7. How many Texans are in golf's World Hall of Fame?

8. Who was the first Texan to win one of golf's four majors?

9. Which Texan has won the most major titles?

10. What is the longest-running professional tournament in Texas?

11. Who's the only Texas pro to win a major championship in his home state?

12. What was the first chartered and recognized country club in Texas?

13. What's the name and city of the first Texas course which features replica golf holes?

14. What year and which three majors did Ben Hogan win in a single season?

15. Which Texas school produced a record sixteen NCAA golf titles?

16. What Texas amateur won a PGA event?

17. What Dallas club pro won a PGA event?

18. Who's the Dallas native who became LPGA commissioner?

19. Which former British Open champion became a Texas golf pro, and where?

20. What is the only Texas course Ben Hogan designed?

Trivia Answers

1. 1913

2. Champions Golf Club, Houston

3. PGA Championship, 1927; U.S. Public Links, 1954

4. Billy Maxwell, Scott Verplank

5. Hardy's Driving Range, Dallas

6. Glen Garden GC, Fort Worth

7. 13

8. Byron Nelson, 1937 Masters

9. Ben Hogan

10. Westin Texas Open, San Antonio

11. Orville Moody

12. Galveston Country Club, 1898

13. Tour 18, Conroe, Texas

14. 1953, Masters, U.S. Open, British Open

15. University of Houston

16. Scott Verplank

17. Earl Stewart Jr.

18. Jim Ritts

19. Bill Rogers, San Antonio Country Club

20. The Trophy Club, Westlake

Course Listings

How to Use This Directory

The Texas Golf Guide is laid out in an easy to understand manner to give you instant information on any of the state's nearly 800 courses. The courses are listed alphabetically by city. There is also an index by course name.

Because prices and other information change on a regular and often rapid basis, you should always call a course before playing to get the most current pricing and other information. Most courses have several specials depending on a person's age, time of day, or part of the year you wish to play. A phone call before you make the trip to the course is always a wise move.

The black bar with the name of the facility indicates members and guests only. The gray bar indicates courses that are open to the public. However, some private courses do allow limited outside play, especially from out-of-town golfers. Check with the specific course.

Many 9-hole courses have double tees, allowing golfers to play 18 holes. The par remains the same for either nine, but its yardage is doubled as shown in the book.

If you have any additions or corrections for the next edition of this golf guide, please send them to Republic of Texas Press, 2320 Los Rios Blvd., Suite 200, Plano, Texas 75074, ATTN: THE TEXAS GOLF GUIDE or fax 972-881-9147. You can also send e-mail to sales@wordware.com and check the web site at www.wordware.com.

Abernathy Country Club   (6,488 yds) 806-328-5261

Highway 2060
Abernathy, TX 79311
Contact: Bobby Sansom
Description: A very tight nine-hole
semiprivate course with no water
hazards and 35-year-old big trees. The
bentgrass greens have strong slopes.
The course is normal length. **Par:** 36.
Rentals: Golf Carts, Driving Range
Open to the public. Walking permitted.

Fees:

Weekday: 18-hole: $9 Cart: $9
9-hole: $5 Cart: $5
Weekend: 18-hole: $10 Cart: $9
9-hole: $5 Cart: $5

Located 15 miles north of Lubbock off
Interstate 27.

Abilene Country Club   (6,310 yds) 915-692-1855

4039 S. Treadway
Abilene, TX 79602
Contact: Allen Botkin
Description: The course was recently
redesigned, making some holes tougher
and with tighter fairways. Water is in
play on nine holes. Clubhouse has
restaurant and pro shop. **Par:** 71.
Rentals: Golf Carts, Driving Range
Members and guests only. Golf lessons
available. Walking permitted.

Fees:

Weekday: 18-hole: $45 Cart: $8.66
9-hole: (N/A) Cart: $4.33
Weekend: 18-hole: $45 Cart: $8.66
9-hole: (N/A) Cart: $4.33

Located southeast of Industrial Blvd.

Fairway Oaks Country Club   (7,020 yds) 915-695-1800

32 Fairway Oaks Blvd.
Abilene, TX 79606
Contact: Doug Fair
Description: Considered one of the
best golf courses west of Dallas/Fort
Worth. Former site of PGA and Senior
PGA tournaments. Top clubhouse and
pro shop. **Par:** 72.
Rentals: Golf Carts, Driving Range
Members and guests only. Golf lessons
available. Walking permitted.

Fees:

Weekday: 18-hole: $35 Cart: $8.50
9-hole: (N/A) Cart: (N/A)
Weekend: 18-hole: $35 Cart: $8.50
9-hole: (N/A) Cart: (N/A)

Take 83/84 south to Antilley Road,
west on Antilley to Fairway Oaks.

Maxwell Municipal Golf Course   (6,129 yds) 915-692-2737

1002 S. 32nd
Abilene, TX 79602
Contact: Dave Hand
Description: A short but tight 18-hole public course with tough par 3s and sharp doglegs. Snack bar and pro shop. **Par:** 71.
Rentals: Golf Carts, Pull Carts, Golf Clubs, Driving Range
Open to the public. Walking permitted. Golf lessons available.

Fees:

Weekday: 18-hole: $11.91 Cart: $8.66 9-hole: $7.74 Cart: $8.66
Weekend: 18-hole: $15.17 Cart: $8.66 9-hole: $8.98 Cart: $8.66

Located next to Abilene Country Club off Winters Freeway, on the south side of town.

Willow Creek Golf Center   (1,163 yds) 915-691-0909

1166 Executive Drive
Abilene, TX 79602
Contact: Ben Richey
Description: An outstanding nine-hole par-3 course with several long holes, lots of water hazards, and trees. Lighted. Clubhouse has bar and pro shop. **Par:** 27.
Open to the public. Walking permitted. Golf lessons available.

Fees:

Weekday: 18-hole: $9.70 Cart: (N/A) 9-hole: $6.50 Cart: (N/A)
Weekend: 18-hole: $10.50 Cart: (N/A) 9-hole: $7.50 Cart: (N/A)

Located on the south side of town off Winters Freeway.

Alamo Country Club   (2,500 yds) 956-787-0910

North Tower Road
Alamo, TX 78514
Contact: Melony Green
Description: A nice nine-hole private course that retired golfers love because it is only 2,500 yards long. There is water and out-of-bounds on seven of the nine holes. **Par:** 35.
Rentals: Club Rentals, Driving Range
Members and guests only. Golf lessons available. Walking permitted.

Fees:

Weekday: 18-hole: $10 Cart: (N/A) 9-hole: $8 Cart: (N/A)
Weekend: 18-hole: $12 Cart: (N/A) 9-hole: $8 Cart: (N/A)

Located one mile north of Hwy 83 on Tower Road.

Albany Golf Club

(3,567 yds) 915-762-3746

P.O. Box 157
Albany, TX 76430
Contact: Club Manager
Description: A rural Texas nine-hole golf course with no sand traps. Lots of wind into the par-5 hole and three tough par 3s. Clubhouse has snack bar. **Par:** 35.
Open to the public. Walking permitted.

Fees:

Weekday: 18-hole: $5 Cart (N/A)
9-hole: (N/A) Cart (N/A)
Weekend: 18-hole: $8 Cart (N/A)
9-hole: (N/A) Cart (N/A)

Located just north of downtown Albany.

Lost Creek Golf Club

(6,338 yds) 817-244-3312

4101 Lost Creek Blvd.
Aledo, TX 76008
Contact: Shannon Cox
Description: A former country club now open to the public. The last two holes are tough and can be a round wrecker. Clubhouse is a public country club with nice amenities. **Par:** 71.
Rentals: Golf Carts, Golf Clubs, Driving Range

Open to the public. Walking permitted. Golf lessons available.

Fees:

Weekday: 18-hole: $15 Cart: $14
9-hole: $15 Cart: $5
Weekend: 18-hole: $25 Cart: $14
9-hole: $25 Cart: $6

Located three miles west of Loop 820 off I-30 West.

Alice Country Club

(6,456 yds) 512-664-3723

Country Club Road
Alice, TX 78332
Contact: Tim Miller
Description: Playing this nine-hole course is like playing in a golfing jungle with doglegs going through mesquite trees and four creeks running through the course. Club has food and drinks. **Par:** 36.
Rentals: Golf Carts, Driving Range

Members and guests only. Golf lessons available. Walking permitted.

Fees:

Weekday: 18-hole: $15 Cart: $9
9-hole: (N/A) Cart: $4
Weekend: 18-hole: $20 Cart: $9
9-hole: (N/A) Cart: $4

Located on Hwy 44.

Alice Municipal Golf Course (6,022 yds) 512-664-7033

Anderson Park
Alice, TX 78332
Contact: Rick Monsevias
Description: A flat South Texas course with no sand traps, wide fairways, and normal greens. Clubhouse sells food and drinks near the pro shop. **Par:** 71.
Rentals: Golf Carts, Pull Carts
Open to the public. Walking permitted. Golf lessons available.

Fees:

Weekday: 18-hole: $6.25 Cart: $7.50
9-hole: (N/A) Cart: $3.50
Weekend: 18-hole: $7 Cart: $7.50
9-hole: (N/A) Cart: $3.50

Located in Anderson Park on North Texas Blvd.

Twin Creeks Golf Club (7,000 yds) 972-390-8888

501 Twin Creeks Drive
Allen, TX 75013
Contact: Pete Witter
Description: Nice Arnold Palmer design. Opened to public in late 1995 in master-planned community. Course features water, trees, ever-present wind, and some very scenic views. Course went to soft spikes in July 1997.
Par: 72.
Rentals: Golf Carts, Golf Clubs, Driving Range

Open to the public. Golf lessons available. Walking permitted.

Fees:

Weekday: 18-hole: $45 Cart (N/A)
9-hole: (N/A) Cart (N/A)
Weekend: 18-hole: $57 Cart (N/A)
9-hole: (N/A) Cart (N/A)

Take U.S. 75 north, exit at McDermott, and turn left. Club is 1½ miles down on the right.

Alpine Country Club (5,808 yds) 915-837-2752

Loop Road
Alpine, TX 79830
Contact: Joe Hutchinson
Description: A short 18-hole course with a tight par-35 front nine with small greens. Back nine is par 35 with more open fairways and no traps. Clubhouse has snacks and pro shop. **Par:** 70.
Rentals: Golf Carts, Pull Carts, Golf Clubs, Driving Range

Open to the public. Walking permitted. Golf lessons available.

Fees:

Weekday: 18-hole: $10 Cart: $14
9-hole: $7 Cart: $7
Weekend: 18-hole: $15 Cart: $14
9-hole: $7 Cart: $7

Located off U.S. 90 off Alpine Road.

Alvin Golf & Country Club   (3,020 yds) 281-331-4541

County Road 539
Alvin, TX 77512
Contact: Frank Vita
Description: An interesting nine-hole
public course with water on seven
holes, trees, and pushed-up greens.
Senior discounts available. Clubhouse
has snack bar and pro shop. **Par:** 35.
Rentals: Golf Carts, Pull Carts
Open to the public. Walking permitted.

Fees:
Weekday: 18-hole: $16 Cart: $8
9-hole: (N/A) Cart (N/A)
Weekend: 18-hole: $21 Cart: $8
9-hole: (N/A) Cart (N/A)

Located off CR 539 two blocks north of
Hwy 6.

Hillcrest Golf Club   (2,358 yds) 281-331-3505

3401 Fairway St.
Alvin, TX 77511
Contact: Dean E. Wilson
Description: A nine-hole course which
revolves around a 25-acre lake and is
totally lighted for night play. Fairways
are wide, but the greens are small.
Par: 33.
Rentals: Golf Carts, Pull Carts, Golf
Clubs, Driving Range

Open to the public. Walking permitted.
Golf lessons available.

Fees:
Weekday: 18-hole: $9.75 Cart: $5.50
9-hole: $6 Cart: $2.75
Weekend: 18-hole: $11 Cart: $5.50
9-hole: $6 Cart: $2.75

Located south of Houston ½ mile off
Hwy 35 on Fairway St.

Amarillo Country Club   (6,501 yds) 806-355-5021

4800 Bushland
Amarillo, TX 79106
Contact: Dale Wood
Description: In 1990 a Ben Hogan
Tour event was played here because it
is one of the best Panhandle courses. It
is very hilly with lots of trees and strong
wind. Great clubhouse. **Par:** 71.
Rentals: Golf Carts, Pull Carts, Golf
Clubs, Driving Range

Members and guests only. Golf lessons
available. Walking permitted.

Fees:
Weekday: 18-hole: $50 Cart: $8
9-hole: (N/A) Cart: $4
Weekend: 18-hole: $50 Cart: $8
9-hole: (N/A) Cart: $4

Located north of town at 45th and
Western, one block to Bushland

Comanche Trail Golf Course

(7,180 yds) 806-378-4281

4200 S. Grand
Amarillo, TX 79103
Contact: George Priolo
Description: Lots of dogleg holes require perfect tee shots. It has one of the best golf holes (par-5 11th) in the state of Texas. A links-style layout with plenty of wind and some water. Great daily-fee golf. **Par:** 72.
Rentals: Golf Carts, Pull Carts, Golf Clubs, Driving Range

Open to the public. Walking permitted. Golf lessons available.

Fees:

Weekday: 18-hole: $10 Cart: $18
9-hole: $8 Cart: $9
Weekend: 18-hole: $12 Cart: $18
9-hole: $10 Cart: $9

Located three miles south of I-40 on South Grand.

La Paloma Golf Club

(3,327 yds) 806-342-9915

4302 Fairway Drive
Amarillo, TX 79124
Contact: Paul Robertson
Description: Tight nine hole semi-private course recently opened in Southwest Amarillo. Be careful of the prevailing West Texas winds which can turn a couple of the par 4s into monsters. Friendly staff and good greens. **Par:** 35.
Rentals: Golf Carts, Golf Clubs, Driving Range

Fees:

Weekday: 18-hole: (N/A) Cart: (N/A)
9-hole: $13 Cart: $9.50
Weekend: 18-hole: (N/A) Cart: (N/A)
9-hole: $25 Cart: $10.50

Take Fairway exit off of I-40 in Southwest Amarillo, go west on Fairway and look for signs to the course.

Preston West Golf Course

(1,773 yds) 806-353-7003

9101 S. Coulter
Amarillo, TX 79119
Contact: Johnny Smith
Description: Good par-3 setting for players to work on their short game. Excellent chance to work on chipping around large greens with trees and some sand. Good practice facilities. **Par:** 27. Open to the public: Driving Range, Putting Green.

Fees:

Weekday: 18-hole: (N/A) Cart: (N/A)
9-hole: $7 Cart: (N/A)
Weekend: 18-hole: (N/A) Cart: (N/A)
9-hole: $10 Cart: (N/A)

Take Coulter exit off I-44, west of downtown. Look for light towers.

Ross Rogers Golf Course   (36 hs) 806-378-3086

722 NW 24th St.
Amarillo, TX 79107
Contact: Sherwin Cox
East Course Description: A wonderful 36-hole public course. The East Course is the toughest of the two courses with more undulating greens and three lakes. Food. **Par:** 72 (6,858 yards).

West Course Description: The West Course is shorter than the East Course but not all that easy. It has wide fairways and tight doglegs. The greens are not as undulating. It is the course to shoot a better score. **Par:** 72 (6,602 yards).

Rentals: Golf Carts, Pull Carts, Golf Clubs, Driving Range
Open to the public. Walking permitted. Golf lessons available.

Fees:

Weekday: 18-hole: $10 Cart: $9
9-hole: (N/A) Cart: $4.50
Weekend: 18-hole: $12 Cart: $9
9-hole: (N/A) Cart: $4.50

Located near Thompson Park on NW 24th St.

Southwest Golf Club   (7,018 yds) 806-355-7161

7490 W. Loop 335 South
Amarillo, TX 79106
Contact: Jim Thomas
Description: Perhaps the longest 18-hole public course in the Panhandle with not much water, no traps, and small trees. Bentgrass greens have slopes and are very tough. **Par:** 72.
Rentals: Golf Carts, Pull Carts, Golf Clubs, Driving Range

Open to the public. Walking permitted. Golf lessons available.

Fees:

Weekday: 18-hole: $10 Cart: $18
9-hole: (N/A) Cart: $5
Weekend: 18-hole: $12 Cart: $18
9-hole: (N/A) Cart: $6

Southwest Amarillo at Hollywood and Coulter Dr.

Tascosa Country Club   (6,492 yds) 806-374-2351

2400 N. Western
P.O. Box 10170
Amarillo, TX 79124
Contact: Alan Coe
Description: A 27-hole private club
with an easier original 18-hole course
and a new nine-hole north layout which
is very hilly with 42 sand traps. **Par:** 72.
Rentals: Golf Carts, Golf Clubs, Driving
Range

Members and guests only. Golf lessons
available. Walking permitted.

Fees:

Weekday: 18-hole: $25 Cart: $9
9-hole: $25 Cart: $4.50
Weekend: 18-hole: $50 Cart: $9
9-hole: $50 Cart: $4.50

Located north of I-40 at Western exit.

Chambers County Golf Course   (6,724 yds) 409-267-8235

1 Pinchback Road
Anahuac, TX 77514
Contact: Hal Underwood
Description: A tight 18-hole course cut
out of the piney woods with water on
eight holes. The greens are tough.
Clubhouse has snack bar and pro shop.
Par: 72.
Rentals: Golf Carts, Pull Carts, Golf
Clubs, Driving Range

Open to the public. Walking permitted.
Golf lessons available.

Fees:

Weekday: 18-hole: $9 Cart: $6.50
9-hole: (N/A) Cart (N/A)
Weekend: 18-hole: $11 Cart: $6.50
9-hole: (N/A) Cart (N/A)

From downtown Houston, take I-10 east
to exit 812; course is ½ mile south.

Andrews County Golf Course   (6,064 yds) 915-524-1462

P.O Box 348
Golf Course Road
Andrews, TX 79714
Contact: Alan C. Pursley
Description: Golfers may think this
18-hole public course is easy because it
is a short course. However, water
comes into play on 13 holes, plus lots
of trees. Food and drinks. **Par:** 70.
Rentals: Golf Carts, Driving Range

Open to the public. Walking permitted.
Golf lessons available.

Fees:

Weekday: 18-hole: $12.50 Cart: $9
9-hole: (N/A) Cart: $3.75
Weekend: 18-hole: $17.50 Cart: $9
9-hole: (N/A) Cart: $3.75

Located east of town on Golf Course
Road.

Hurricane Creek Country Club   (7,052 yds) 972-924-3247

1800 Fairway Lane
Anna, TX 75003
Contact: Lance Awe
Description: A long 18-hole private club with tough par 3s. The shortest par 3 is 180 yards long. Very fast bentgrass greens and trees on the back nine. Clubhouse recently built. **Par:** 72.
Rentals: Golf Carts, Pull Carts, Driving Range

Members and guests only. Golf lessons available. Walking permitted.

Fees:

Weekday: 18-hole: $25 Cart: $8
9-hole: (N/A) Cart: $4
Weekend: 18-hole: $40 Cart: $8
9-hole: (N/A) Cart: $4

Take Hwy 75 to exit 48 west, then north 1¾ mi. on service road.

Anson Municipal Golf Course   (3,205 yds) 915-823-2822

Route 1 Box 1
Anson, TX 79501
Contact: Lanny Ivy
Description: A typical rural Texas nine-hole course that is enjoyable to play. The course is average length with double tees. First come/first serve. **Par:** 36.
Rentals: Golf Carts
Open to the public. Walking permitted.

Fees:

Weekday: 18-hole: $4 Cart: $5 9-hole: (N/A) Cart (N/A)
Weekend: 18-hole: $5 Cart: $5 9-hole: (N/A) Cart (N/A)

Located near city park in the middle of town.

Archer City Country Club   (5,719 yds) 940-574-4332

1007 S. Ash St.
Archer City, TX 76351
Contact: Paul Wylie
Description: No sand traps but a fair nine-hole test of golf because of four uphill dogleg holes and small fairways. Semiprivate with pro shop and club. **Par:** 35.
Rentals: Golf Carts
Members and guests only. Walking permitted.

Fees:

Weekday: 18-hole: $7.50 Cart: $8
9-hole: (N/A) Cart (N/A)
Weekend: 18-hole: $9 Cart: $8 9-hole: (N/A) Cart (N/A)

Located in the south part of town off Main and Ash Street.

Chester W. Ditto Golf Course   (6,661 yds) 817-275-5941

801 Brown Blvd.
Arlington, TX 76011
Contact: Michael Krsnak
Description: One of the tightest golf
courses in Texas. The back nine
fairways are narrow and undulating.
City clubhouse has a pro shop and
snack bar. **Par:** 72.
Rentals: Golf Carts, Pull Carts, Golf
Clubs, Driving Range
Open to the public. Walking permitted.

Golf lessons available.

Fees:

Weekday: 18-hole: $12 Cart: $16
9-hole: $8 Cart: $8
Weekend: 18-hole: $14 Cart: $16
9-hole: $8 Cart: $8

Located north of I-30 on Collins Ave. to
Brown Blvd.

Lake Arlington Municipal   (6,637 yds) 817-451-6101

1516 W. Green Oaks Blvd.
Arlington, TX 76013
Contact: Gary Dennis
Description: A challenging 18-hole
public course near Lake Arlington. The
lake is not on the course, but its creeks
create hazards. The course is very hilly.
Par: 71.
Rentals: Golf Carts, Pull Carts, Golf
Clubs

Open to the public. Walking permitted.
Golf lessons available.

Fees:

Weekday: 18-hole: $12 Cart: $16
9-hole: $8 Cart: $8
Weekend: 18-hole: $14 Cart: $16
9-hole: $8 Cart: $8

Located off Spur 303 south on Green
Oaks Blvd.

Meadowbrook Park Golf Course   (2,000 yds) 817-275-0221

1300 E. Dugan
Arlington, TX 76010
Contact: Craig Beasley
Description: A great golf course for
beginners. It is a nine-hole par 33
course with the longest hole a 304-yard
par 4. Great short iron practice layout.
Par: 33.
Open to the public. Walking permitted.

Fees:

Weekday: 18-hole: $8 Cart (N/A)
9-hole: $8 Cart (N/A)
Weekend: 18-hole: $9.50 Cart (N/A)
9-hole: $9.50 Cart (N/A)

Located south of I-30 off Collins to
Abrams, then to Dugan.

Rolling Hills Country Club
(6,117 yds) 817-261-6221

401 W. Lamar
Arlington, TX 76011
Contact: Lamar East
Description: It looks short on the scorecard, 6,117 yards from the back tees, but is so hilly, it plays longer. Ten of the holes have out-of-bounds, so your score can go higher. **Par:** 71.
Rentals: Golf Carts, Pull Carts, Golf Clubs, Driving Range

Members and guests only. Golf lessons available. Walking permitted.

Fees:

Weekday: 18-hole: $15 Cart: $9
9-hole: $4.50 Cart: $4.50
Weekend: 18-hole: $30 Cart: $9
9-hole: $4.50 Cart: $4.50

Located north of I-30 off Cooper St.

Shady Valley Golf Club
(6,800 yds) 817-275-8771

4001 W. Park Row
Arlington, TX 76013
Contact: David Hersman
Description: A creek runs all through the golf course requiring a lot of go-for-broke shots. Lots of trees and out-of-bounds add penalty strokes. Very nice clubhouse. **Par:** 70.
Rentals: Golf Carts, Golf Clubs, Driving Range

Members and guests only. Golf lessons available. Walking permitted.

Fees:

Weekday: 18-hole: $30 Cart: $10
9-hole: (N/A) Cart: $5
Weekend: 18-hole: $45 Cart: $10
9-hole: (N/A) Cart: $5

Located north of Spur 303 off Park Springs Road.

Tierra Verde Golf Club
(7,000 yds) 817-572-1300

7005 Golf Club Drive
Arlington, TX 76063
Contact: Mike Krsnak
Description: Challenging new addition for DFW area which opened in November '98. Daily-fee offers plenty of wooded terrain with bunkers and water on several holes. Two reachable par-5s and par-3s of varying length. Located in fast growing Tarrant County area. **Par:** 72.

Fees:

Weekday: 18-hole: $40 Cart: included
9-hole: (N/A) Cart: (N/A)
Weekend: 18-hole: $55 Cart: included
9-hole: (N/A) Cart: (N/A)

Located at intersection of Highway 287 and Eden Road, in southwest Arlington. Follow signs.

Aspermont City Golf Course   (5,730 yds) 940-989-3381

P.O. Box 419
Aspermont, TX 79502
Contact: Pro Shop
Description: Golfers can post their career low score on this nine-hole public course thanks to wide fairways and short holes. There are 15 tees and nine greens. **Par:** 36.
Rentals: Golf Carts

Open to the public. Walking permitted.

Fees:

Weekday: 18-hole: $5 Cart: $10
9-hole: (N/A) Cart (N/A)
Weekend: 18-hole: $5 Cart: $10
9-hole: (N/A) Cart (N/A)

Located 1½ miles southwest of city.

Atascocita Country Club   (27 hs) 713-852-8115

20114 Pinehurst Road
Atascocita, TX 77346
Contact: Scott Shelby
Description: An excellent 27-hole private club. Lots of gulf coast trees, traps, and hilly doglegs. The nine-hole course has more water. Plenty of water views from pro shop. **Par:** 71.
Rentals: Golf Carts, Pull Carts, Golf Clubs, Driving Range

Members and guests only. Golf lessons available. Mandatory carts.

Fees:

Weekday: 18-hole: $40 Cart: $10
9-hole: (N/A) Cart: $5
Weekend: 18-hole: $50 Cart: $10
9-hole: (N/A) Cart: $5

Located east of I-45 on FM 1960.

Athens Country Club   (5,873 yds) 903-677-3844

Park Lane
Athens, TX 75751
Contact: Gaylord Walden
Description: Pretty East Texas semiprivate course. Course has plenty of trees, water, and traps. Back nine has thick trees lining fairway. Out-of-county golfers are welcome. **Par:** 71.
Rentals: Golf Carts, Pull Carts, Golf Clubs

Members and guests only. Golf lessons available. Walking permitted.

Fees:

Weekday: 18-hole: $15 Cart: $9
9-hole: (N/A) Cart: $4.50
Weekend: 18-hole: $25 Cart: $9
9-hole: (N/A) Cart: $4.50

Located off Prairieville Road to Park Lane.

Indian Hills Country Club   (5,695 yds) 903-796-4146

O'Farrell Road
Atlanta, TX 75551
Contact: Ronnie Hailey
Description: A semiprivate nine-hole course that has lots of pine trees, a pond, and sand traps. The greens are large. Golfers play two sets of tees to make 18 holes on this Northeast Texas layout. **Par:** 36.
Rentals: Golf Carts, Golf Clubs, Driving Range

Members and guests only. Walking permitted.

Fees:

Weekday: 18-hole: $12 Cart: $7.50
9-hole: (N/A) Cart: $3.75
Weekend: 18-hole: $20 Cart: $7.50
9-hole: (N/A) Cart: $3.75

Located on O'Farrell Road off Hwy 59.

Austin Country Club   (6,848 yds) 512-328-0090

4408 Long Champ Drive
Austin, TX 78746
Contact: Dale Morgan
Description: Legendary home of pros Harvey and Tinsley Penicks. A very difficult Pete Dye design along the Colorado River with spectacular back nine views. Tom Kite a member. One of the best in Texas. **Par:** 72.
Rentals: Golf Carts, Driving Range
Members and guests only. Golf lessons available. Walking permitted.

Fees:

Weekday: 18-hole: $35 Cart: $10
9-hole: (N/A) Cart: $6
Weekend: 18-hole: $50 Cart: $10
9-hole: (N/A) Cart: $6

Take Loop 360 north to Westlake Drive, right to Long Champ Drive, and left to club entrance.

Balcones Country Club-Balcones (6,649 yds) 512-258-2775

8600 Balcones Club Drive
Austin, TX 78750
Contact: Philip Miranda
Balcones Course Description: A 36-hole private club. The Balcones Course is mid-length with two different nines. The front nine has Spanish oak trees, the back nine has out-of-bounds, hills, and small greens. Great clubhouse. **Par:** 70.
Rentals: Golf Carts, Pull Carts, Golf Clubs, Driving Range

Members and guests only. Golf lessons available. Walking permitted.

Fees:

Weekday: 18-hole: $22.50 Cart: $10
9-hole: (N/A) Cart: $5
Weekend: 18-hole: $30 Cart: $10
9-hole: (N/A) Cart: $5

Located west of Hwy 183 on Balcones Club Drive.

Balcones Country Club-Spicewood (6,706 yds) 512-258-6763

11210 Spicewood Club Drive
Austin, TX 78750
Contact: Tina Bradley
Spicewood Course Description: The newer Spicewood Course is longer with lots of trees, hills, and holes set around water. The greens are larger than the older Balcones Course. **Par:** 72.
Rentals: Golf Carts, Pull Carts, Golf Clubs, Driving Range

Members and guests only. Golf lessons available. Walking permitted.

Fees:

Weekday: 18-hole: $22.50 Cart: $10
9-hole: (N/A) Cart: $5
Weekend: 18-hole: $30 Cart: $10
9-hole: (N/A) Cart: $5

Located west of Hwy 183, 5 miles west of Highway 360.

Barton Creek Resort & Country Club   (36 hs) 512-329-4000

8212 Barton Club Drive
Austin, TX 78735
Contact: Chip Gist
Fazio Course Description: The former site of The Legends of Golf. An excellent resort with fine rooms, health club, spas. Constantly ranked as one of the top five courses in Texas, with a highly scenic back nine. A third 18-hole course is located in Spicewood, Texas with a fourth layout scheduled for 1999. **Par:** 72 (6,956 yards).

Fees:

Weekday: 18-hole: $135 Cart: (N/A)
9-hole: (N/A) Cart: (N/A)
Weekend: 18-hole: $135 Cart: (N/A)
9-hole: (N/A) Cart: (N/A)

Crenshaw Course Description: Ben Crenshaw designed this course in 1991 with 18 large greens. You can set a personal record for most greens hit, but most are three putts. Great Hill Country scenery. Favorite hangout of UT's Darrell Royal. **Par:** 71 (6,678 yards).
Rentals: Golf Carts, Golf Clubs, Driving Range
Open to the public. Walking permitted. Golf lessons available.

Fees:

Weekday: 18-hole: $95 Cart: (N/A)
9-hole: (N/A) Cart: (N/A)
Weekend: 18-hole: $95 Cart: (N/A)
9-hole: (N/A) Cart: (N/A)

> Located off Barton Creek Blvd. west of FM 2244.

Bluebonnet Hill Golf Club   (6,500 yds) 512-272-4228

9100 Decker Lane
Austin, TX 78724
Contact: Jeff Wilson
Description: A nice Hill Country 18-hole public course with lots of natural land hazards instead of water. Course located atop hill with wind a factor. **Par:** 72.
Rentals: Golf Carts, Golf Clubs, Driving Range

Open to the public. Walking permitted. Golf lessons available.

Fees:

Weekday: 18-hole: $12 Cart: $7.50
9-hole: (N/A) Cart: $4.25
Weekend: 18-hole: $18 Cart: $7.50
9-hole: (N/A) Cart: $4.25

> Located east of Austin off I-35 to 290 east to South Decker.

Butler Park Pitch & Putt Course　　(2,300 yds) 512-477-9025

201 Lee Barton Drive
Austin, TX 78704
Contact: Winston Kinser
Description: A nine-hole par-3 course
which helps make your short game
better thanks to demand for accurate
tee shots off elevated tees. There are
traps and trees. **Par:** 27.
Rentals: Golf Clubs
Open to the public. Walking permitted.

Fees:

Weekday: 18-hole: $8 Cart: (N/A)
9-hole: (N/A) Cart: $3.75
Weekend: 18-hole: $8 Cart: (N/A)
9-hole: (N/A) Cart: $3.75

Located on Riverside east of South
Lamar.

Circle C Ranch Golf Club　　(6,858 yds) 512-288-4297

7401 Hwy. 45
Austin, TX 78739
Contact: Rob Shields
Description: Built in 1992, Circle C is
a classic Jay Morrish/Tom Weiskopf
course with short par 4s with severe
water hazards and sand traps. Great
South Austin location with native trees,
rock outcroppings, and water. **Par:** 72.
Rentals: Golf Carts, Golf Clubs, Driving
Range

Open to the public. Golf lessons
available. Mandatory carts.

Fees:

Weekday: 18-hole: $39 Cart: (N/A)
9-hole: (N/A) Cart: (N/A)
Weekend: 18-hole: $49 Cart: (N/A)
9-hole: (N/A) Cart: (N/A)

Take FM 1826; turn right on
Whisperwood Drive and follow sign.

Great Hills Golf Club　　(6,599 yds) 512-345-0505

5914 Lost Horizon
Austin, TX 78759
Contact: Chance Blythe
Description: This 18-hole private
course will be redesigned by 1998.
Currently it is hilly with lots of blind
shots. It requires accurate shots. **Par:**
71.
Rentals: Golf Carts, Pull Carts, Golf
Clubs, Driving Range

Members and guests only. Golf lessons
available. Walking permitted.

Fees:

Weekday: 18-hole: $25 Cart: $8
9-hole: (N/A) Cart: $5
Weekend: 18-hole: $45 Cart: $8
9-hole: (N/A) Cart: $5

½ mi. south of Loop 360 and Hwy
183. Take Great Hills Drive to Lost
Horizon.

Hancock Park Golf Course   (2,643 yds) 512-453-0276

811 E. 41st St.
Austin, TX 78751
Contact: Steve Darby
Description: The original Austin
Country Club built in 1899. Now a
nine-hole public course and the oldest
continually operated nine holes in the
state. Once the site of a round by
President William Howard Taft. **Par:** 35.
Rentals: Golf Carts, Pull Carts, Golf
Clubs

Open to the public. Walking permitted.
Golf lessons available.

Fees:

Weekday: 18-hole: $11.50 Cart:
$6.90 9-hole: $6.50 Cart: $4.16
Weekend: 18-hole: $12 Cart: $6.90
9-hole: $7 Cart: $4.16

> Take access road from I-35; course is
> two blocks west of I-35 on 41st St.

Jimmy Clay Golf Course   (6,857 yds) 512-444-0999

5400 Jimmy Clay Drive
Austin, TX 78744
Contact: Jana Balander-Benton
Description: A really neat 18-hole
public course. Longtime site of Texas
girls high school championship. The
course has very long par 4s and par 5s.
Part of 36-hole complex. **Par:** 72.
Rentals: Golf Carts, Pull Carts, Golf
Clubs, Driving Range

Open to the public. Walking permitted.
Golf lessons available.

Fees:

Weekday: 18-hole: $12 Cart: $8.25
9-hole: (N/A) Cart: $4.50
Weekend: 18-hole: $13.50 Cart:
$8.25 9-hole: (N/A) Cart: $4.50

> Located in south Austin on Stassney
> Lane off I-35.

Lakeway Golf Course

(36 hs) 512-261-7572

602 Lakeway Drive
Austin, TX 78734
Contact: Joey Yadouga
Live Oak Course Description: Part of excellent 36-hole combination at scenic Lakeway layout. Live Oak layout is very tight with water. Live Oak has no traps but has several holes near Lake Travis with some great views. **Par:** 72 (6,643 yards).
Rentals: Golf Carts, Golf Clubs, Driving Range
Open to the public. Golf lessons available. Mandatory carts.

Yaupon Course Description: The Live Oak and Yaupon courses are open to hotel guests. The 562-yard par-5 first hole on the Yaupon Course is one of the hilliest holes in Texas. **Par:** 72 (6,565 yards).
Rentals: Golf Carts, Driving Range
Open to the public. Walking permitted.

Fees:

Weekday: 18-hole: $38 Cart: $12
9-hole: (N/A) Cart: $7
Weekend: 18-hole: $45 Cart: $12
9-hole: (N/A) Cart: $7

Located off RR 620 in scenic Lakeway.

Lions Municipal Golf Course

(6,001 yds) 512-477-6963

2901 Enfield Road
Austin, TX 78703
Contact: Lloyd Morrison
Description: Not a long 18-hole public course, but Ben Hogan once said the par-4 16th hole (then seventh) was great. It's an uphill dogleg where golfers have to lay up short of the hill. City course, founded by Lions Club.
Par: 71.
Rentals: Golf Carts, Pull Carts, Golf Clubs, Driving Range

Open to the public. Walking permitted. Golf lessons available.

Fees:

Weekday: 18-hole: $12 Cart: $8.25
9-hole: (N/A) Cart: $4.25
Weekend: 18-hole: $13.50 Cart: $8.25 9-hole: (N/A) Cart: $4.25

Located in west Austin, less than two miles west of Mopac Expwy (Loop 1).

Lost Creek Country Club — (6,570 yds) 512-892-2032

2612 Lost Creek Blvd.
Austin, TX 78746
Contact: Jim Terry
Description: Very hilly and tough 18 holes below Crenshaw Course at Barton Creek. Lots of trees, water, and sand traps. Clubhouse has a restaurant, nice lockers. Scenery takes any pain out of high scores. **Par:** 72.
Rentals: Golf Carts, Pull Carts, Golf Clubs, Driving Range

Members and guests only. Golf lessons available. Walking permitted.

Fees:

Weekday: 18-hole: $25 Cart: $20
9-hole: (N/A) Cart: $10
Weekend: 18-hole: $45 Cart: $20
9-hole: (N/A) Cart: $10

Take Lost Creek Drive Blvd. off Loop 360; course is 2½ miles on the right.

Morris Williams Golf Center — (6,636 yds) 512-926-1298

4305 Manor Road
Austin, TX 78723
Contact: Gib Kizer
Description: The fairways are very tight on this recently remodeled 18-hole public course. That means the tee shot has to be well placed to be able to reach the small greens. **Par:** 72.
Rentals: Golf Carts, Pull Carts, Golf Clubs, Driving Range

Open to the public. Walking permitted. Golf lessons available.

Fees:

Weekday: 18-hole: $12 Cart: $8.50
9-hole: (N/A) Cart: $4.25
Weekend: 18-hole: $13.50 Cart: $8.50 9-hole: (N/A) Cart: $4.25

Located east of the Austin Airport.

Onion Creek Golf Club — (27 hs) 512-282-2162

2510 Onion Creek Parkway
Austin, TX 78747
Contact: Matt Jones
Description: The Senior PGA Tour was born at Onion Creek because of the start of The Legends of Golf. It is a classic tight up-and-down course with a new nine holes in 1996. Will host LPGA Tour event in 1999. **Par:** 70 (6,367 yards).
Rentals: Golf Carts, Golf Clubs, Driving Range

Members and guests only. Golf lessons available. Walking permitted.

Fees:

Weekday: 18-hole: $53.13 Cart: $10
9-hole: (N/A) Cart: $5
Weekend: 18-hole: $67.76 Cart: $10
9-hole: (N/A) Cart: $5

Located off I-35 south of Austin.

River Place Country Club

(6,611 yds) 512-346-6784

4207 River Place Blvd.
Austin, TX 78730
Contact: Darrell Eskelman
Description: Great public course redesigned by Tom Kite. A former country club now open to the public. Great views of hills, lakes, and trees with scenic 19th hole. **Par:** 71.
Rentals: Golf Carts, Golf Clubs, Driving Range

Open to the public. Golf lessons available. Mandatory carts.

Fees:

Weekday: 18-hole: $50 Cart: (N/A)
9-hole: (N/A) Cart: (N/A)
Weekend: 18-hole: $65 Cart: (N/A)
9-hole: (N/A) Cart: (N/A)

Located four miles west of Loop 360 on RR 2222 to River Place Blvd.

Riverside Golf Course

(6,500 yds) 512-389-1070

5712 E. Riverside Drive
Austin, TX 78741
Contact: Jack Haby
Description: The former Austin C.C. where Tom Kite and Ben Crenshaw learned to play golf. It is not the same, but it's still tight, hilly, and historic. Owned by Austin Community College. **Par:** 71.
Rentals: Golf Carts, Pull Carts, Golf Clubs

Open to the public. Walking permitted.

Fees:

Weekday: 18-hole: $14 Cart: $10
9-hole: (N/A) Cart: $5
Weekend: 18-hole: $18 Cart: $10
9-hole: (N/A) Cart: $5

Take Riverside exit east off I-35 to Grove Blvd., then left on Grove near college.

Roy Kizer Golf Course

(6,749 yds) 512-444-0999

5400 Jimmy Clay Drive
Austin, TX 78744
Contact: Kevin Gomillion
Description: Very scenic 18-hole addition to public Jimmy Clay layout. Both courses owned by city, but Kizer includes native trees, brush, and birds. Named for local longtime course superintendent. **Par:** 71.
Rentals: Golf Carts, Pull Carts, Driving Range

Open to the public. Walking permitted. Golf lessons available.

Fees:

Weekday: 18-hole: $16 Cart: $16.50
9-hole: (N/A) Cart: $8.75
Weekend: 18-hole: $21 Cart: $16.50
9-hole: (N/A) Cart: $8.75

Located in south Austin off Stassney Lane West and I-35.

Cross Timbers Golf Course
(7,100 yds) 817-444-4940

1181 S. Stewart St.
Azle, TX 76020
Contact: Carl Fisher
Description: New city-owned course which opened in 1995. Inspired by local golf hero Robert Landers, who had stint on Senior PGA Tour. Layout takes advantage of local scenery with trees, traps, and brush. **Par:** 72.
Rentals: Golf Carts, Golf Clubs, Driving Range

Open to the public. Golf lessons available. Mandatory carts.

Fees:

Weekday: 18-hole: $25.80 Cart: (N/A)
9-hole: (N/A) Cart: (N/A)
Weekend: 18-hole: $33.00 Cart: (N/A)
9-hole: (N/A) Cart: (N/A)

Located 30 minutes northwest of downtown Fort Worth. From Loop 820, take Hwy 199 west to Stewart Street.

Shady Oaks Golf Club
(6,455 yds) 915-854-1757

Route 1
Baird, TX 79504
Contact: Derrick Long
Description: A former nine-hole public course that added a new nine in 1993. The new nine is more difficult with rolling fairways, water, and traps. Clubhouse has restaurant and bar. **Par:** 70.
Rentals: Golf Carts, Pull Carts, Golf Clubs, Driving Range

Open to the public. Walking permitted. Golf lessons available.

Fees:

Weekday: 18-hole: $10 Cart: $7
9-hole: (N/A) Cart: $4
Weekend: 18-hole: $13 Cart: $7
9-hole: (N/A) Cart: $4

Exit I-20 on Union Hill.

Ballinger Country Club
(5,752 yds) 915-365-3214

Box 641
Ballinger, TX 76821
Contact: Wayne Herrmann
Description: A classic nine-hole rural Texas private course. It is short with good scores possible. Out-of-county golfers are welcome to play the course. **Par:** 36.
Rentals: Golf Carts, Driving Range
Members and guests only. Walking permitted.

Fees:

Weekday: 18-hole: $11 Cart: $15
9-hole: $7.50 Cart: $7.50
Weekend: 18-hole: $15 Cart: $15
9-hole: $7.50 Cart: $7.50

Located west on Country Club Road off Hwy 158.

Flying L Ranch Golf Course (6,646 yds) 830-796-8466

P.O. Box 1959
Bandera, TX 78003
Contact: Carl Worley Jr.
Description: A mid-length 18-hole public course that requires playing well on the hilly front nine to post a good score. The back nine is open. Nice, new clubhouse. **Par:** 72.
Rentals: Golf Carts, Pull Carts, Golf Clubs, Driving Range

Open to the public. Walking permitted. Golf lessons available.

Fees:

Weekday: 18-hole: $21.50 Cart: $8
9-hole: (N/A) Cart: $4.50
Weekend: 18-hole: $27.75 Cart: $8
9-hole: (N/A) Cart: $4.50

Located one mile west of Bandera on Hwy 173, follow signs.

Lost Valley Resort Ranch (6,210 yds) 830-460-7958

P.O. Box 2170
Bandera, TX 78003
Contact: Will Heardon
Description: The front nine is called the "Senior Nine" because it is short but tight. The back nine is longer with larger water hazards. On-site lodging and clubhouse. **Par:** 72.
Rentals: Golf Carts, Pull Carts, Golf Clubs

Open to the public. Walking permitted.

Fees:

Weekday: 18-hole: $19.50 Cart: (N/A)
9-hole: (N/A) Cart: $3.50
Weekend: 18-hole: $24.50 Cart: (N/A)
9-hole: (N/A) Cart: $5.50

Located 2½ miles south of Bandera on Hwy 16.

ColoVista Country Club (6,966 yds) 512-303-1665

One Country Club Drive
Bastrop, TX 78602
Contact: Moore McDonough
Description: Promising new course located on prime riverside property. Will be private but is allowing public play after first opening in summer of 1997. Great Hill Country views with some holes by Colorado River and huge, first-class facilities. **Par:** 72.
Rentals: Golf Carts, Driving Range

Open to the public. Walking permitted. Golf lessons available.

Fees:

Weekday: 18-hole: $40 Cart: $10
9-hole: (N/A) Cart: (N/A)
Weekend: 18-hole: $50 Cart: $10
9-hole: (N/A) Cart: (N/A)

Located on Hwy 71 four miles east of town.

Lost Pines Golf Club   (5,017 yds) 512-321-2327

Park Road 1A
Bastrop, TX 78602
Contact: Rudy Belmares
Description: The pines are not lost on this beautiful public course. They make the fairways very narrow. A new nine holes opened in late 1997 at this former WPA project. **Par:** 71.
Rentals: Golf Carts, Pull Carts, Golf Clubs, Driving Range

Open to the public. Walking permitted. Golf lessons available.

Fees:

Weekday: 18-hole: $14.34 Cart: $18.50 9-hole: (N/A) Cart: $9.20
Weekend: 18-hole: $16.51 Cart: $19.50 9-hole: (N/A) Cart: $9.20

Located off Hwy 21 at Bastrop State Park.

Pine Forest Golf Club   (6,600 yds) 512-321-1181

2509 Riverside Drive
Bastrop, TX 78602
Contact: Tom Belobraydic
Description: An extremely hilly 18-hole public course with trees surrounding the fairways and very undulating greens. Great location near banks of Colorado River with top pro shop. **Par:** 72.
Rentals: Golf Carts, Golf Clubs, Driving Range

Open to the public. Walking permitted. Golf lessons available.

Fees:

Weekday: 18-hole: $21 Cart: (N/A) 9-hole: (N/A) Cart: (N/A)
Weekend: 18-hole: $31 Cart: (N/A) 9-hole: (N/A) Cart: (N/A)

Located off Hwy 71 one mile east of town.

Bay City Country Club   (3,215 yds) 409-245-3577

P.O. Box 1606
Bay City, TX 77414
Contact: Jim Williams
Description: A real testy nine-hole private course with lots of oak trees, and tight fairways with sand traps. Colorado River comes into play on several holes. **Par:** 36.
Rentals: Golf Carts, Driving Range
Members and guests only. Golf lessons available. Walking permitted.

Fees:

Weekday: 18-hole: $17 Cart: $9 9-hole: $12.75 Cart: $5
Weekend: 18-hole: $21 Cart: $9 9-hole: $12.75 Cart: $5

Located southwest of Houston on Hwy 35.

Baycel Golf Club   (3,200 yds) 409-245-4871

Celanese Road
Bay City, TX 77414
Contact: Ben Kiker
Description: The Colorado River runs
through the first hole of this short
nine-hole corporate course. The next
eight holes have trees but no traps.
Par: 35.
Members and guests only. Walking
permitted.

Fees:

Weekday: 18-hole: $4 Cart: (N/A)
9-hole: (N/A) Cart: (N/A)
Weekend: 18-hole: $8 Cart: (N/A)
9-hole: (N/A) Cart: (N/A)

Located southwest of Houston on
Celanese Road off Hwy 35.

Rio Colorado Golf Course   (6,834 yds) 409-244-2955

P.O. Box 576
FM 2668 @ Riverside Park Drive
Bay City, TX 77414
Contact: Doug Firestone
Description: The Colorado River runs
alongside this 18-hole upscale public
course. Hooks and slices off the fairway
can get wet in a hurry. Fourteen holes
have water hazards with 57 sand traps.
Worth the drive. **Par:** 72.
Rentals: Golf Carts, Pull Carts, Golf
Clubs, Driving Range

Open to the public. Walking permitted.
Golf lessons available.

Fees:

Weekday: 18-hole: $26 Cart: $8.50
9-hole: (N/A) Cart: $4.50
Weekend: 18-hole: $36 Cart: $8.50
9-hole: (N/A) Cart: $4.50

Located off FM 2668 in Bay City.

Evergreen Point Golf Course   (7,000 yds) 281-837-9000

1530 Evergreen Road
Baytown, TX 77520
Contact: Fred Marti
Description: Strong combination of
rolling hills, native trees, and brush
with plenty of water. Led by local golf
veteran Fred Marti, who has worked at
several local courses. **Par:** 72.
Rentals: Golf Carts, Driving Range
Open to the public. Walking permitted.
Golf lessons available.

Fees:

Weekday: 18-hole: $20 Cart: $9
9-hole: (N/A) Cart: (N/A)
Weekend: 18-hole: $27 Cart: $9
9-hole: (N/A) Cart: (N/A)

Take 146 north to Business 80, go two
miles, and turn right on Spur 55. Turn
right on Tri-Cities Beach Road and then
turn right on Evergreen.

Goose Creek Country Club   (6,530 yds) 281-424-5565

5000 Country Club View
Baytown, TX 77521
Contact: Glenn VonBieberstein
Description: Both nines of the private 18-hole course are different. The front nine has trees and lots of water. The back nine has Goose Creek and three lakes. Five par 3s and five par 5s. **Par:** 72.
Rentals: Golf Carts, Golf Clubs, Driving Range
Members and guests only. Golf lessons available. Walking permitted.

Fees:

Weekday: 18-hole: $25 Cart: $9
9-hole: (N/A) Cart: $7
Weekend: 18-hole: $30 Cart: $9
9-hole: (N/A) Cart: $7

> From Houston, take I-10 east to Spur 330, turn left on Baker Road, and turn right on Country Club View.

Bayou Din Golf Club   (27 hrs) 409-796-1327

8537 La Belle Road
Beaumont, TX 77705
Contact: Donnie Allen
Description: A 27-hole public course with a third nine added in July 1993. The Old Course is fun with no traps and an island green. The new nine is long with sand, mounds, and water. **Par:** 71 (6,285 yards).
Rentals: Golf Carts, Pull Carts, Golf Clubs, Driving Range
Open to the public. Walking permitted. Golf lessons available.

Fees:

Weekday: 18-hole: $8 Cart: $7 9-hole: $5 Cart: $5
Weekend: 18-hole: $10 Cart: $7
9-hole: $7.50 Cart: $5

> Located in the southwest part of the city, off Fannett Road to LaBelle Road.

Beaumont Country Club   (6,414 yds) 409-892-9431

5355 Pine St.
Beaumont, TX 77704
Contact: Brian White
Description: Even though there are tight fairways with lots of trees, some golfers consider this 18-hole private course to be easy with few water hazards and small greens. **Par:** 72.
Rentals: Golf Carts, Pull Carts, Golf Clubs, Driving Range
Members and guests only. Golf lessons available. Walking permitted.

Fees:

Weekday: 18-hole: $20 Cart: $19
9-hole: (N/A) Cart: $10
Weekend: 18-hole: $30 Cart: $19
9-hole: (N/A) Cart: $10

> Located off I-10; take 11th St. to Pine.

Belle Oaks Golf Club   (6,875 yds)　409-796-1311

15075 Country Club Road
Beaumont, TX 77640
Contact: Scott Goebel
Description: Fairly new public course
in golf-rich Golden Triangle. Plenty of
trees, as name would suggest, with
brush, moss, water and several holes
and bermuda grass greens. Good
challenge for weekend player. **Par:** 72.
Rentals: Golf Carts, Golf Clubs, Driving
Range

Open to public.

Fees:

Weekday: 18-hole: $10 Cart: $10
9-hole: (N/A) Cart: (N/A)
Weekend: 18-hole: $17 Cart: $10.50
9-hole: (N/A) Cart: (N/A)

From Houston, take Hwy 73 toward
Port Arthur, go right at Country Club
Road exit, approx. 15 miles from Hwy
73 Winnie Exit.

Brentwood Country Club   (7,100 yds)　409-840-9440

4201 S. Major
Beaumont, TX 77707
Contact: Jeff Johnson
Description: A very difficult 18-hole
private course that is 7,100 yards long
with tight fairways, out-of-bounds, traps,
and big greens. Nice clubhouse. **Par:**
71.
Rentals: Golf Carts, Pull Carts, Golf
Clubs, Driving Range

Members and guests only. Golf lessons
available. Walking permitted.

Fees:

Weekday: 18-hole: $20 Cart: $8.50
9-hole: (N/A) Cart: $3.75
Weekend: 18-hole: $25 Cart: $8.50
9-hole: (N/A) Cart: $3.75

Located in the west part of the city off
I-10.

Henry Homberg Golf Course   (6,846 yds)　409-842-3220

Babe Zaharias Drive (Tyrrell Park)
Beaumont, TX 77720
Contact: Andy Hebert
Description: Historic 18-hole public
layout dedicated to longtime pro and
local female pro golfer. Tee shots go a
long way on firm fairways. Only five
water hazards. **Par:** 72.
Rentals: Golf Carts, Pull Carts, Golf
Clubs

Open to the public. Walking permitted.
Golf lessons available.

Fees:

Weekday: 18-hole: $7 Cart: $7.50
9-hole: $5 Cart: $3.75
Weekend: 18-hole: $8 Cart: $7.50
9-hole: $5 Cart: $3.75

Located southwest of town in Tyrrell
Park.

Rabbit Run Golf Course (6,300 yds) 409-866-7545

1805 Brooks Road
Beaumont, TX 77713
Contact: Johnny Barlow
Description: One of the best new public courses in the Golden Triangle area. Opened in 1995 to rave reviews. Good test for golfers with trees, water, only two par 5s, but several long par 4s. Come prepared. **Par:** 70.

Fees:

Weekday: 18-hole: $8 Cart: $15
9-hole: (N/A) Cart: (N/A)
Weedend: 18-hole: $10 Cart: $15
9-hole: (N/A) Cart: (N/A)

One mile north of I-10, take Major Drive exit to Brooks Road.

Beeville Country Club (6,338 yds) 512-358-1216

Business Highway 181 North
Beeville, TX 78104
Contact: Bobby Schauer
Description: A very tight nine-hole private course that has oak trees, water hazards, and small greens. No sand traps. Clubhouse recently rebuilt. **Par:** 36.
Rentals: Golf Carts, Golf Clubs, Driving Range

Members and guests only. Golf lessons available. Walking permitted.

Fees:

Weekday: 18-hole: $10 Cart: $7.50
9-hole: (N/A) Cart: (N/A)
Weekend: 18-hole: $20 Cart: $7.50
9-hole: (N/A) Cart: (N/A)

Located 50 miles southwest of Victoria on Business 181.

John C. Beasley Municipal Course (7,100 yds) 512-358-4295

400 N. Washington
Beeville, TX 78102
Contact: Victor Trujillo
Description: A very simple nine-hole public course with big greens, tight, flat fairways, no traps, and little water. Clubhouse has small pro shop. **Par:** 36.
Rentals: Golf Carts, Pull Carts, Golf Clubs, Driving Range
Open to the public. Walking permitted.

Fees:

Weekday: 18-hole: $8.66 Cart: $8.12
9-hole: (N/A) Cart: $4.33
Weekend: 18-hole: $10.83 Cart: $8.12 9-hole: (N/A) Cart: $4.33

Located 50 miles southwest of Victoria off Hwy 59.

Bellville Golf & Recreation Club   (6,100 yds)   409-865-9058

P.O. Box 117
Highway 36
Bellville, TX 77418
Contact: Tim Lewis
Description: Out-of-town golfers are welcome on weekdays. This nine-hole course has tiny greens, hilly but wide fairways, and only one sand trap. Food. **Par:** 36.
Open to the public. Walking permitted. Golf lessons available.

Fees:

Weekday: 18-hole: $12 Cart: $16
9-hole: (N/A) Cart: $8
Weekend: 18-hole: $15 Cart: $16
9-hole: (N/A) Cart: $8

Located west of Houston on I-10 to Hwy 36 north.

Leon Valley Golf Course   (6,900 yds)   254-939-5271

709 East 24th St.
Belton, TX 76513
Contact: Golf Shop
Description: The difference between the blue and white tees is dramatic. Par is 72 from the blues and 71 from the whites with a 1,300-yard difference. **Par:** 72.
Rentals: Golf Carts, Pull Carts, Golf Clubs

Open to the public. Walking permitted. Golf lessons available.

Fees:

Weekday: 18-hole: $8 Cart: $8 9-hole: (N/A) Cart: $4
Weekend: 18-hole: $10 Cart: $8
9-hole: (N/A) Cart: $4

Located off I-35 south to exit 294B and right on 6th St. to Hwy 317. Right to East 24th St.

Big Lake Golf Assn. Golf Course   (5,792 yds)   915-884-2633

Highway 67
Big Lake, TX 76932
Contact: Wade Daughtery
Description: Good scores are common on this short nine-hole private course thanks to no sand traps, no water, and flat, wide fairways. Clubhouse has snack bar and pro shop. **Par:** 35.
Rentals: Club Rentals, Driving Range

Members and guests only. Golf lessons available. Walking permitted.

Fees:

Weekday: 18-hole: $7.50 Cart: (N/A)
9-hole: (N/A) Cart: (N/A)
Weekend: 18-hole: $10.50 Cart: (N/A)
9-hole: (N/A) Cart: (N/A)

Located on Hwy 67 one mile east of town.

Ambassador College Golf Course (5,000 yds) 903-636-2000

Highway 80
Big Sandy, TX 75755
Contact: Kevin Hemsley
Description: A nine-hole semiprivate college golf course. Course is hilly and tight with small greens and marked hazards. Usually open only during school year. **Par:** 35.
Rentals: Driving Range

Open to the public. Walking permitted.

Fees:

Weekday: 18-hole: $5 Cart: $4 9-hole: (N/A) Cart: (N/A)
Weekend: 18-hole: $10 Cart: $4 9-hole: (N/A) Cart: (N/A)

> Located on Hwy 80 in Big Sandy at college, follow signs

Holly Lake Ranch Golf Course (6,700 yds) 903-769-2397

Rt. 1 Box 973
FM 2869
Big Sandy, TX 75755
Contact: Jeff Davis
Description: A rather long 18-hole public course that is very hilly with narrow fairways through pine trees. Few traps and no water but requires hard shots. Nearby houses for rent. **Par:** 72.
Rentals: Golf Carts, Golf Clubs, Driving Range

Open to the public. Walking permitted. Golf lessons available.

Fees:

Weekday: 18-hole: $14 Cart: $9 9-hole: $10 Cart: $6
Weekend: 18-hole: $18 Cart: $9 9-hole: $13 Cart: $6

> From Hwy 80, take FM 14 north five miles to FM 2869.

Big Spring Country Club (6,920 yds) 915-267-5354

P.O. Box 3686
East Driver Road
Big Spring, TX 79721
Contact: Larry Bryan
Description: May be easy to post a good score on this 18-hole private course. The fairways are wide open and putts often fall into the cup on the nice bentgrass greens. **Par:** 71.
Rentals: Golf Carts, Driving Range

Members and guests only. Golf lessons available. Walking permitted.

Fees:

Weekday: 18-hole: $13 Cart: $6.75 9-hole: (N/A) Cart: $3.50
Weekend: 18-hole: $20 Cart: $6.75 9-hole: (N/A) Cart: $3.50

> Located south of town off Hwy 87 to East Driver Road.

Comanche Trail Golf Course　　(6,327 yds)　915-263-7271

800 Commanche Park Road
Big Spring, TX 79720
Contact: Jack Birdwell
Description: A somewhat short 18-hole public course that is more difficult because of hilly and tight fairways, sand traps, and fast bentgrass greens. Clubhouse and pro shop. **Par:** 71.
Rentals: Golf Carts, Pull Carts, Clubs

Open to the public. Walking permitted.

Fees:

Weekday: 18-hole: $9 Cart: $17.50
9-hole: (N/A) Cart: $9
Weekend: 18-hole: $14 Cart: $17.50
9-hole: (N/A) Cart: $9

Located south of town off Hwy 87.

Chemcel Golf Club　　(3,503 yds)　512-584-3511

Business Hwy 77
Bishop, TX 78343
Contact: Roger Edge
Description: This nine-hole private course is open only to Chemcel corporate employees and their guests. The course has out-of-bounds and a creek runs through three holes. **Par:** 36.
Rentals: Driving Range

Fees:

Weekday: 18-hole: $5 Cart: (N/A)
9-hole: (N/A) Cart: (N/A)
Weekend: 18-hole: $5 Cart: (N/A)
9-hole: (N/A) Cart: (N/A)

Located behind the chemical plant in Bishop.

Fair Oaks Ranch Golf & Country Club　　(36 hs)　830-981-9604

7900 Fair Oaks Parkway
Boerne, TX 78006
Contact: Bill Keys
Blackjack Course Description: A 36-hole private club, located northwest of San Antonio. The Blackjack 18 is the longer, tougher, and newer layout, but both courses have plenty of hills, trees, and great views. Huge clubhouse. **Par:** 72 (7,077 yards).
Live Oak Course Description: The Live Oak 18 is the oldest and designed in part by golf legend Gary Player. Live Oak is shorter and may be a stroke easier. **Par:** 72 (6,884 yards).

Rentals: Golf Carts, Pull Carts, Golf Clubs, Driving Range
Members and guests only. Golf lessons available. Walking permitted.

Fees:

Weekday: 18-hole: $55 Cart: $10
9-hole: (N/A) Cart: (N/A)
Weekend: 18-hole: $65 Cart: $10
9-hole: (N/A) Cart: (N/A)

Located approximately 25 miles northwest of San Antonio off I-10. Take Fair Oaks Pkwy exit.

Tapatio Springs Resort & Club   (6,472 yds) 800-999-3299

End of Johns Road, West
Boerne, TX 78006
Contact: Jess Hawkins
Description: A beautiful 18-hole
layout, along with a short executive
course on the side of a mountain.
Hidden Hill Country gem. Large,
well-stocked pro shop and friendly
service. **Par:** 72.
Rentals: Golf Carts, Golf Clubs, Driving
Range

Open to the resort guests. Golf lessons
available.

Fees:

Weekday: 18-hole: $73 Cart: (N/A)
9-hole: (N/A) Cart: (N/A)
Weekend: 18-hole: $83 Cart: (N/A)
9-hole: (N/A) Cart: (N/A)

Located approximately 20 miles
northwest of San Antonio. Take Johns
Road exit West off I-10 and follow signs
five miles to the course

Bonham Golf Course   (3,300 yds) 903-583-8815

500 W. Russell Street
Bonham, TX 75418
Contact: Mark Wright
Description: An old, 1914, rural
nine-hole course that is short but very
tight with seven holes with water, lots
of trees, and slick bentgrass greens.
Visiting golfers OK. **Par:** 35.
Rentals: Golf Carts, Driving Range

Members and guests only. Walking
permitted.

Fees:

Weekday: 18-hole: $9 Cart: $15
9-hole: (N/A) Cart: (N/A)
Weekend: 18-hole: $10 Cart: $15
9-hole: (N/A) Cart: (N/A)

Located off Hwy 121 to Russell Ave.

Booker Country Club   (3,633 yds) 806-658-9663

Highway 15
Booker, TX 79005
Contact: Club Manager
Description: This nine-hole public
course, the northernmost golf course in
Texas, is located in the upper east
corner of the Panhandle. The course is
reasonably long. First come/first serve.
Par: 36.
Rentals: Golf Carts, Pull Carts

Open to the public. Walking permitted.

Fees:

Weekday: 18-hole: $4.50 Cart: $5
9-hole: (N/A) Cart: (N/A)
Weekend: 18-hole: $6 Cart: $5 9-hole:
(N/A) Cart: (N/A)

Located off Hwy 15 in Booker.

Huber Golf Course (6,199 yds) 806-273-2231

Broadmore Street
Borger, TX 79007-2831
Contact: Richard M. Hale
Description: One of the shortest 18-hole public courses in the Panhandle. The greens are bentgrass with lots of trees and traps. Clubhouse has a snack bar and pro shop. **Par:** 72.
Rentals: Golf Carts, Pull Carts, Driving Range

Open to the public. Walking permitted. Golf lessons available.

Fees:

Weekday: 18-hole: $9.50 Cart: $16
9-hole: $6 Cart: $11
Weekend: 18-hole: $13.75 Cart: $16
9-hole: $9 Cart: $11

Located 4½ miles south of town.

Phillips Municipal Golf Course (6,300 yds) 806-274-6812

1609 N. Sterling Street
Borger, TX 79007
Contact: Larry Joe Reed
Description: One of the easier 18-hole public courses in the Panhandle with few traps, wide fairways, and short holes. Clubhouse recently remodeled. Pro shop. **Par:** 72.
Rentals: Golf Carts, Pull Carts, Golf Clubs, Driving Range

Open to the public. Walking permitted. Golf lessons available.

Fees:

Weekday: 18-hole: $9.50 Cart: $16
9-hole: $6 Cart: $11
Weekend: 18-hole: $13.75 Cart: $16
9-hole: $9 Cart: $11

Located on the northwest side of town off Hwy 207 at Country Club Road.

Top-O-The-Lake Country Club (6,400 yds) 940-872-5401

Route 2 Box 829
Bowie, TX 76230
Contact: Ken Rhoades
Description: A short nine-hole semiprivate course that is open to the public on weekdays. The greens are championship bermuda and good putting is vital to shoot a low score. **Par:** 35.
Rentals: Golf Carts, Pull Carts, Golf Clubs, Driving Range

Open to the public. Walking permitted. Golf lessons available.

Fees:

Weekday: 18-hole: $10 Cart: $8
9-hole: (N/A) Cart: $4
Weekend: 18-hole: (N/A) Cart: (N/A)
9-hole: (N/A) Cart: (N/A)

Located off Hwy 287 to FM 1125.

Fort Clark Springs Country Club   (5,752 yds) 830-563-9204

345 Fort Clark Road
Brackettville, TX 78832
Contact: Bob De La Rossa
Description: It may be easy to post a good score on this short 18-hole semiprivate course with flat fairways, no water, and few bunkers. Out-of-bounds can add penalty strokes. **Par:** 70.
Rentals: Golf Carts, Pull Carts, Golf Clubs

Open to the public. Walking permitted.

Fees:

Weekday: 18-hole: $14 Cart: $16
9-hole: $9 Cart: $8
Weekend: 18-hole: $18 Cart: $16
9-hole: $9 Cart: $8

Located off Hwy 90 in Bracketville

Brady Municipal Country Club   (5,815 yds) 915-597-6010

Highway 87 West
Brady, TX 76825
Contact: Wendell Frankie
Description: A short nine-hole public course with small bentgrass greens and narrow doglegs demanding shots over corner trees and water. Clubhouse has nice pro shop. **Par:** 36.
Rentals: Golf Carts, Pull Carts, Golf Clubs, Driving Range

Open to the public. Walking permitted.
Golf lessons available.

Fees:

Weekday: 18-hole: $8 Cart: $8 9-hole: $5 Cart: $4
Weekend: 18-hole: $12 Cart: $8
9-hole: $7 Cart: $4

Located northwest of town on Hwy 87.

Breckenridge Country Club   (6,614 yds) 254-559-3466

W. Walker Street
Breckenridge, TX 76424
Contact: Paul Blackerby
Description: A nine-hole public course that has a rare par-6 hole in Texas. It is 625 yards into the wind. Clubhouse has a snack bar and pro shop. **Par:** 36.
Rentals: Golf Carts, Golf Clubs, Driving Range

Open to the public. Walking permitted.
Golf lessons available.

Fees:

Weekday: 18-hole: $8.08 Cart: $6.09
9-hole: (N/A) Cart: $3
Weekend: 18-hole: $10.75 Cart: $6.09 9-hole: (N/A) Cart: $3

Located just west of the city, south of Hwy 180.

Brenham Country Club   (6,789 yds) 409-836-1733

P.O. Box 223
Brenham, TX 77833
Contact: Mark Gray
Description: A former nine-hole
private course that added a new nine.
Small greens, ponds, and mounds.
Private club members from out of town
welcome. **Par:** 72.
Members and guests only. Golf lessons
available. Walking permitted.

Fees:

Weekday: 18-hole: $15 Cart: $9
9-hole: (N/A) Cart: (N/A)
Weekend: 18-hole: $20 Cart: $9
9-hole: (N/A) Cart: (N/A)

Take Hwy 290 to 105.

Bridgeport Golf & Country Club   (5,983 yds) 940-683-9438

P.O. Box 305
Bridgeport, TX 76426
Contact: Lonny Benham
Description: A short nine-hole course
open to the public on weekdays. Scenic
lake views. Clubhouse has a bar, pro
shop, and meeting rooms. **Par:** 35.
Rentals: Golf Carts, Pull Carts, Golf
Clubs, Driving Range

Open to the public. Walking permitted.
Golf lessons available.

Fees:

Weekday: 18-hole: $10.68 Cart: $16
9-hole: $8 Cart: $8
Weekend: 18-hole: (N/A) Cart: (N/A)
9-hole: (N/A) Cart: (N/A)

Located off Hwy 114 to FM 2123.

Club at Runaway Bay   (6,900 yds) 940-575-2228

400 Half Moon Way
Bridgeport, TX 76426
Contact: Randy Brittain
Description: Your score on the front
nine may be better than the back nine
since there are lots of out-of-bounds on
the back side. New owners improving
all facilities. **Par:** 71.
Rentals: Golf Carts, Pull Carts, Golf
Clubs, Driving Range

Open to the public. Walking permitted.
Golf lessons available.

Fees:

Weekday: 18-hole: $32.48 Cart: (N/A)
9-hole: $15 Cart: $4.50
Weekend: 18-hole: $54.93 Cart: (N/A)
9-hole: $20 Cart: $4.50

Located six miles west of Bridgeport on
Hwy 380.

Singing Winds Golf Course

(2,896 yds) 915-473-2156

County Park Road
Bronte, TX 76933
Contact: Debra Ingram
Description: A nine-hole public course located in retirement village. Designed to let seniors play well, thanks to short holes, no traps, and rolling hills. **Par:** 36.
Rentals: Golf Carts, Pull Carts, Golf Clubs, Driving Range

Open to the public. Walking permitted. Golf lessons available.

Fees:

Weekday: 18-hole: $5 Cart: $12
9-hole: (N/A) Cart: $6
Weekend: 18-hole: $10 Cart: $12
9-hole: (N/A) Cart: $6

Located on Hwy 277 halfway between Abilene and San Angelo in city park.

Brownfield Country Club

(3,187 yds) 806-637-3656

Tahoka Highway
Brownfield, TX 79316
Contact: Chuck Fletcher
Description: Even though there are double tees on this nine-hole semi-private course, it is possible to shoot a good score thanks to few trees, flat fairways, bentgrass greens, and one water hazard. **Par:** 36.
Rentals: Golf Carts, Driving Range

Open to the public. Walking permitted.

Fees:

Weekday: 18-hole: $9.50 Cart: $8.50
9-hole: (N/A) Cart: $4.25
Weekend: 18-hole: $13.50 Cart: $8.50 9-hole: (N/A) Cart: $4.25

Located east of town, south of U.S. 380 (Tahoka Hwy).

Brownsville Country Club

(6,050 yds) 956-541-2582

1800 W. San Marcelo
Brownsville, TX 78520
Contact: Scott Blundell
Description: Recreation is quite common on this 18-hole public course because it is a short course with some water, and the center also offers tennis, games, and a sauna to relax and have fun. **Par:** 70.
Rentals: Golf Carts, Pull Carts, Golf Clubs

Open to the public. Walking permitted. Golf lessons available.

Fees:

Weekday: 18-hole: $8.50 Cart: $8
9-hole: (N/A) Cart: $4
Weekend: 18-hole: $8.50 Cart: $8
9-hole: (N/A) Cart: $4

Located off FM 802 to San Marcelo.

Fort Brown Municipal Golf Course   (6,072 yds) 956-541-0394

P.O. Box 3027
Brownsville, TX 78520
Contact: Robert Lucio
Description: The fairways were renovated, making them smoother and dry. That means your drive goes longer on the ground of the wide fairways. Food. **Par:** 72.
Rentals: Golf Carts, Pull Carts, Golf Clubs, Driving Range

Open to the public. Walking permitted. Golf lessons available.

Fees:

Weekday: 18-hole: $7.50 Cart: $8
9-hole: (N/A) Cart: $4
Weekend: 18-hole: $7.50 Cart: $8
9-hole: (N/A) Cart: $4

Located off International Bridge on Elizabeth St.

River Bend Resort & Country Club   (6,828 yds) 956-548-0192

Route 8, Box 649
Brownsville, TX 78520
Contact: Eric Christensen
Description: This 18-hole public course is next to the Rio Grande. Golfers who hit hooks may hit their ball into Mexico. With 14 water holes on a pretty long course, it's a tough test. **Par:** 72.
Rentals: Golf Carts, Pull Carts, Golf Clubs, Driving Range

Open to the public. Walking permitted. Golf lessons available.

Fees:

Weekday: 18-hole: $18.33 Cart: $9.17 9-hole: $13.75 Cart: $6.87
Weekend: 18-hole: $23.91 Cart: $9.17 9-hole: $13.75 Cart: $6.87

Located on Hwy 281 North.

Valley Inn & Country Club   (6,538 yds) 956-546-5331

300 Country Club Drive
Brownsville, TX 78520
Contact: Jerry Klinger
Description: Lots of trees, sand traps, and water on this mid-length semiprivate course. Mandatory carts December through March. Out-of-bounds causes penalty strokes. Food and drinks. **Par:** 70.

Open to the public. Walking permitted at certain times. Golf lessons available.

Fees:

Weekday: 18-hole: $13.25 Cart: $10.57 9-hole: $5 Cart: $8
Weekend: 18-hole: $16.50 Cart: $10.83 9-hole: $5 Cart: $8

Located north on FM 802.

Brownwood Country Club (6,228 yds) 915-646-1086

Country Club Road
Brownwood, TX 76804
Contact: Steve McNabb
Description: A short 18-hole private course constructed around a lake with bentgrass greens. Par is 35 on the front nine and 37 on the back nine. Food and drinks. **Par:** 72.
Rentals: Golf Carts, Golf Clubs, Driving Range

Members and guests only. Golf lessons available. Walking permitted.

Fees:

Weekday: 18-hole: $20 Cart: $8
9-hole: $12 Cart: $5
Weekend: 18-hole: $25 Cart: $8
9-hole: $15 Cart: $5

Located south of town on Hwy 377.

Briarcrest Country Club (6,783 yds) 409-776-1490

1929 Country Club Drive
Bryan, TX 77802
Contact: Jim Bear
Description: Rolling hills and lots of trees, traps, and a creek make this 18-hole private course tough. The creek crosses five holes. Modern clubhouse. **Par:** 72.
Rentals: Golf Carts, Pull Carts, Golf Clubs, Driving Range

Members and guests only. Golf lessons available. Walking permitted.

Fees:

Weekday: 18-hole: $20 Cart: $9.50
9-hole: (N/A) Cart: $5.50
Weekend: 18-hole: $30 Cart: $9.50
9-hole: (N/A) Cart: $5.50

Located near College Station off Hwy 6 East bypass.

Bryan Municipal Golf Course (6,228 yds) 409-823-0126

206 West Villa Maria
Bryan, TX 77801
Contact: Billy Bob Lane
Description: An 18-hole public course built in 1925. It is short but has lots of water, trees, hills, and small undulating greens. Par-3 third is signature hole. **Par:** 70.
Rentals: Golf Carts, Pull Carts, Golf Clubs, Driving Range

Open to the public. Walking permitted. Golf lessons available.

Fees:

Weekday: 18-hole: $15 Cart: $10
9-hole: (N/A) Cart: (N/A)
Weekend: 18-hole: $18 Cart: $10
9-hole: (N/A) Cart: (N/A)

Located off Hwy 6 to West Villa Maria one mile.

Highland Lakes Golf Course

(3,200 yds) 512-793-2859

P.O. Box 194
Buchanan Dam, TX 78609
Contact: Johnny Tyson
Description: Slicers and hookers will always hit tee shots into Inks Lake, which guards all nine holes. No traps but small greens. **Par:** 36.
Rentals: Golf Carts, Pull Carts, Golf Clubs
Open to the public. Walking permitted. Golf lessons available.

Fees:

Weekday: 18-hole: $10 Cart: $6
9-hole: (N/A) Cart: $6
Weekend: 18-hole: $12 Cart: $6
9-hole: (N/A) Cart: $6

> Located northwest of Austin, nine miles west of Burnet on Hwy 29 in state park.

Emerald Bay Club

(6,622 yds) 903-825-3444

208 S. Bay
Bullard, TX 75757
Contact: Tom Campbell
Description: A long 18-hole private course that has a fairly open front nine and a tight, hilly back nine. Bentgrass greens. The clubhouse was recently expanded. **Par:** 71.
Rentals: Golf Carts, Driving Range

Members and guests only. Golf lessons available. Walking permitted.

Fees:

Weekday: 18-hole: $15 Cart: $18
9-hole: (N/A) Cart: $9
Weekend: 18-hole: $20 Cart: $18
9-hole: (N/A) Cart: $9

> Located south of Tyler from Hwy 155 to FM 344 on Lake Palestine.

Peach Tree Golf Club

(36 hs) 903-894-7079

County Road 152 West
Bullard, TX 75757
Contact: Darrell Chase
Oak Hurst Course Description: The
expansion of Peach Tree Golf Club has
added a longer 18-hole course with lots
of water, large, easy-to-three-putt
greens, and traps. **Par:** 72 (6,813
yards).

Peach Tree Course Description: An
18-hole semiprivate course which
opened a new 18 holes in August
1993. Peach Tree's original 18 holes is
a short course good for beginners and
seniors. Great East Texas setting with
trees. **Par:** 70 (5,556 yards).

Contact: Darrell Chase
Rentals: Golf Carts, Pull Carts, Golf
Clubs, Driving Range
Open to the public. Walking permitted.
Golf lessons available.

Fees:

Weekday: 18-hole: $18.50 Cart: $10
9-hole: (N/A) Cart: $5
Weekend: 18-hole: $26.50 Cart: $10
9-hole: (N/A) Cart: $5

> Take Hwy 69 south off Loop 323 in
> Tyler. Courses are nine miles south of
> Loop at Hwy 69 and County Road 152
> West.

River Creek Golf Course

(6,727 yds) 940-855-3361

FM 1177
Burkburnett, TX 76354
Contact: Tom Swiney
Description: An 18-hole public course
that has the front nine alongside the
Red River. Golfers can see Oklahoma.
Open fairways and no traps but hilly
holes. Food, drinks, and pro shop.
Par: 70.
Rentals: Golf Carts, Pull Carts, Golf
Clubs, Driving Range

Open to the public. Walking permitted.
Golf lessons available.

Fees:

Weekday: 18-hole: $8 Cart: $10
9-hole: (N/A) Cart: $5
Weekend: 18-hole: $9.05 Cart: $10
9-hole: (N/A) Cart: $5

> Located on FM 1177 South near
> Texas-Oklahoma border.

Hidden Creek Golf Course   (6,743 yds) 817-447-4444

700 S. Burleson Blvd.
Burleson, Texas, 76028
Contact: Andy Franks
Description: New daily-fee course opened in January 1997. Steve Plummer design features lush bentgrass greens. The 6,743-yard layout is lined by thick trees which provide a narrow landing path on some shots. **Par:** 71.
Rentals: Golf Carts, Pull Carts, Golf Clubs, Driving Range

Open to the public. Walking permitted. Golf lessons available.

Fees:

Weekday: 18-hole: $25 Cart: $20
9-hole: (N/A) Cart: $10
Weekend: 18-hole: $35 Cart: $20
9-hole: (N/A) Cart: $10

Located south of Fort Worth off I-35 W at Renfro.

Delaware Springs Golf Course   (6,817 yds) 512-756-8471

127 E. Jackson
Burnet, TX 78611
Contact: Al Pryor
Description: A nice public 18-hole course which is very challenging because it is 6,817 yards long. Also very pretty. Rustic clubhouse, restaurant, and pro shop. **Par:** 72.
Rentals: Golf Carts, Pull Carts, Golf Clubs, Driving Range

Open to the public. Walking permitted. Golf lessons available.

Fees:

Weekday: 18-hole: $40 Cart: (N/A)
9-hole: (N/A) Cart: (N/A)
Weekend: 18-hole: $55 Cart: (N/A)
9-hole: (N/A) Cart: (N/A)

Take Hwy 29 exit off I-35 west to Burnet; course is just off Hwy 281 S.

Copperas Hollow Country Club   (6,400 yds) 409-567-4422

Highway 26
P.O. Box 316A
Caldwell, TX 77836
Contact: David McNeely
Description: A nine-hole private course that allows out-of-town golfers to play on weekdays. Well-maintained course with trees, creeks, and big greens. Food and drinks. **Par:** 36.
Rentals: Golf Carts, Pull Carts, Golf Clubs, Driving Range

Members and guests only. Walking permitted.

Fees:

Weekday: 18-hole: $10 Cart: $8
9-hole: $4 Cart: $4
Weekend: 18-hole: $12 Cart: $8
9-hole: (N/A) Cart: $4

Located southwest of Bryan on Hwy 26.

Calvert Country Club   (3,327 yds) 409-364-8803

P.O. Box 244
Calvert, TX 77837
Contact: Golf Shop
Description: Small, challenging
nine-hole layout through trees on this
Brazos Valley site. Keep the ball in the
fairway or you could have plenty of
trouble. **Par:** 35.
Rentals: Golf Carts

Fees:

Weekday: 18-hole: $15 Cart: $10
9-hole: (N/A) Cart: (N/A)
Weekend: 18-hole: $20 Cart: $5
9-hole: (N/A) Cart: (N/A)

Take Calvert Rd. east off Main St. past
railroad station to course.

Cameron Country Club   (5,562 yds) 254-697-2371

Marlow Road
Cameron, TX 76520
Contact: C.E. Woodum
Description: A rather tight nine-hole
private course that has four holes over
water, small greens, traps, and rolling
fairways. Food and drinks. **Par:** 35.
Rentals: Golf Carts, Driving Range
Members and guests only. Walking
permitted.

Fees:

Weekday: 18-hole: $10 Cart: $20
9-hole: (N/A) Cart: $11
Weekend: 18-hole: $10 Cart: $20
9-hole: (N/A) Cart: $11

Located off Hwy 77 east on 22nd St. to
Marlow Road.

Canadian Golf Course   (6,306 yds) 806-323-5512

P.O. Box 1
Highway 83
Canadian, TX 79014
Contact: Kirk Morrow
Description: Golfers playing this
nine-hole public course face lots of
blind tee shots, tough second shots over
trees, and out-of-bounds. Bentgrass
greens and only two traps. Food and
pro shop. **Par:** 36.

Rentals: Golf Carts, Pull Carts, Golf
Clubs
Open to the public. Walking permitted.
Golf lessons available.

Fees:

Weekday: 18-hole: $10 Cart: $16
9-hole: $6 Cart: $8
Weekend: 18-hole: $12 Cart: $16
9-hole: $6 Cart: $8

Located on Hwy 83 North.

Van Zandt Country Club   (6,760 yds) 903-567-2336

I-20 Service Road
Canton, TX 75103
Contact: Ed Gatlin
Description: Excellent golf course east of Dallas. Clubhouse has pro shop and food. Very visible course from interstate between Dallas and Tyler. **Par:** 72.
Rentals: Golf Carts, Pull Carts, Golf Clubs, Driving Range

Members and guests only. Golf lessons available. Walking permitted.

Fees:

Weekday: 18-hole: $21.75 Cart: $16.25 9-hole: (N/A) Cart: $9
Weekend: 18-hole: $32.50 Cart: $16.25 9-hole: (N/A) Cart: $9

Located ½ mile from Canton on I-20 service road.

Canyon Country Club   (5,838 yds) 806-499-3397

Route 1 Box 213
Canyon, TX 79015
Contact: Larry Squier
Description: A short nine-hole public course constructed in the bottom of a canyon with lots of slopes, trees, and small greens. Food, drinks, and pro shop. **Par:** 35.
Rentals: Golf Carts, Pull Carts, Golf Clubs, Driving Range

Open to the public. Walking permitted. Golf lessons available.

Fees:

Weekday: 18-hole: $10.65 Cart: $8 9-hole: (N/A) Cart: $4
Weekend: 18-hole: $12.75 Cart: $8 9-hole: (N/A) Cart: $4

Located four miles west of Canyon on Hwy 60.

Palo Duro Creek Golf Course   (6,900 yds) 806-655-1106

50 Country Club Drive
Canyon, TX 79015
Contact: Emil Hale
Description: The front nine is easier, but the back nine has a lot of water and fast greens. Posting a good score requires good back nine shots. Food and drinks. **Par:** 72.
Rentals: Golf Carts, Pull Carts, Golf Clubs, Driving Range

Open to the public. Walking permitted. Golf lessons available.

Fees:

Weekday: 18-hole: $9.65 Cart: $8.66 9-hole: (N/A) Cart: $4.29
Weekend: 18-hole: $11.80 Cart: $8.66 9-hole: (N/A) Cart: $4.29

Located off I-27 to Hunsley Hills Road.

Canyon Lake Golf & Country Club   (6,132 yds) 830-899-3372

405 Watts Lane
P.O. Box 185K
Canyon Lake, TX 78133
Contact: Don Aken
Description: An 18-hole public course surrounding Canyon Lake with ponds formed from the lake. Narrow fairways with undulating greens. Great Canyon Lake views. **Par:** 72.
Rentals: Golf Carts, Pull Carts, Golf Clubs, Driving Range

Open to the public. Walking permitted. Golf lessons available.

Fees:

Weekday: 18-hole: $22.95 Cart: $7
9-hole: $9 Cart: $5.50
Weekend: 18-hole: $26.95 Cart: $7
9-hole: $11 Cart: $5.50

Located 14 miles north of New Braunfels on FM 3159.

Carrizo Springs Municipal Course   (3,420 yds) 830-876-2596

Highway 85
P.O. Box 44
Carrizo Springs, TX 78834
Contact: Lester Wetzeg
Description: A rather long nine-hole public course with lots of trees, water on all nine holes, large greens, and no sand traps. Clubhouse has a good pro shop. **Par:** 36.
Rentals: Golf Carts, Pull Carts, Golf Clubs, Driving Range

Open to the public. Walking permitted.

Fees:

Weekday: 18-hole: $9 Cart: $8 9-hole: (N/A) Cart: $4
Weekend: 18-hole: $14 Cart: $8
9-hole: (N/A) Cart: $4

Located on Hwy 85 south of the town's airport.

Columbian Country Club   (6,760 yds) 972-416-6496

2525 Country Club Drive
Carrollton, TX 75006
Contact: Tom Strueber
Description: Lee Trevino was a construction worker at Columbian before he turned pro. The course is hilly and filled with water. Clubhouse is very nice. **Par:** 71.
Rentals: Golf Carts, Golf Clubs, Driving Range

Members and guests only. Golf lessons available. Walking permitted.

Fees:

Weekday: 18-hole: $50 Cart: $10
9-hole: (N/A) Cart: $6
Weekend: 18-hole: $75 Cart: $10
9-hole: (N/A) Cart: $6

Located north of Belt Line on Columbian Road to Country Club Drive.

Country Place Golf Club   (1,100 yds) 972-416-0660

2727 Country Place
Carrollton, TX 75006
Contact: Duff Stammer
Description: Very good par-3 course in
Dallas area. Most holes are between
100 and 138 yards, but the fourth hole
is 210 yards over water. Course is
private club for Country Place home
owners. **Par:** 27.

Members and guests only. Golf lessons
available. Walking permitted.

Fees:

Weekday: 18-hole: $6 Cart: (N/A)
9-hole: $6 Cart: (N/A)
Weekend: 18-hole: $8 Cart: (N/A)
9-hole: $8 Cart: (N/A)

Located off Marsh Lane.

Coyote Ridge Golf Club   (6,795 yds) 972-939-0666

1680 Bandera Road
Carrollton, TX 75010
Contact: Devin Thomas
Description: New Dallas area course
scheduled to open in summer of 1999.
Trees with some elevation change over
scenic Denton County landscape. Water
on seven holes including par 4 ninth
hole, which is surrounded on three
sides. **Par:** 71.

Rentals: Golf Cart, Golf Clubs

Fees:

Weekday: 18-hole: $49 w/ cart 9-hole:
(N/A)
Weekend: 18-hole: $59 w/ cart
9-hole: (N/A)

Located east of Vista Ridge Mall off
Hebron Pkwy. on Bandera Rd.

Indian Creek Golf Course

(36 hs) 972-492-3620

1650 E. Frankford Road
Carrollton, TX 75011
Contact: Steve Hibbison
Creek Course Description: The Creek Course was the original course. Creeks replace the lakes as water hazards and come into play on 14 holes. Back nine is really special with public golf at its best. Nice clubhouse. **Par:** 72 (7,218 yards).
Rentals: Golf Carts, Pull Carts, Golf Clubs, Driving Range
Open to the public. Walking permitted. Golf lessons available.

Fees:

Weekday: 18-hole: $20 Cart: NA
9-hole: (N/A) Cart: $10
Weekend: 18-hole: $29 Cart: NA
9-hole: (N/A) Cart: $10

Lakes Course Description: Part of a strong 36-hole public course with so much water on the Lakes Course, it's a great round not to lose any golf balls. **Par:** 72 (7,060 yards).

Fees:

Weekday: 18-hole: $20 Cart: NA
9-hole: (N/A) Cart: (N/A)
Weekend: 18-hole: $29 Cart: NA
9-hole: (N/A) Cart: (N/A)

Located north of Trinity Mills Road, and just east of I-35E.

Carthage Country Club

(6,341 yds) 903-693-9062

Highway 59
Carthage, TX 75633
Contact: L.H. Chandler/ J.W. Thompson
Description: Water dominates this nine-hole private course. The par-3 second hole is an island green. There are four lakes, traps, and trees. Out-of-town golfers welcome. **Par:** 36. Members and guests only. Walking permitted.

Fees:

Weekday: 18-hole: $15 Cart: $16
9-hole: (N/A) Cart: $8
Weekend: 18-hole: $15 Cart: $16
9-hole: (N/A) Cart: $8

Located on Hwy 59 31 miles south of Marshall.

Alsatian Golf Course   (6,835 yds) 830-931-3100

County Road 4516
Castroville, TX 78009
Contact: Richard Russell
Description: Charming public course in historic Hill Country town. Course owned by local golfers who felt town needed golf outlet. Back nine tougher than front, with water, trees, and out-of-bounds factors. **Par:** 72.
Rentals: Golf Carts, Pull Carts, Driving Range

Open to the public. Walking permitted. Golf lessons available.

Fees:

Weekday: 18-hole: $25 Cart: (N/A)
9-hole: (N/A) Cart: (N/A)
Weekend: 18-hole: $30 Cart: (N/A)
9-hole: (N/A) Cart: (N/A)

> Located one mile west of Castroville. Turn right at blinking traffic light, then turn left on FM 4516 to Quihi Road.

Center Country Club   (6,438 yds) 409-598-5513

P.O. Box 2106
Highway 96 North
Center, TX 75935
Contact: Joe Whittlesey
Description: A nice nine-hole private course with double tees and two lakes on the course. In excellent condition with hilly fairways and trees. Clubhouse has food, drinks, and pro shop. **Par:** 36.
Rentals: Golf Carts, Pull Carts, Golf Clubs, Driving Range

Members and guests only. Golf lessons available. Walking permitted.

Fees:

Weekday: 18-hole: $21.55 Cart: $8
9-hole: (N/A) Cart: $6
Weekend: 18-hole: $31.19 Cart: $8
9-hole: (N/A) Cart: $6

> Located on Hwy 96 north of town.

Channelview Golf Course   (6,214 yds) 281-452-2183

8306 Sheldon Road
Channelview, TX 77530
Contact: Damon LaBouve
Description: Wide, flat fairways with not many trees make this 18-hole public course play well. There are three lakes and sand traps. Snack bar and pro shop. **Par:** 72.
Rentals: Golf Carts, Pull Carts, Golf Clubs, Driving Range

Open to the public. Walking permitted.

Fees:

Weekday: 18-hole: $10 Cart: $8
9-hole: (N/A) Cart: $4
Weekend: 18-hole: $16 Cart: $8
9-hole: (N/A) Cart: $4

> Located on Sheldon Road north of I-10 east of Houston.

Childress Country Club   (3,330 yds)   940-937-8552

Route 1 Box 125A
Childress, TX 79201
Contact: Clint Crawford
Description: One of the easier nine-hole courses in area. Very short with flat, wide fairways, bentgrass greens, and only one water hazard. Pro shop and 19th hole bar. **Par:** 35.
Rentals: Golf Carts

Members and guests only. Walking permitted.

Fees:

Weekday: 18-hole: $5 Cart: $7 9-hole: (N/A) Cart: $3.50
Weekend: 18-hole: $10 Cart: $7 9-hole: (N/A) Cart: $3.50

Located northwest of town on Hwy 83.

Northcliffe Country Club   (6,532 yds)   830-606-7351

5301 Country Club Blvd.
Cibolo, TX 78108
Contact: Ken Whitaker
Description: Every green on this 18-hole semiprivate course is protected by sand traps. The back nine is rolling with water on five holes. Friendly staff. **Par:** 72.
Rentals: Golf Carts, Golf Clubs, Driving Range

Open to the public. Walking permitted. Golf lessons available.

Fees:

Weekday: 18-hole: $20 Cart: (N/A) 9-hole: (N/A) Cart: (N/A)
Weekend: 18-hole: $29 Cart: (N/A) 9-hole: (N/A) Cart: (N/A)

Take I-35 to exit 178 in Cibolo. Course is to the right on access road.

Lake Cisco Country Club   (2,598 yds)   254-442-2725

P.O. Box 389
Cisco, TX 76437
Contact: Tonya Vaughn
Description: A very short nine-hole golf course that attracts a lot of senior golfers who enjoy it. No par 5s, no water, and no sand traps. Snacks available. **Par:** 34.
Rentals: Golf Carts, Pull Carts
Open to the public. Walking permitted. Golf lessons available.

Fees:

Weekday: 18-hole: $8 Cart: $7 9-hole: $5 Cart: $3
Weekend: 18-hole: $10 Cart: $7 9-hole: $5 Cart: $3

Located three miles north of Cisco on Hwy 6.

Clarendon Country Club   (6,745 yds) 806-874-2166

Star Route 2 Box 48A
Clarendon, TX 79226
Contact: Nobel Watson
Description: A hilly 18-hole public
course with lots of trees, wide fairways,
and not a lot of sand traps. Food,
drinks, and pro shop. **Par:** 72.
Rentals: Golf Carts, Pull Carts, Driving
Range
Open to the public. Walking permitted.
Golf lessons available.

Fees:

Weekday: 18-hole: $8 Cart: $15
9-hole: $9 Cart: $7.50
Weekend: 18-hole: $10 Cart: $15
9-hole: $9 Cart: $7.50

Located five miles north of Hwy 70 next
to Lake Greenbelt on Country Club
Drive.

Clarksville Country Club   (6,129 yds) 903-427-3450

P.O. Box 801
Clarksville, TX 75426
Contact: Allan Norton
Description: A traditonal nine-hole
semiprivate course with double tees
that make a second nine longer. Lots of
trees, small greens, and no sand traps.
Out-of-county golfers welcome. **Par:** 36.
Rentals: Golf Carts, Driving Range

Open to the public. Walking permitted.
Golf lessons available.

Fees:

Weekday: 18-hole: $10.68 Cart:
$7.50 9-hole: (N/A) Cart: $5
Weekend: 18-hole: $16 Cart: $7.50
9-hole: (N/A) Cart: $5

Located on Hwy 37 north of town.

Pat Cleburne Municipal Golf Course (6,326 yds) 817-645-9078

2500 Country Club Road
Cleburne, TX 76031
Contact: Ronnie O. Humphrey
Description: A short 18-hole rural
public course that is not too difficult
because there are no trees, no sand
traps, and wide fairways. **Par:** 71.
Rentals: Golf Carts, Pull Carts, Golf
Clubs
Open to the public. Walking permitted.
Golf lessons available.

Fees:

Weekday: 18-hole: $8 Cart: $8 9-hole:
(N/A) Cart: $4
Weekend: 18-hole: $10 Cart: $8
9-hole: (N/A) Cart: $4

Located by Lake Pat Cleburne, three
miles off Hwy 67.

Riverview Golf Club (6,605 yds) 817-641-2580

2501 S. Nolan River Road
Cleburne, TX 76031
Contact: Scott Aten
Description: A nice 18-hole semiprivate golf course with wide fairways, some sand traps, and good greens. 13 holes have Buffalo Creek trouble. **Par:** 72.
Rentals: Golf Carts, Golf Clubs, Driving Range

Open to the public. Walking permitted.

Fees:

Weekday: 18-hole: $23 Cart: $9
9-hole: $9.48 Cart: $4.50
Weekend: 18-hole: $28 Cart: $9
9-hole: $9.48 Cart: $4.50

Located three miles south of Hwy 67 on Nolan River Road.

Kirbywood Golf (6,500 yds) 281-593-3303

P.O. 657
Cleveland, TX 77328
Contact: Jay Dugas
Description: An excellent nine-hole public course that is tight with tall pine and oak trees, double tees, and rolling hills. Food, drinks, and pro shop. **Par:** 36.
Rentals: Golf Carts, Golf Clubs, Driving Range

Open to the public. Walking permitted. Golf lessons available.

Fees:

Weekday: 18-hole: $8 Cart: $10
9-hole: (N/A) Cart: $5
Weekend: 18-hole: $10 Cart: $10
9-hole: (N/A) Cart: $5

Located north of Houston on Hwy 59, FM 321 at Kirbywood.

Cape Royale Golf Club (6,200 yds) 409-653-2388

FM 224
P.O. Box 1670
Coldspring, TX 77331
Contact: Paul Hendrix
Description: This 18-hole public course is short, but the fairways are tight and hilly. The course is on Lake Livingston, which provides a lot of water hazards. Snack bar, drinks, and pro shop. **Par:** 70.
Rentals: Golf Carts, Pull Carts, Golf Clubs, Driving Range

Open to the public. Walking permitted. Golf lessons available.

Fees:

Weekday: 18-hole: $17.50 Cart: $19
9-hole: (N/A) Cart: $10
Weekend: 18-hole: $22.50 Cart: $19
9-hole: (N/A) Cart: $10

Located off Hwy 156, five miles from town on FM 224.

Coleman Country Club

(6,140 yds) 915-625-2922

206 San Angelo Hwy
Coleman, TX 76834
Contact: Dany Birdwell
Description: All golfers will have a lot of fun on this nine-hole public course thanks to short holes, no water hazards, and small one-putt greens. Snack bar and pro shop. **Par:** 36.
Rentals: Golf Carts, Pull Carts, Golf Clubs

Open to the public. Walking permitted.

Fees:

Weekday: 18-hole: $10 Cart: $7
9-hole: $8 Cart: $4
Weekend: 18-hole: $12 Cart: $7
9-hole: $10 Cart: $4

Located five miles south of town.

Pebble Creek Country Club

(6,513 yds) 409-690-0990

4500 Pebble Creek Parkway
College Station, TX 77845
Contact: Jim Baetge
Description: First-class country club, one of the best between Dallas and Houston area for a private course. Built in a creek bottom with lots of trees and large undulating greens. New clubhouse completes super setup. **Par:** 72.
Rentals: Golf Carts, Golf Clubs, Driving Range

Members and guests only. Golf lessons available. Walking permitted.

Fees:

Weekday: 18-hole: $20 Cart: $9
9-hole: $10 Cart: $4.50
Weekend: 18-hole: $30 Cart: $9
9-hole: $15 Cart: $4.50

Located north of Bryan off Hwy 6. Go east on Greens Prairie Road for one mile; turn right into Pebble Creek development.

Texas A&M Golf Course

(6,532 yds) 409-845-1723

Bizzella Street
College Station, TX 77843
Contact: Johnny Andrews
Description: The five par 3s on this 18-hole public course are considered to be very tough because they are long with small greens. Water hazards on nine holes. Open fairways with live oak trees. Food and pro shop. **Par:** 70.
Rentals: Golf Carts, Pull Carts, Golf Clubs

Open to the public. Walking permitted.

Fees:

Weekday: 18-hole: $13 Cart: $8
9-hole: (N/A) Cart: $5
Weekend: 18-hole: $16 Cart: $8
9-hole: (N/A) Cart: $5

Located on Texas A&M campus just off University Drive.

Wolf Creek Golf Course

(6,900 yds) 915-728-5514

Route 3 Box 445
Colorado City, TX 79512
Contact: Abel Alvarez
Description: Looking at the scorecard, golfers would think they would dominate this short nine-hole course. However, there are out-of-bounds and five creeks to make it tough. **Par:** 35.
Rentals: Golf Carts, Pull Carts, Golf Clubs, Driving Range

Open to the public. Walking permitted. Golf lessons available.

Fees:

Weekday: 18-hole: $12 Cart: $7.50
9-hole: $5 Cart: $3.75
Weekend: 18-hole: $16 Cart: $7.50
9-hole: $7.50 Cart: $3.75

Located east of town off I-20 on Country Club Road.

Columbus Golf Course

(5,620 yds) 409-732-5575

1617 Walnut St.
Columbus, TX 78934
Contact: Jeff Steger
Description: Six holes of this nine-hole public course have water hazards, and there are lots of trees on the tight, flat fairways but no traps. Small greens. Food and drinks. **Par:** 35.
Rentals: Golf Carts, Pull Carts

Open to the public. Walking permitted. Golf lessons available.

Fees:

Weekday: 18-hole: $10 Cart: $5
9-hole: (N/A) Cart: $6.50
Weekend: 18-hole: $15 Cart: $5
9-hole: (N/A) Cart: $7.55

Located on I-10 west of Houston.

P.A.R. Country Club

(6,300 yds) 254-879-2296

P.O. Box 12
Comanche, TX 76442
Contact: David Widner
Description: A short semiprivate 18-hole course that has no sand traps, wide fairways, few trees, and only four water hazards. Clubhouse has pool, restaurant, bar, and pro shop. **Par:** 72.
Rentals: Golf Carts, Pull Carts, Golf Clubs, Driving Range

Open to the public. Walking permitted. Golf lessons available.

Fees:

Weekday: 18-hole: $10 Cart: $7.50
9-hole: $5 Cart: $5
Weekend: 18-hole: $15.92 Cart: $7.50 9-hole: (N/A) Cart: $5

Located off Hwy 377 to FM 2861.

Sand Hills Country Club

(6,090 yds) 903-886-4455

P.O. Box 255
Commerce, TX 75429
Contact: Mel Fox
Description: A nine-hole semiprivate course that was constructed on a flat, open farm field. Some trees are fairly new, but the course is short and wide with no traps and one water hazard. **Par:** 36.

Rentals: Golf Carts, Pull Carts, Golf Clubs
Open to the public. Walking permitted.

Fees:

Weekday: 18-hole: $10 Cart: $7
9-hole: (N/A) Cart: (N/A)
Weekend: 18-hole: $20 Cart: $7
9-hole: (N/A) Cart: (N/A)

South off FM 1568.

Conroe Country Club

(3,246 yds) 409-756-5222

3051 N. Loop 336 West
Conroe, TX 77303
Contact: Debbie Williams
Description: All nine holes on this private nine-hole course have water. Fairways are narrow with big traps around small greens. Food. **Par:** 35.
Rentals: Golf Carts, Driving Range
Members and guests only. Walking permitted.

Fees:

Weekday: 18-hole: $10 Cart: $6.50
9-hole: (N/A) Cart: $5
Weekend: 18-hole: $15 Cart: $6.50
9-hole: (N/A) Cart: $5

Located southwest of town off I-45 on Loop 336 to Hwy 105.

Panorama Country Club

(27 hs) 409-856-5533

73 Greenbrier Drive
Conroe, TX 77304
Contact: Larry Davis
Description: This 27-hole private course has the hardest, tallest trees in town. Lakes, creeks, and traps make this course tough, and it is rather long. **Par:** 72.
Rentals: Golf Carts, Golf Clubs, Driving Range

Members and guests only. Golf lessons available. Walking permitted.

Fees:

Weekday: 18-hole: $15 Cart: $11
9-hole: $9 Cart: $5.50
Weekend: 18-hole: $25 Cart: $11
9-hole: $15 Cart: $5.50

Located north of town off I-45 on League Line Road.

River Plantation Country Club

(27 hs) 409-321-5833

1 Country Club Drive
Conroe, TX 77302
Contact: Bruce Springer
Description: A 27-hole public course. Golfers can play any two nines for an 18-hole round. The Charleston nine is tighter with doglegs and creek. The Augusta and Biloxi nines are longer and open. **Par:** 72.
Rentals: Golf Carts, Pull Carts, Golf Clubs, Driving Range

Open to the public. Walking permitted. Golf lessons available.

Fees:

Weekday: 18-hole: $10.50 Cart: $16
9-hole: (N/A) Cart: $7
Weekend: 18-hole: $13.50 Cart: $16
9-hole: (N/A) Cart: $7

Take I-45 exit 83 east.

Wedgewood Golf Course

(6,817 yds) 409-539-4653

5454 Hwy 105 West
Conroe, TX 77304
Contact: Jeff Bellnap
Description: An excellent 18-hole public course north of Houston. Lots of trees, good greens, water and great views. A solid clubhouse with a snack bar and pro shop. **Par:** 72.
Rentals: Golf Carts, Golf Clubs, Driving Range

Open to the public. Walking permitted. Golf lessons available.

Fees:

Weekday: 18-hole: $32 Cart: (N/A)
9-hole: (N/A) Cart: (N/A)
Weekend: 18-hole: $46 Cart: (N/A)
9-hole: (N/A) Cart: (N/A)

Located 3½ miles west of I-45 on Hwy 105 West.

Carmack Lake Golf Course

(5,891 yds) 210-658-3806

Route 1
Box 228
Converse, TX 78109
Contact: Don Carmack
Description: This is a short 18-hole executive course, but it can be somewhat tough with very rolling greens, holes over water, and out-of-bounds. Food and drinks. **Par:** 59.

Rentals: Golf Carts, Pull Carts, Golf Clubs
Open to the public. Walking permitted.

Fees:

Weekday: 18-hole: $8 Cart: $7 9-hole: $4 Cart: (N/A)
Weekend: 18-hole: $8 Cart: $7 9-hole: (N/A) Cart: (N/A)

Located north of I-10 on FM 1518.

Delta Country Club   (2,548 yds) 903-395-4712

FM 1529
Cooper, TX 75432
Contact: Benny Davis
Description: A good nine-hole private golf course that is open to out-of-county golfers. Only one water hazard, a lake on the third hole, and only one bunker. **Par:** 35.
Rentals: Golf Carts

Members and guests only. Walking permitted.

Fees:

Weekday: 18-hole: $10 Cart: $6
9-hole: $9 Cart: $4.25
Weekend: 18-hole: $13 Cart: $6
9-hole: $10 Cart: $4.25

Located on FM 1529 east of Cooper.

Riverchase Golf Club   (6,595 yds) 972-462-8281

700 Riverchase Drive
Coppell, TX 75019
Contact: Bob Archer
Description: A neat George Fazio-designed public course with strong water hazards and tough par 3s. Clubhouse has a snack bar and pro shop. **Par:** 71.
Rentals: Golf Carts, Golf Clubs, Driving Range

Open to the public. Walking permitted. Golf lessons available.

Fees:

Weekday: 18-hole: $40 Cart: (N/A)
9-hole: (N/A) Cart: (N/A)
Weekend: 18-hole: $59.50 Cart: (N/A)
9-hole: (N/A) Cart: (N/A)

Located north of Beltline Road; turn north on MacArthur to Riverchase.

Copperas Cove Golf Course   (3,264 yds) 254-547-2606

Golf Course Road
Copperas Cove, TX 76522
Contact: Dave Kaesheimer
Description: A nice nine-hole rural public course with very wide fairways. The large greens are easy to hit in regulation but also three-putt. Hooks tend to go out of bounds. **Par:** 36.
Rentals: Golf Carts, Pull Carts, Golf Clubs
Open to the public. Walking permitted.

Fees:

Weekday: 18-hole: $8 Cart: $15.50
9-hole: (N/A) Cart: $11
Weekend: 18-hole: $10 Cart: $15.50
9-hole: (N/A) Cart: $11

Located in the northeast corner of town.

Oakmont Country Club   (6,908 yds)   940-321-5599

1200 Clubhouse Drive
Corinth, TX 76205
Contact: John Ericson
Description: A semiprivate club with a difficult, long into-the-wind par-5 sixth hole. A new clubhouse opened in April 1994. Very pretty North Texas setting. **Par:** 72.
Rentals: Golf Carts, Golf Clubs, Driving Range

Members and guests only. Golf lessons available. Mandatory carts.

Fees:

Weekday: 18-hole: $55 Cart: (N/A)
9-hole: (N/A) Cart: (N/A)
Weekend: 18-hole: $60 Cart: (N/A)
9-hole: (N/A) Cart: (N/A)

Located east of I-35E south of Denton off exit 461.

Corpus Christi Country Club   (6,506 yds)   512-991-7870

6300 Everhart
Corpus Christi, TX 78413
Contact: Doug DeSive
Description: Many members of this 18-hole private course shoot some good scores because the course is short and wide with only three water hazards. Fast greens. Well-appointed clubhouse. **Par:** 72.
Rentals: Golf Carts, Golf Clubs, Driving Range

Members and guests only. Golf lessons available. Walking permitted.

Fees:

Weekday: 18-hole: $50 Cart: $10
9-hole: (N/A) Cart: $4.50
Weekend: 18-hole: $75 Cart: $10
9-hole: (N/A) Cart: $4.50

Located on Everhart Road south of Padre Island Drive.

Gabe Lozano Senior Golf Center   (6,953 yds)   512-883-3696

4401 Old Brownsville Road
Corpus Christi, TX 78405
Contact: Bruce M. Haddad
Description: Senior golfers prefer the nine-hole executive course as opposed to playing the long 18-hole public course. Both courses have water and not many bunkers. Wide fairways. Snack bar and pro shop. **Par:** 72.
Rentals: Golf Carts, Pull Carts, Golf Clubs, Driving Range

Open to the public. Walking permitted. Golf lessons available.

Fees:

Weekday: 18-hole: $10 Cart: $8
9-hole: $4.50 Cart: $5
Weekend: 18-hole: $12 Cart: $8
9-hole: $6 Cart: $5

Take Hwy 37 to NAS/SPID Expressway. Exit left to Old Brownsville Road.

Gulf Winds Golf Shop — (6,316 yds) 512-939-3250

U.S. Naval Air Station
Bldg 1272
Corpus Christi, TX 78419
Contact: Gene Marr
Description: The small greens on this 18-hole private military course are very difficult to hit in regulation. Protected by water and traps, and the rough is thick. Snack bar. **Par:** 70.
Rentals: Golf Carts, Pull Carts, Golf Clubs, Driving Range

Members and guests only. Walking permitted.

Fees:

Weekday: 18-hole: $8 Cart: $6 9-hole: (N/A) Cart: $3
Weekend: 18-hole: $9 Cart: $6 9-hole: (N/A) Cart: $3

Located on the Naval Air Station.

Kings Crossing Golf & Country Club (6,762 yds) 512-994-1395

6201 Oso Parkway
Corpus Christi, TX 78414
Contact: David Preston
Description: Water is a big deal in this links-style 18-hole private course. Anybody who hits a wild shot will see the ball sink with the fish. Not many trees. Clubhouse has restaurant, bar, and pro shop. **Par:** 71.
Rentals: Golf Carts, Driving Range

Members and guests only. Golf lessons available. Walking permitted.

Fees:

Weekday: 18-hole: $15 Cart: (N/A) 9-hole: (N/A) Cart: $4
Weekend: 18-hole: $35 Cart: (N/A) 9-hole: (N/A) Cart: $4

Take Hwy 37 to NAS/SPID Expwy. Exit right on Staples; course is six to seven miles on the left.

Oso Beach Municipal Golf Course (6,223 yds) 512-991-5351

5601 S. Alameda
Corpus Christi, TX 78412
Contact: Jimmie Taylor
Description: The back nine on this 18-hole public course is a short par 34 but has lots of water. The front nine is solid with flat fairways and traps. Senior discount. **Par:** 70.
Rentals: Golf Carts, Pull Carts, Golf Clubs

Open to the public. Walking permitted. Golf lessons available.

Fees:

Weekday: 18-hole: $10 Cart: $8 9-hole: (N/A) Cart: $4.45
Weekend: 18-hole: $12 Cart: $8 9-hole: (N/A) Cart: $4.45

Located off Ocean Drive at South Alameda.

Padre Isles Country Club (6,223 yds) 512-949-8006

14353 Commodore Drive
Corpus Christi, TX 78418
Contact: Robert Smith
Description: Members of private clubs associated with the USGA are welcome on this 18-hole private course. It has heather rough and water on 16 holes. One of the best with great seaside views. Food and drinks. **Par:** 72.
Rentals: Golf Carts, Golf Clubs, Driving Range

Members and guests only. Golf lessons available. Walking permitted.

Fees:

Weekday: 18-hole: $39 Cart: (N/A)
9-hole: (N/A) Cart: (N/A)
Weekend: 18-hole: $49 Cart: (N/A)
9-hole: (N/A) Cart: (N/A)

Located on North Padre Island on Commodore Drive.

Pharaoh's Golf Club (6,187 yds) 512-991-1490

7111 Pharaoh's Drive
Corpus Christi, TX 78412
Contact: Randy Walker
Description: There is nothing difficult about this short 18-hole public course. Only the wind can cause a problem. Fairways are flat and open and there are not many bunkers. **Par:** 70.
Rentals: Golf Carts, Golf Clubs, Driving Range

Open to the public. Walking permitted. Golf lessons available.

Fees:

Weekday: 18-hole: $25 Cart: (N/A)
9-hole: $20 Cart: (N/A)
Weekend: 18-hole: $35 Cart: (N/A)
9-hole: $25 Cart: (N/A)

Located north of South Padre Island Drive.

River Hills Country Club (6,096 yds) 512-387-3563

River Hills Drive
Corpus Christi, TX 78426
Contact: Tom Inman
Description: This 18-hole private course was originally built by a farmer many years ago. Now it is modern with hilly fairways, eight water hazards, 20 traps, and fast, undulating greens. **Par:** 70.
Rentals: Golf Carts, Golf Clubs, Driving Range

Members and guests only. Golf lessons available. Walking permitted.

Fees:

Weekday: 18-hole: $17.50 Cart: $8
9-hole: (N/A) Cart: $4
Weekend: 18-hole: $25 Cart: $8
9-hole: (N/A) Cart: $4

Located west of Hwy 77.

Corsicana Country Club   (6,541 yds) 903-874-2441

5000 Emhouse Road
Corsicana, TX 75110
Contact: Matt Child
Description: An outstanding 18-hole
rural Texas private club designed by
A.W. Tillinghast. Big greens are very
easy to three-putt. Clubhouse is great.
Par: 71.
Rentals: Golf Carts, Golf Clubs, Driving
Range

Members and guests only. Golf lessons
available. Walking permitted.

Fees:

Weekday: 18-hole: $15 Cart: $9
9-hole: (N/A) Cart: (N/A)
Weekend: 18-hole: $25 Cart: $9
9-hole: (N/A) Cart: (N/A)

Located off I-45 exit 31 to Beeton Rd.

New Oaks Golf Course   (3,456 yds) 903-872-7252

2501 N. Highway 75
Corsicana, TX 75110
Contact: John Sikes
Description: A former sand green golf
course that is the only public course in
the city of Corsicana. A short and easy
nine-hole course. **Par:** 35.
Rentals: Golf Carts
Open to the public. Walking permitted.

Fees:

Weekday: 18-hole: $10 Cart: $6.50
9-hole: (N/A) Cart: (N/A)
Weekend: 18-hole: $15 Cart: $6.50
9-hole: (N/A) Cart: (N/A)

Located east of I-45 south of Ennis on
Business 45.

Creekview Golf Club   (7,238 yds) 972-427-3811

1602 E. Hwy 175
Crandall, TX 75114
Contact: Danny Silianoff
Description: Lush bentgrass greens
highlight this solid daily-fee layout,
designed by architect Dick Phelps, who
also did highly popular Firewheel in
Garland. Creekview features trees,
traps, and scenic views. **Par:** 72.
Rentals: Golf Carts, Golf Clubs, Driving
Range

Open to the public. Walking permitted.
Golf lessons available.

Fees:

Weekday: 18-hole: $31 Cart: (N/A)
9-hole: (N/A) Cart: (N/A)
Weekend: 18-hole: $43 Cart: (N/A)
9-hole: (N/A) Cart: (N/A)

Located southeast of Dallas on Highway
175.

Crane Country Club

(6,184 yds) 915-558-2651

300 E. 20th St.
Crane, TX 79731
Contact: Brian Renfro
Description: An interesting nine-hole public course with no water hazards or sand traps. The fairways are wide open with hunchback greens. Good pro shop. **Par:** 36.
Rentals: Golf Carts, Driving Range
Open to the public. Walking permitted.

Fees:

Weekday: 18-hole: $8 Cart: $14
9-hole: (N/A) Cart: $6.38
Weekend: 18-hole: $13.50 Cart: $14
9-hole: (N/A) Cart: $6.38

Located two miles north of the city on Hwy 385.

Spring Creek Country Club

(5,665 yds) 409-544-7848

P.O. Box 492
Crockett, TX 75835
Contact: Barry Truelove
Description: Nice semiprivate course which combines pleasant setting with some challenge with water and trees. It is short with wide holes and some water. Food and drinks. **Par:** 35.
Rentals: Golf Carts, Driving Range

Members and guests only. Walking permitted.

Fees:

Weekday: 18-hole: $10 Cart: $10
9-hole: $8 Cart: $6
Weekend: 18-hole: $15 Cart: $10
9-hole: $16 Cart: $6

Located off Hwy 19 North and west on FM 2160.

Indian Shores Golf Club

(6,610 yds) 281-324-2592

2141 White Feather Trail
Crosby, TX 77532
Contact: Sammy Borden
Description: Out-of-bounds on all nine holes of this public course make the fairways tight despite no sand traps or water hazards. Small greens. Pro shop. **Par:** 36.
Rentals: Golf Carts, Pull Carts, Driving Range

Open to the public. Walking permitted. Golf lessons available.

Fees:

Weekday: 18-hole: $6.38 Cart: $7.50
9-hole: (N/A) Cart: $3.75
Weekend: 18-hole: $12.75 Cart: $7.50 9-hole: (N/A) Cart: $3.75

Located northeast of Houston on Hwy 90.

Newport Golf & Country Club (6,496 yds) 281-328-2541

P.O. Box 191
16401 Golf Club Drive
Crosby, TX 77532
Contact: Scott Cannon
Description: This 18-hole private course is kind of long with lots of sand traps and trees but only two water hazards. The greens are flat. Food, drinks, tennis, and pool. **Par:** 72.
Rentals: Golf Carts, Golf Clubs, Driving Range

Members and guests only. Golf lessons available. Walking permitted.

Fees:

Weekday: 18-hole: $20 Cart: $9
9-hole: $9 Cart: $5
Weekend: 18-hole: $28 Cart: $9
9-hole: $12 Cart: $5

Located on FM 2100 between Hwy 90 and FM 1960.

Rancho Carribe (3,063 yds) 409-684-1600

1605 Ranch Road
Crystal Beach, TX 77650
Contact: Robby Sharpless
Description: Scenic new addition to Southeast TX area. Golfers play among trees, sand, and some water. Rough and native grasses complete the challenge picture. Good test for all golfers. **Par:** 36.

Fees:

Weekday: 18-hole: $10 Cart: $10
9-hole: $7 Cart: $5
Weekend: 18-hole: $13 Cart: $10
9-hole: $9 Cart: $5

Located at intersection of Highway 87 and Ranch Road in Crystal Beach.

Cuero Municipal Golf Course (3,600 yds) 512-275-3233

1200 E. Main
Cuero, TX 77954
Contact: Keith Krueger
Description: Even though this nine-hole public course is reasonably short, the elevated greens and water on five holes make it play a lot tougher. Double tees. Snack bar and pro shop.
Par: 36.
Rentals: Golf Carts, Pull Carts, Golf Clubs

Open to the public. Walking permitted. Golf lessons available.

Fees:

Weekday: 18-hole: $5 Cart: $6.50
9-hole: (N/A) Cart: $3.75
Weekend: 18-hole: $8 Cart: $6.50
9-hole: (N/A) Cart: $3.75

Located on Hwy 87.

Cypress Golf Club

(5,371 yds) 281-373-0727

P.O. Box 248
14914 Spring-Cypress Road
Cypress, TX 77429
Contact: Bobby Westfall
Description: This nine-hole semiprivate
course is open to the public during
weekdays. Double tees result in the
176-yard par-3 third hole playing as a
245-yard par-4 12th hole. Very pretty
setting. **Par:** 35.
Rentals: Golf Carts, Pull Carts, Golf
Clubs, Driving Range

Open to the public. Walking permitted.
Golf lessons available.

Fees:

Weekday: 18-hole: $25 Cart: (N/A)
9-hole: (N/A) Cart: $3.50
Weekend: 18-hole: $25 Cart: (N/A)
9-hole: (N/A) Cart: $3.50

Located northwest of Houston,
Spring-Cypress at Huffmeister.

Longwood Golf Club

(7,010 yds) 281-373-4100

13300 Longwood Trace
Cypress, TX 77429
Contact: Billy Haynes
Description: New daily-fee layout in
fast-growing golfers market. Jack
Montgomery and Keith Fergus, who
designed wildly popular Old Orchard
Course, did this one as well which
opened in 1995 in very scenic setting.
Par: 72.
Rentals: Golf Carts, Pull Carts, Golf
Clubs, Driving Range

Open to the public. Walking permitted.
Golf lessons available.

Fees:

Weekday: 18-hole: $35 Cart: (N/A)
9-hole: (N/A) Cart: (N/A)
Weekend: 18-hole: $50 Cart: (N/A)
9-hole: (N/A) Cart: (N/A)

Take Hwy 290 to Telge, right on Telge
to Huffmeister.

Hyatt Bear Creek Golf Club   (36 hs) 972-615-6800

West Airfield Drive & Bear Creek
DFW Airport, TX 75261
Contact: Larry Box
West Course Description: The West
Course is very hilly and tight with lots
of trees and a few water hazards. The
clubhouse has a restaurant, locker
room, and very nice pro shop. **Par:** 72
(6,670 yards).

East Course Description: A great
36-hole public course. The fifth hole on
the East Course is signature hole. **Par:**
72 (6,609 yards).

Rentals: Golf Carts, Golf Clubs, Driving
Range
Open to the public. Walking permitted.
Golf lessons available.

Fees:

Weekday: 18-hole: $75 Cart: (N/A)
9-hole: (N/A) Cart: (N/A)
Weekend: 18-hole: $85 Cart: (N/A)
9-hole: (N/A) Cart: (N/A)

> Located in the southwest section of
> DFW Airport. Turn left before entering
> the south entrance of the airport.

Beaver Brook Country Club   (5,768 yds) 903-645-2976

Route 1 Box 313G
Daingerfield, TX 75638
Contact: Christy Wayne
Description: A wide open nine-hole
semiprivate course that has very short
trees, only two bunkers, and a creek.
Open to golfers living more than 20
miles away. Club has bar and pro shop.
Par: 36.
Rentals: Golf Carts, Pull Carts

Members and guests only. Walking
permitted.

Fees:

Weekday: 18-hole: $10 Cart: $15
9-hole: (N/A) Cart: (N/A)
Weekend: 18-hole: $12.50 Cart: $15
9-hole: (N/A) Cart: (N/A)

> Located on Hwy 11 east of town.

Dalhart Country Club   (6,539 yds) 806-249-5596

Box 130
Dalhart, TX 79022
Contact: David Britton
Description: A very long 18-hole private course with bentgrass greens that are very easy to three-putt. Only one pond but tight fairways. Food, drinks, and pro shop. **Par:** 72.
Rentals: Golf Carts, Pull Carts, Golf Clubs, Driving Range

Members and guests only. Walking permitted.

Fees:

Weekday: 18-hole: $20 Cart: $14
9-hole: $10 Cart: $7
Weekend: 18-hole: $20 Cart: $14
9-hole: $10 Cart: $7

Located two miles west of town on Hwy 54.

Bent Tree Country Club   (7,113 yds) 972-931-7326

5201 Westgrove
Dallas, TX 75248
Contact: David Price
Description: Redesigned in 1991, Bent Tree has many outstanding holes. The par 3s are very difficult. The Senior PGA Reunion Pro Am was started at Bent Tree. **Par:** 72.
Rentals: Golf Carts, Driving Range

Members and guests only. Golf lessons available. Walking permitted.

Fees:

Weekday: 18-hole: $75 Cart: $11
9-hole: (N/A) Cart: $5.50
Weekend: 18-hole: $100 Cart: $11
9-hole: (N/A) Cart: $5.50

Located one block east of Dallas Tollway off Westgrove.

Brookhaven Country Club   (54 hs) 972-488-4896

3333 Golfing Green Drive
Dallas, TX 75234
Contact: Phillip Wiese
Masters Course Description: The
largest private club in Dallas with 54
holes, five swimming pools, 50 tennis
courts, fitness center, child care center,
and a restaurant. Fairways converted to
Tift-94 in 1998. Masters Course is the
best of the three courses. **Par:** 72
(6,866 yards).

Championship Course Description:
Championship Course is a traditional
style course with many sand traps and
water hazards. It is nearly as tough as
the Masters Course. Fairways converted
to Tift-94 in 1999. **Par:** 72 (6,535
yards).

Presidents Course Description:
Presidents Course is the easiest 18-hole
course of the trio. The 5,527-yard
par-72 course is popular with seniors,
kids, and beginners. Low handicap
golfers can improve their short game
here. Fairways will be converted to
Tift-94 in 2000. **Par:** 72 (5,527 yards).
Rentals: Golf Carts, Driving Range
Members and guests only. Golf lessons
available. Walking permitted.

Fees:

Weekday: 18-hole: $40 Cart: $24
9-hole: (N/A) Cart: (N/A)
Weekend: 18-hole: $60 Cart: $24
9-hole: (N/A) Cart: (N/A)

Located north of I-635 off Marsh Lane
then left to Brookhaven, on Golfing
Green Drive.

Brook Hollow Golf Club   (6,743 yds) 214-637-1914

8301 Harry Hines Blvd.
Dallas, TX 75235
Contact: Jerry Smith
Description: One of the oldest and
best courses in Dallas recently
redesigned by Ben Crenshaw and Bill
Coore. Originally designed by A.W.
Tillinghast. Elite setting. **Par:** 71.
Rentals: Golf Carts, Driving Range
Members and guests only. Golf lessons
available. Walking permitted.

Fees:

Weekday: 18-hole: $100 Cart: (N/A)
9-hole: (N/A) Cart: (N/A)
Weekend: 18-hole: $100 Cart: (N/A)
9-hole: (N/A) Cart: (N/A)

Located on Harry Hines Blvd. west of
Love Field near downtown.

Cedar Crest Park Golf Course   (6,550 yds) 214-670-7615

1800 Southerland
Dallas, TX 75203
Contact: Leonard Jones
Description: Dallas' most historic golf course, the site of the 1927 PGA won by Walter Hagen. The base of a good score is doing well on the tough par 3s. **Par:** 71.
Rentals: Golf Carts, Pull Carts, Golf Clubs

Open to the public. Walking permitted. Golf lessons available.

Fees:

Weekday: 18-hole: $14 Cart: $18.40
9-hole: (N/A) Cart: $8
Weekend: 18-hole: $17 Cart: $18.40
9-hole: (N/A) Cart: $8

Located west of I-35E off Illinois Ave to Southerland.

Dallas Athletic Club   (36 hs) 972-279-6517

4111 LaPrada
Dallas, TX 75228
Contact: Dennis Ewing
Blue Course Description: Site of the 1963 PGA Championship, the first PGA won by Nicklaus. He redesigned both courses in 1980s. Blue Course hosted 1997 USGA Mid-Am championship. **Par:** 72 (6,710 yards).

Gold Course Description: The 18th hole on the Gold Course is one of the most difficult par 5s in Texas with sand and water. Clubhouse has restaurant, bar, lockers, showers, meeting rooms, and tennis courts. **Par:** 72 (6,993 yards).
Rentals: Golf Carts, Golf Clubs, Driving Range
Members and guests only. Golf lessons available. Walking permitted.

Fees:

Weekday: 18-hole: $55 Cart: $11
9-hole: (N/A) Cart: (N/A)
Weekend: 18-hole: $80 Cart: $11
9-hole: (N/A) Cart: (N/A)

Located off I-635 LaPrada exit in Mesquite.

Dallas Country Club   (6,250 yds) 214-521-2151

4100 Beverly Drive
Dallas, TX 75205
Contact: Billy Harris
Description: The first country club in
Dallas is very exclusive. The course is
short but tight with trees, bunkers, and
water. Clubhouse is great. **Par:** 70.
Rentals: Golf Carts, Driving Range
Members and guests only. Golf lessons
available. Walking permitted.

Fees:

Weekday: 18-hole: $75 Cart: $9
9-hole: (N/A) Cart: $4.50
Weekend: 18-hole: $100 Cart: $9
9-hole: (N/A) Cart: $4.50

Located just south of Preston Road and
Mockingbird Lane in Highland Park.

Family Golf Center   (989 yds) 214-341-9600

8787 Park Lane
Dallas, TX 75231
Contact: Golf Shop
Description: A perfect place to learn
golf and for kids to have fun. It has a
four-hole par-3 course and a great
driving range. There is a 54-hole
miniature golf course, batting cage, and
pro shop. **Par:** 12.

Rentals: Club Rentals, Driving Range
Open to the public. Walking permitted.
Golf lessons available.

Fees:

Weekday: 4-hole: $6 Cart: (N/A)
Weekend: 4-hole: $8 Cart: (N/A)

Located at Park and Abrams.

Keeton Park Golf Course   (6,520 yds) 214-670-8784

2323 Jim Miller Rd.
Dallas, TX 75227
Contact: Kim Brown
Description: To post a good score,
golfers must play well on the tight first
six holes. The last three are also
difficult. Clubhouse has a snack bar and
a pro shop. **Par:** 72.
Rentals: Golf Carts, Pull Carts, Golf
Clubs, Driving Range

Open to the public. Walking permitted.
Golf lessons available.

Fees:

Weekday: 18-hole: $14 Cart: $9.20
9-hole: (N/A) Cart: $4
Weekend: 18-hole: $17 Cart: $9.20
9-hole: (N/A) Cart: $4

Located south of I-30 off Jim Miller
Road.

L.B. Houston Municipal Golf Course (6,705 yds) 214-670-6322

11223 Luna Road
Dallas, TX 75229
Contact: Leonard Jones
Description: A very tight 18-hole public course. The back nine has more trees that demand straight tee shots. Clubhouse has a pro shop, snack bar, and tennis courts. **Par:** 72.
Rentals: Golf Carts, Pull Carts, Golf Clubs, Driving Range

Open to the public. Walking permitted. Golf lessons available.

Fees:

Weekday: 18-hole: $14 Cart: $9.20
9-hole: (N/A) Cart: $4
Weekend: 18-hole: $17 Cart: $9.20
9-hole: (N/A) Cart: $4

Located off Luna Road south of I-635.

Lakewood Country Club (6,518 yds) 214-821-7690

6430 Gaston Ave.
Dallas, TX 75214
Contact: James Williams Jr.
Description: Site of first Dallas Open in 1944. A traditional style design from 1912. Great redesigned greens and traditional shot values make this very nice. **Par:** 71.
Rentals: Golf Carts, Driving Range

Members and guests only. Golf lessons available. Walking permitted.

Fees:

Weekday: 18-hole: $75 Cart: $10
9-hole: $50 Cart: $5
Weekend: 18-hole: $100 Cart: $10
9-hole: $75 Cart: $5

Located north of I-30 in East Dallas at Gaston and Abrams.

Lone Star Golf Center (1,300 yds) 214-247-4653

2101 Walnut Hill
Dallas, TX 75229
Contact: O.B. Nelson
Description: The best nine-hole par-3 course in Dallas with sand traps, mounds, and bentgrass greens. A rare lighted par-3 course in Dallas. **Par:** 27.
Rentals: Golf Clubs, Driving Range
Open to the public. Walking permitted. Golf lessons available.

Fees:

Weekday: 18-hole: $13 Cart: (N/A)
9-hole: $8 Cart: (N/A)
Weekend: 18-hole: $16.25 Cart: (N/A)
9-hole: $10 Cart: (N/A)

Located west of I-35E at the dead end of Walnut Hill Lane.

Northwest Pitch and Putt

(1,050 yds) 214-348-3693

10726 E. Northwest Hwy
Dallas, TX 75238
Contact: Golf Shop
Description: A good lighted par-3
course with holes ranging from 45 to
95 yards. There are bunkers, hills, and
creeks. A good place to improve your
short game. **Par:** 27.
Rentals: Golf Clubs, Driving Range

Open to the public. Walking permitted.
Golf lessons available.

Fees:

Weekday: 18-hole: $8 Cart: (N/A)
9-hole: $5 Cart: (N/A)
Weekend: 18-hole: $10 Cart: (N/A)
9-hole: $5 Cart: (N/A)

Located on the corner of Northwest
Hwy and Plano Road.

Northwood Club

(6,835 yds) 972-934-0544

6524 Alpha Road
Dallas, TX 75240
Contact: Bob Elliot
Description: The site of the 1952 U.S.
Open, the first tournament Julius Boros
ever won. It is one of the best courses
in Dallas with fast bentgrass greens.
Exclusive private club setting. **Par:** 71.
Rentals: Golf Carts, Golf Clubs, Driving
Range

Members and guests only. Golf lessons
available. Walking permitted.

Fees:

Weekday: 18-hole: $85 Cart: $10
9-hole: (N/A) Cart: $5
Weekend: 18-hole: $100 Cart: $10
9-hole: (N/A) Cart: $5

Located north of I-635 off Preston
Road and Alpha Road.

Oak Cliff Country Club

(6,579 yds) 214-333-3595

2200 N. Redbird Lane
Dallas, TX 75232
Contact: Russell Orth
Description: One of Dallas' most
historic courses, site of the Dallas Open
in the 1950s and '60s. A beautiful golf
course with trees and water. **Par:** 70.
Rentals: Golf Carts, Pull Carts, Golf
Clubs, Driving Range
Members and guests only. Golf lessons
available. Walking permitted.

Fees:

Weekday: 18-hole: $40 Cart: $10
9-hole: (N/A) Cart: (N/A)
Weekend: 18-hole: $60 Cart: $10
9-hole: (N/A) Cart: (N/A)

Located south of downtown Dallas off
Hwy 67 to Hampton Road; east to
Redbird Lane.

Preston Trail Golf Club   (7,091 yds) 972-248-8448

17201 Preston Trail Drive
Dallas, TX 75248
Contact: Gordon Johnson
Description: The site of the Byron Nelson Classic from 1968 to 1982. It is a very tough, hilly golf course with male-only membership. A very luxurious clubhouse. **Par:** 72.
Rentals: Golf Carts, Driving Range

Members and guests only. Golf lessons available. Walking permitted.

Fees:

Weekday: 18-hole: $100 Cart: $10
9-hole: (N/A) Cart: $6.25
Weekend: 18-hole: $175 Cart: $10
9-hole: (N/A) Cart: $6.25

Located west of Preston Road off Campbell Road.

Prestonwood Country Club   (36 hs) 972-307-1508

972-307-1508
15909 Preston Road
Dallas, TX 75240
Contact: Cotton Dunn
Hills Course Description: A 36-hole private club with the newer Hills Course located 10 miles northwest of the Creek Course. Hills Course is hilly and tight.
Par: 72 (6,484 yards).
Rentals: Golf Carts, Golf Clubs, Driving Range
Members and guests only. Golf lessons available. Walking permitted.

Fees:

Weekday: 18-hole: $55 Cart: $10
9-hole: (N/A) Cart: $6.50
Weekend: 18-hole: $76.86 Cart: $10
9-hole: (N/A) Cart: $6.50

Hills Course is located off Columbine Road north of FM 544 in Plano.

972-233-6166
15909 Preston Road
Dallas, TX 75240
Contact: Cotton Dunn
Creek Course Description: The Creek Course, the original course, has creeks running through several holes. Clubhouse has food, fun, and pro shop.
Par: 71 (6,484 yards).
Rentals: Golf Carts, Golf Clubs, Driving Range
Members and guests only. Golf lessons available. Walking permitted.

Fees:

Weekday: 18-hole: $55 Cart: $10
9-hole: (N/A) Cart: $6.50
Weekend: 18-hole: $76.86 Cart: $10
9-hole: (N/A) Cart: $6.50

Located near Prestonwood Mall between Preston Road and Arapaho.

Royal Oaks Country Club   (6,949 yds) 214-691-0339

7915 Greenville Ave.
Dallas, TX 75231
Contact: Randy Smith
Description: The tightest golf course
in Dallas demands perfect tee shots.
Home course of PGA superstar Justin
Leonard, who learned his game here.
Par: 71.
Rentals: Golf Carts, Driving Range
Members and guests only. Golf lessons
available. Walking permitted.

Fees:

Weekday: 18-hole: $50 Cart: $10
9-hole: (N/A) Cart: $5
Weekend: 18-hole: $60 Cart: $10
9-hole: (N/A) Cart: $5

> Located on Greenville Ave., just south
> of Royal Lane.

Sleepy Hollow Golf & Country Club   (36 hs) 214-371-3430

4747 S. Loop 12
Dallas, TX 75216
Contact: Chuck Tabor
Lake Course Description: The Lake
Course has an extra par 3 on each nine
to make it a fast round of golf. Historic
and highly popular south Dallas semiprivate club. Clubhouse has nice pro
shop. Mayor Ron Kirk an active
member. **Par:** 70 (6,052 yards).

River Course Description: A 36-hole
semiprivate club. River Course is a
7,100-yard par 71, which makes it the

toughest of the two courses and a good
test for all. **Par:** 71 (7,031 yards).
Rentals: Golf Carts, Driving Range
Open to the public. Walking permitted.
Golf lessons available.

Fees:

Weekday: 18-hole: $20 Cart: $11
9-hole: (N/A) Cart: (N/A)
Weekend: 18-hole: $30 Cart: $11
9-hole: (N/A) Cart: (N/A)

> Located south of downtown off I-45 at
> Loop 12 West,

Stevens Park Golf Club (6,005 yds) 214-670-7506

1005 N. Montclair
Dallas, TX 75208
Contact: Jim Henderson
Description: A short 18-hole public course. Golfers hitting good tee shots and putts will post a great score. There are hills and trees. **Par:** 71.
Rentals: Golf Carts, Pull Carts, Golf Clubs
Open to the public. Walking permitted. Golf lessons available.

Fees:

Weekday: 18-hole: $14 Cart: $9
9-hole: (N/A) Cart: $4.33
Weekend: 18-hole: $17 Cart: $9
9-hole: (N/A) Cart: $4.33

Located west of downtown, south of I-30 off Colorado Blvd.

Tenison Park Golf Course (36 hs) 214-670-1402

3501 Samuell Blvd.
Dallas, TX 75223
Contact: Jack Neumann
East Course Description: An outstanding 36-hole public course in Dallas. The East Course has water and trees that require accurate tee shots. Lee Trevino started here. **Par:** 72 (6,802 yards).

West Course Description: The West Course is the hilliest course in Dallas. Two par 4s go up and down hills making them play extra long or extra short. Not much water, but hills and trees are challenging. Renovations start in 1999. **Par:** 71 (6,902 yards).

Rentals: Golf Carts, Pull Carts, Golf Clubs
Open to the public. Walking permitted.

Fees:

Weekday: 18-hole: $14 Cart: $18.40
9-hole: (N/A) Cart: (N/A)
Weekend: 18-hole: $17 Cart: $18.40
9-hole: (N/A) Cart: (N/A)

Located off I-30 just east of downtown off Grand Ave.

Decatur Golf Club

(6,518 yds) 940-627-3789

Route 3, Box 208
Decatur, TX 76234
Contact: Carol Wells
Description: A typical rural Texas nine-hole course with lots of trees, a creek, a pond, and small rolling hills. Clubhouse has food, drinks, and pro shop. **Par:** 36.
Rentals: Golf Carts

Open to the public. Walking permitted.

Fees:

Weekday: 18-hole: $15 Cart: $7.50
9-hole: $9 Cart: $4
Weekend: 18-hole: $25 Cart: $7.50
9-hole: $11 Cart: $4

Located off Hwy 730 north.

Battleground at Deer Park

(6,943 yds) 281-478-4653

1600 Georgia Parkway
Deer Park, TX 77356
Contact: Ken Kelley
Description: City course built on historic Texas battleground site. Course, which opened in 1996, gives golfers a chance to play on site of Texas independence battles. Outstanding design with 38 sand traps. **Par:** 72.
Rentals: Golf Carts, Pull Carts, Golf Clubs, Driving Range

Open to the public. Walking permitted. Golf lessons available.

Fees:

Weekday: 18-hole: $22 Cart: $17
9-hole: (N/A) Cart: (N/A)
Weekend: 18-hole: $30 Cart: $17
9-hole: (N/A) Cart: (N/A)

Off Hwy 225, exit Center Street right to Georgia Parkway.

San Felipe Country Club

(6,300 yds) 830-775-3953

P.O. Box 1228
Del Rio, TX 78840
Contact: Clint Black
Description: Springs from the San Felipe River run through seven holes of this nine-hole public course. Tight trees on fairways and double tees demand good tee shots to avoid traps. Snack bar, bar, and pro shop. **Par:** 36.
Rentals: Golf Carts, Pull Carts, Golf Clubs, Driving Range

Open to the public. Walking permitted. Golf lessons available.

Fees:

Weekday: 18-hole: $20 Cart: $7.50
9-hole: $11 Cart: $4
Weekend: 18-hole: $25 Cart: $7.50
9-hole: $15 Cart: $4

Located east of town.

Bergstrom Cedars Golf Course   (6,576 yds) 512-385-4653

Bldg 3711
Del Valle, TX 78617
Contact: Troy Gann
Description: The former Bergstrom
AFB course opened to the public with
several improvements, especially on the
back side with added water. Small
greens and good par 3s over water. Site
of new Austin Airport. **Par:** 71.
Rentals: Golf Carts, Pull Carts, Golf
Clubs

Open to the public. Walking permitted.
Golf lessons available.

Fees:

Weekday: 18-hole: $9 Cart: $8 9-hole:
(N/A) Cart: $4
Weekend: 18-hole: $12 Cart: $8
9-hole: (N/A) Cart: $4

Located off Hwy 71 in southeast
Austin.

Denison Country Club   (6,134 yds) 903-465-4488

Box 96
Denison, TX 75020
Contact: Poke Horsfall
Description: A neat 18-hole private
club with a heavy tree-lined front nine
and a back nine around a lake.
Clubhouse has restaurant, bar, lockers,
fishing, tennis courts, and pro shop.
Par: 71.
Rentals: Golf Carts, Driving Range

Open to the public. Walking permitted.
Golf lessons available.

Fees:

Weekday: 18-hole: $40 Cart: (N/A)
9-hole: $20 Cart: $7.50
Weekend: 18-hole: $40 Cart: (N/A)
9-hole: $20 Cart: $7.50

Located west of U.S. 75 on Hwy 84.

Grayson County College Golf Course (6,358 yds) 903-786-9719

7109 Dinn Street
Denison, TX 75020
Contact: Mike Hurley
Description: A former Air Force base
nine-hole course. The college added a
second nine. The old nine is tough, and
golfers will hit all clubs in 18 holes.
Clubhouse has food and pro shop.
Par: 71.
Rentals: Golf Carts, Pull Carts, Driving
Range

Open to the public. Walking permitted.
Golf lessons available.

Fees:

Weekday: 18-hole: $8.50 Cart: $17
9-hole: $4 Cart: $8.50
Weekend: 18-hole: $13 Cart: $17
9-hole: $5 Cart: $8.50

Located west of U.S. 75 on FM 691.

Sugartree Golf & Country Club   (6,726 yds) 817-594-5435

Highway 1189
Dennis, TX 76037
Contact: Joe Henshaw
Description: An outstanding 18-hole
rural public course. Lots of trees, hills,
and water. Very scenic country setting;
worth the drive. **Par:** 71.
Rentals: Golf Carts, Pull Carts, Driving
Range
Open to the public. Walking permitted.
Golf lessons available.

Fees:

Weekday: 18-hole: $31 Cart: $10.58
9-hole: $10.40 Cart: $10.58
Weekend: 18-hole: $42 Cart: $11.47
9-hole: $14.42 Cart: $11.47

Located 10 miles south of I-20 on FM
1189 west of Fort Worth. Take exit
403.

Denton Country Club   (6,303 yds) 940-387-2812

Box 1069
Denton, TX 76202
Contact: Alan Poyner
Description: A great Ralph
Plummer-designed course with a lake
between the nines to set up 15 holes
with water hazards. Lots of hilly dogleg
holes. Nice clubhouse. **Par:** 71.
Rentals: Golf Carts, Driving Range

Members and guests only. Golf lessons
available. Walking permitted.

Fees:

Weekday: 18-hole: $17.50 Cart: $8
9-hole: (N/A) Cart: $5
Weekend: 18-hole: $50 Cart: $8
9-hole: (N/A) Cart: $5

Located five miles south of Denton off
Hwy 1830.

Eagle Point Golf Club   (6,647 yds) 940-387-5180

2211 I-35 North
Denton, TX 76205
Contact: Coleman Gulley
Description: The course was
redesigned in 1993 with 300 more
yards and par up to 72 from 70. Very
hilly golf course with more water
hazards. Part of a local hotel. **Par:** 72.
Rentals: Golf Carts, Pull Carts, Golf
Clubs, Driving Range

Open to the public. Walking permitted.
Golf lessons available.

Fees:

Weekday: 18-hole: $18 Cart: $10
9-hole: (N/A) Cart: (N/A)
Weekend: 18-hole: $24 Cart: $10
9-hole: (N/A) Cart: (N/A)

Located at I-35E exit Ave. D.

Texas Woman's Univ. Golf Course (6,647 yds) 940-898-3163

University Hill Station
Denton, TX 76204
Contact: Shari Cotton
Description: Short course near Texas
Woman's University but enjoyable for
men and women as well as children. A
good course for those just getting into
the game. **Par:** 69.
Rentals: Golf Carts, Pull Carts, Golf
Clubs

Open to the public. Walking permitted.

Fees:

Weekday: 18-hole: $11 Cart: $15
9-hole: (N/A) Cart: $8
Weekend: 18-hole: $13 Cart: $15
9-hole: (N/A) Cart: $8

Located off Smith St. near TWU.

Yoakum County Golf Course (6,292 yds) 806-592-2947

Box 1259
Denver City, TX 79323
Contact: Wiley Osborne
Description: Like many Texas
nine-hole courses, this semiprivate
course has double tees to set up a good
18-hole round. The length of the course
is favorable. **Par:** 36.
Rentals: Golf Carts
Open to the public. Walking permitted.

Fees:

Weekday: 18-hole: $10.63 Cart: $16
9-hole: (N/A) Cart: $8
Weekend: 18-hole: $13.28 Cart: $16
9-hole: (N/A) Cart: $8

Located six miles north of town on Hwy
214.

Thorntree Country Club (7,050 yds) 972-296-7317

825 W. Wintergreen Road
DeSoto, TX 75115
Contact: Ron King
Description: An outstanding private
club south of downtown Dallas. At 666
yards, the first hole is the longest par 5
in North Texas. The clubhouse is tops.
Par: 72.
Rentals: Golf Carts, Golf Clubs, Driving
Range
Members and guests only. Golf lessons

available. Walking permitted.

Fees:

Weekday: 18-hole: $45 Cart: $11
9-hole: (N/A) Cart: $5
Weekend: 18-hole: $65 Cart: $11
9-hole: (N/A) Cart: $5

Located west of I-35, 3½ miles west on
Wintergreen Road.

Devine Golf Course (6,503 yds) 830-663-9943

116 Malone Drive
Devine, TX 78016
Contact: Kevin Yanity
Description: Many golfers playing this 18-hole semiprivate course can hit good shots but still make bogey after three-putting the fast, undulating greens. **Par:** 72.
Rentals: Golf Carts, Pull Carts
Open to the public. Walking permitted. Golf lessons available.

Fees:

Weekday: 18-hole: $10 Cart: $7.50
9-hole: $6 Cart: $4
Weekend: 18-hole: $13.85 Cart: $7.50 9-hole: $7 Cart: $4

Located at the intersection of I-35 and Hwy 173 south of San Antonio.

Neches Pines Golf Course (7,014 yds) 409-829-5086

900 Harris St.
Diboll, TX 75941
Contact: Jimmy Medlin
Description: A former nine-hole course that added a second nine in 1991. The newer nine is tight with water hazards, hills, and many trees. Clubhouse has a pro shop. **Par:** 72.
Rentals: Golf Carts, Pull Carts, Driving Range

Open to the public. Walking permitted. Golf lessons available.

Fees:

Weekday: 18-hole: $15 Cart: $10.83
9-hole: (N/A) Cart: $4.87
Weekend: 18-hole: $20 Cart: $10.83
9-hole: (N/A) Cart: $4.87

Located east of Hwy 59 on Harris St.

Dickinson Country Club (6,425 yds) 281-337-3031

P.O. Box 432
Dickinson, TX 77539
Contact: Bobby Tillison
Description: A nine-hole private course constructed in a wooded area that has lots of trees and water hazards on seven holes. Double tees make 18 holes great. Food and drinks. **Par:** 36.
Members and guests only. Walking permitted.

Fees:

Weekday: 18-hole: $10 Cart: $7
9-hole: (N/A) Cart: $5
Weekend: 18-hole: $15 Cart: $7
9-hole: (N/A) Cart: $5

Located on I-45 southwest of Houston.

Green River Golf Club

(1,800 yds) 281-337-2021

2415 Caroline
Dickinson, TX 77539
Contact: Alan Howard
Description: Lighted par 3 good for practice or first-time golfers. Several challenging holes with sand and rough. Can be busy on summer nights or weekends. Closed Monday. **Par:** 27.

Fees:

Weekday: 9-hole: $4.50 Cart: $3
Weekend: 9-hole: $6 Cart: $3.50

From Houston, take exit 517 off I-45, go past Highway 3, and turn right on Caroline to course.

Dimmitt Country Club

(3,306 yds) 806-647-4502

West Halsell
Dimmitt, TX 79027
Contact: Kevin Gwyn
Description: A nice nine-hole course that swirls around a lake and has several out-of-bounds. It is semiprivate, but out-of-county golfers can play the course at a higher rate. **Par:** 36.
Rentals: Golf Carts, Driving Range

Members and guests only. Golf lessons available. Walking permitted.

Fees:

Weekday: 18-hole: $10 Cart: $10
9-hole: (N/A) Cart: $4
Weekend: 18-hole: $20 Cart: $10
9-hole: (N/A) Cart: $4

Located west of town.

North Plains Country Club

(6,656 yds) 806-935-7375

Sunray Highway
Dumas, TX 79029
Contact: Golf Shop
Description: Fairly new private course in small West Texas setting. Course has some water and has trees and traps. Keep the ball in the fairways if you wish to be successfull. **Par:** 72.
Rentals: Golf Carts

Fees:

Weekday: 18-hole: $10 Cart: $7
9-hole: (N/A) Cart: (N/A)
Weekend: 18-hole: $12 Cart: $7
9-hole: (N/A) Cart: (N/A)

One mile north of Dumas on Sunray Hwy (119).

Pheasant Trails Golf Course   (6,481 yds) 806-935-7375

Highway 119
Dumas, TX 79029
Contact: Charlie Nelson
Description: Converted to 18 holes in 1991 after original nine holes were built in 1950. Course has swimming pool, restaurant, bar, meeting room, and lockers. **Par:** 71.
Rentals: Golf Carts, Pull Carts, Golf Clubs, Driving Range

Open to the public. Walking permitted. Golf lessons available.

Fees:

Weekday: 18-hole: $8.50 Cart: $9.03 9-hole: $7.50 Cart: $4.50
Weekend: 18-hole: $11.69 Cart: $9.03 9-hole: $10 Cart: $4.50

Located four miles north of Dumas on Maddox Road.

Mesquite Grove Golf Course   (7,005 yds) 915-692-4405

766 Mesquite Trail
Dyess AFB, TX 79607
Contact: Paul Carlile
Description: A very long 18-hole military course that has elevated bentgrass greens that are easy to three-putt. Large sand traps and a creek. One of the best Texas military layouts. **Par:** 72.
Rentals: Golf Carts, Pull Carts, Golf Clubs, Driving Range

Members and guests only. Golf lessons available. Walking permitted.

Fees:

Weekday: 18-hole: $12 Cart: $15 9-hole: (N/A) Cart: $10
Weekend: 18-hole: $16.50 Cart: $15 9-hole: (N/A) Cart: $10

Located west of Abilene.

Eagle Lake Recreation Center   (3,300 yds) 409-234-5981

P.O. Box 845
Eagle Lake, TX 77434
Contact: Larry Broesche
Description: There are trees in the middle of the fairways on this nine-hole public course, which make for difficult tee shots. Also, the ninth hole is a long watered par 3. Food. **Par:** 35.
Rentals: Golf Carts, Pull Carts

Open to the public. Walking permitted.

Fees:

Weekday: 18-hole: $7 Cart: $13 9-hole: $5 Cart: $3
Weekend: 18-hole: $9 Cart: $13 9-hole: $8 Cart: $3

Located off Hwy 90A West.

Eagle Pass Golf Course

(6,163 yds) 830-773-9761

483 Bliss St.
Fort Duncan Park
Eagle Pass, TX 78852
Contact: Bill Hickey
Description: The Rio Grande runs along this nine-hole public course but doesn't come into play. A creek from the river does on one hole. Large greens and three-putts. **Par:** 36.
Rentals: Golf Carts, Pull Carts, Driving Range

Open to the public. Walking permitted. Golf lessons available.

Fees:

Weekday: 18-hole: $10 Cart: $10.83
9-hole: (N/A) Cart: $2.50
Weekend: 18-hole: $15 Cart: $16.84
9-hole: (N/A) Cart: $2.50

Located in Fort Duncan Park.

Lakeside Country Club

(6,174 yds) 254-629-2892

109 Connella
Eastland, TX 76448
Contact: Rod Straw
Description: A public nine-hole course that has a very tough par 5 with trees in the middle of the fairway 200 yards off the tee. Three creeks run through the course. Snacks. **Par:** 36.
Rentals: Golf Carts, Pull Carts, Golf Clubs

Open to the public. Walking permitted. Golf lessons available.

Fees:

Weekday: 18-hole: $7.50 Cart: $6.50
9-hole: (N/A) Cart: $3.25
Weekend: 18-hole: $9 Cart: $6.50
9-hole: (N/A) Cart: $3.25

Located on FM 3101 northwest of town.

Lone Cedar Country Club

(6,333 yds) 254-647-3613

Route 2, Box 152
Eastland, TX 76448
Contact: Jerry Doyle
Description: A nine-hole public course with holes that change from par 4 to par 5 on the second nine. Flat course with few trees. Clubhouse has food, drinks, and pro shop. **Par:** 35.
Open to the public. Walking permitted. Golf lessons available.

Fees:

Weekday: 18-hole: $10 Cart: $6.50
9-hole: (N/A) Cart: $4
Weekend: 18-hole: $15 Cart: $6.50
9-hole: (N/A) Cart: $4

Located off Hwy 570 north of Lake Leon.

Ebony Golf Course   (3,000 yds) 956-381-1244

300 W. Palms
Edinburg, TX 78539
Contact: Walter Shirah
Description: This is a 10-hole public course. Golfers play the original nine as the front nine, then skip the ninth hole and play the 10th hole as the 18th hole. Not long, the 10th hole is a 326-yard par 4. **Par:** 39.
Rentals: Golf Carts, Pull Carts, Golf Clubs

Open to the public. Walking permitted.

Fees:

Weekday: 18-hole: $9 Cart: $7.58
9-hole: $7 Cart: $3.75
Weekend: 18-hole: $9 Cart: $7.58
9-hole: $7 Cart: $3.75

Take Hwy 281 south to Palms Drive.

Monte Cristo Golf Course   (6,204 yds) 956-381-0965

Route 8, Box 985 D
Edinburg, TX 78539
Contact: Andy Garza
Description: The back nine on this 18-hole public course is a target nine with water surrounding fairways and greens. The front nine is wide open with young trees. Food, drinks, and pro shop. **Par:** 72.
Rentals: Golf Carts, Pull Carts, Golf Clubs

Open to the public. Walking permitted. Golf lessons available.

Fees:

Weekday: 18-hole: $12 Cart: $8
9-hole: $9 Cart: $8
Weekend: 18-hole: $12 Cart: $8
9-hole: $9 Cart: $8

Located on FM 1925 off route Route 8 in south Edinburg

Edna Country Club   (3,434 yds) 512-782-3010

P.O. Box 563
Edna, TX 77957
Contact: Charles Reithmeir
Description: The fairways on this nine-hole semiprivate course are extremely undulating, providing lots of uneven lies even after a good tee shot. Double tees. Food, pro shop, and big TV. **Par:** 36.
Rentals: Golf Carts, Pull Carts, Driving Range

Open to the public. Walking permitted. Golf lessons available.

Fees:

Weekday: 18-hole: $5 Cart: $10
9-hole: (N/A) Cart: $5
Weekend: 18-hole: $15 Cart: $15
9-hole: (N/A) Cart: $7.50

Located on Hwy 59 northeast of Victoria.

El Campo Country Club

(3,603 yds) 409-543-6592

Route 4, Box 47B
El Campo, TX 77437
Contact: Tim Supak
Description: Out-of-town golfers are welcome at this nine-hole private course. It is open with young trees and has water on eight holes. Double tees. Food and drinks. **Par:** 36.
Rentals: Golf Carts

Members and guests only. Golf lessons available. Walking permitted.

Fees:

Weekday: 18-hole: $15 Cart: $7.50
9-hole: (N/A) Cart: $4
Weekend: 18-hole: $15 Cart: $7.50
9-hole: (N/A) Cart: $4

> Located southwest of Houston on Hwy 59.

Eldorado Golf Club

(3,063 yds) 915-853-2036

P.O. Box 1116
Eldorado, TX 76936
Contact: Jim Nance
Description: This nine-hole public course has only one par 5, three par 4s, and five par 3s. The small greens and trees make the holes play tight. No water. **Par:** 32.
Rentals: Golf Carts
Open to the public. Walking permitted.

Fees:

Weekday: 18-hole: $9 Cart: $6 9-hole: (N/A) Cart: $2.50
Weekend: 18-hole: $9 Cart: $6 9-hole: (N/A) Cart: $2.50

> Located near middle of town near the stop sign.

Crooked Creek Country Club

(3,201 yds) 940-495-3832

Route 2
Electra, TX 76360
Contact: David Simon
Description: A nice nine-hole golf course with tight fairways and two creeks that run through the course. Clubhouse has snack bar and pro shop. **Par:** 36.
Rentals: Golf Carts

Open to the public. Walking permitted. Golf lessons available.

Fees:

Weekday: 18-hole: $7.50 Cart: $8
9-hole: (N/A) Cart: $4
Weekend: 18-hole: $10 Cart: $8
9-hole: (N/A) Cart: $4

> Located north on Hwy 25; east on Hwy 240.

Elkhart Golf Club

(6,100 yds) 903-764-2461

FM 1817
Elkhart, TX 75839
Contact: Darrell Thomas
Description: A short, very good public course that expanded to 18 holes in 1995. The course is tight with water on five holes. **Par:** 70.
Open to the public. Walking permitted. Golf lessons available.

Fees:

Weekday: 18-hole: $10.50 Cart: $7.50 9-hole: (N/A) Cart: $4
Weekend: 18-hole: $12.50 Cart: $7.50 9-hole: (N/A) Cart: $4

Located 25 miles north of Crockett.

Ascarate Golf Course

(6,500 yds) 915-772-7381

6900 Delta Drive
El Paso, TX 79905
Contact: Pat Alderoton
Description: Considered one of the toughest 18-hole courses in El Paso with undulating greens and a back nine filled with lots of water hazards. It has an easy nine-hole executive course with driveable par 4s. **Par:** 71.
Rentals: Golf Carts, Pull Carts, Golf Clubs, Driving Range

Open to the public. Walking permitted. Golf lessons available.

Fees:

Weekday: 18-hole: $10 Cart: $8 9-hole: $5 Cart: $8
Weekend: 18-hole: $13 Cart: $8 9-hole: $5 Cart: $8

Located east of El Paso at Alameda and Delta.

Cielo Vista Golf Course

(6,411 yds) 915-591-4927

1510 Hawkins
El Paso, TX 79925
Contact: Mark Pelletier
Description: Considered to be the fairest 18-hole course in El Paso with wide fairways, light bunkers, and only two small ponds. The driving range is lighted for lessons. **Par:** 71.
Rentals: Golf Carts, Pull Carts, Golf Clubs, Driving Range

Open to the public. Walking permitted. Golf lessons available.

Fees:

Weekday: 18-hole: $14 Cart: $8.66 9-hole: $7.04 Cart: $3.75
Weekend: 18-hole: $19.49 Cart: $8.66 9-hole: $7.58 Cart: $3.75

Located off I-10; north on Hawkins Road.

Coronado Country Club · (6,500 yds) 915-584-3841

1044 Broadmoor Drive
El Paso, TX 79912
Contact: Danny Swain
Description: A mid-length 18-hole private course that has very fast greens, no water hazards, and 14 out-of-bounds holes. Food, drinks, and pro shop. **Par:** 70.
Rentals: Golf Carts, Golf Clubs, Driving Range

Members and guests only. Golf lessons available. Walking permitted.

Fees:

Weekday: 18-hole: $40 Cart: $10
9-hole: $20 Cart: $4.50
Weekend: 18-hole: $50 Cart: $10
9-hole: $25 Cart: $4.50

> Located off I-10 on the Sunland Park exit to Thunderbird Road.

El Paso Country Club · (7,040 yds) 915-584-0511

5000 Country Club Place
El Paso, TX 79922
Contact: Cameron Doan
Description: An excellent 18-hole private course with fast, undulating bentgrass greens, water hazards, and bunkers. Course bends around Rio Grande. Food, drinks, and pro shop. **Par:** 71.
Rentals: Golf Carts, Golf Clubs, Driving Range

Members and guests only. Golf lessons available. Walking permitted.

Fees:

Weekday: 18-hole: $40 Cart: (N/A)
9-hole: (N/A) Cart: (N/A)
Weekend: 18-hole: $100 Cart: (N/A)
9-hole: (N/A) Cart: (N/A)

> Located south of I-10 off Mesa Road; left at Country Club Place.

Emerald Springs Golf & Conf. Ctr. · (7,000 yds) 915-852-3150

16000 Ashford St.
El Paso, TX 79927
Contact: Ignacio Vela
Description: A rather long 18-hole semiprivate course that has flat, wide open fairways lined with trees. Lots of water hazards and sand traps. Lee Trevino was once an assistant pro here. **Par:** 71.
Rentals: Golf Carts, Pull Carts, Golf Clubs, Driving Range

Open to the public. Walking permitted. Golf lessons available.

Fees:

Weekday: 18-hole: $19.50 Cart: (N/A)
9-hole: (N/A) Cart: $4.62
Weekend: 18-hole: $28.50 Cart: (N/A)
9-hole: (N/A) Cart: $4.62

> Located 2½ miles off I-10.

Painted Dunes Desert Golf Course (6,925 yds) 915-821-2122

12000 McCombs Road
El Paso, TX 79934
Contact: Bill Barnard
Description: The only golf course in Texas that is built on desert land with a demand for straight tee shots. Spectacular mountainside views ease the sting of any bad shots **Par:** 72.
Rentals: Golf Carts, Pull Carts, Golf Clubs, Driving Range

Open to the public. Walking permitted. Golf lessons available.

Fees:

Weekday: 18-hole: $19 Cart: $9.75
9-hole: $7.50 Cart: $5
Weekend: 18-hole: $27 Cart: $9.75
9-hole: $9 Cart: $8

Located northeast of El Paso on Hwy 54 East 10 miles from I-10. Turn left on McCombs; one mile on right.

Underwood Golf Course (36 hs) 915-562-2066

3200 Coe Avenue
El Paso, TX 79916
Contact: Bobby Kaerwer
Description: A 36-hole military course which added a new 18-hole course in November 1994. The original course is 40 years old with elevated bentgrass greens and flat fairways. **Par:** 72.
Rentals: Golf Carts, Pull Carts, Golf Clubs, Driving Range

Members and guests only. Golf lessons available. Walking permitted.

Fees:

Weekday: 18-hole: $15 Cart: $8
9-hole: $5.50 Cart: $4
Weekend: 18-hole: $18 Cart: $8
9-hole: $7 Cart: $4

Take I-10 to Gateway.

Vista Hills Country Club (7,200 yds) 915-592-6565

2210 Trawood Drive
El Paso, TX 79935
Contact: Terry Jennings
Description: A very long 18-hole private course with fast bentgrass greens, out-of-bounds, hilly fairways, and a lake. Club has food, tennis, pools, and pro shop. **Par:** 72.
Rentals: Golf Carts, Golf Clubs, Driving Range

Members and guests only. Golf lessons available. Walking permitted.

Fees:

Weekday: 18-hole: $25 Cart: $10.50
9-hole: $15 Cart: $4.33
Weekend: 18-hole: $35 Cart: $10.50
9-hole: $17.50 Cart: $4.33

Located off I-10 at the Lee Trevino exit.

Lakeside Country Club   (6,000 yds) 972-875-3641

Box 238
Country Club Drive
Ennis, TX 75119
Contact: Club Manager
Description: A nice nine-hole course with lots of water hazards and a very long par-5 seventh hole over water. Out-of-town golfers are welcome.
Par: 36.

Members and guests only. Walking permitted.

Fees:

Weekday: 18-hole: $15 Cart: (N/A)
9-hole: (N/A) Cart: (N/A)
Weekend: 18-hole: $20 Cart: (N/A)
9-hole: (N/A) Cart: (N/A)

> Located east of downtown Ennis off Hwy 287.

Summit at Eagle's View   (6,702 yds) 972-878-4653

102 Crescent View Drive
Ennis, TX 75119
Contact: Benny Passons
Description: An interesting public golf course that rolls around the hills. There are weekday discounts for seniors and all week discounts for women. **Par:** 72.
Rentals: Golf Carts, Pull Carts, Golf Clubs, Driving Range

Open to the public. Walking permitted. Golf lessons available.

Fees:

Weekday: 18-hole: $10 Cart: $8.50
9-hole: (N/A) Cart: (N/A)
Weekend: 18-hole: $17 Cart: $8.50
9-hole: (N/A) Cart: (N/A)

> Take exit 258 off I-45 south of Dallas.

Texas Star Golf Club   (7,100 yds) 888-Tex-star

1400 Texas Star Parkway
Euless, TX 76040
Contact: Duff Cunningham
Description: New daily-fee course designed by Keith Foster, architect of The Quarry in San Antonio. Each hole features beautiful mounding and is named for its particular charm. Owned by City of Euless. **Par:** 71.
Rentals: Golf Carts, Golf Clubs, Driving Range

Open to the public. Walking permitted. Golf lessons available.

Fees:

Weekday: 18-hole: $34 Cart: $12
9-hole: (N/A) Cart: (N/A)
Weekend: 18-hole: $47 Cart: $12
9-hole: (N/A) Cart: (N/A)

> Located in Euless Industrial Park. Take Hwy 10 to Euless and South Pipeline Road.

Falfurrias Golf Course

(6,480 yds) 512-325-5348

400 E. Travis
Falfurrias, TX 78355
Contact: George Heitz
Description: One of the most popular nine-hole courses in South Texas because of no sand traps, hills, wide fairways, small greens, and only two water hazards. Snack bar and pro shop. **Par:** 36.
Rentals: Golf Carts

Open to the public. Walking permitted.

Fees:

Weekday: 18-hole: $7 Cart: $7.54
9-hole: (N/A) Cart: $3.23
Weekend: 18-hole: $8 Cart: $7.54
9-hole: (N/A) Cart: $3.23

Located on Hwy 281 East.

Farwell Country Club

(6,700 yds) 806-481-9210

Route 2
Farwell, TX 79325
Contact: Chris Fontanilla
Description: Double tees make this nine-hole semiprivate course really nice for an 18-hole round. The course is normal length, however, thanks to the Panhandle wind, it plays longer. **Par:** 36.
Rentals: Golf Carts, Pull Carts

Open to the public. Walking permitted.

Fees:

Weekday: 18-hole: $7 Cart: $8 9-hole: (N/A) Cart: $4
Weekend: 18-hole: $12 Cart: $8
9-hole: (N/A) Cart: $4

Located off Hwy 60 West.

Flatonia Golf Course

(6,112 yds) 512-865-2922

P.O. Box 391
Flatonia, TX 78941
Contact: Ed Husley
Description: Deep grass bunkers make this nine-hole public course play tough. With undulating greens, bunker recovery shots often end up with a three-putt double bogey. **Par:** 36.
Rentals: Golf Carts, Pull Carts, Driving Range

Open to the public. Walking permitted.

Fees:

Weekday: 18-hole: $7.50 Cart: $6.50
9-hole: (N/A) Cart: $4
Weekend: 18-hole: $12.50 Cart: $6.50 9-hole: (N/A) Cart: $4

Located one mile east of town on U.S. 90.

Bridlewood Golf Club

(7,036 yds) 972-355-4800

4000 Windsor
Flower Mound, TX 75028
Contact: Courtney Connell
Description: First design effort from PGA Tour veteran D.A. Weiberg. A solid daily-fee layout through gentle hills and trees. Back nine especially strong with golfers forced to think on each shot. Soft spikes only. **Par:** 72.
Rentals: Golf Carts, Golf Clubs, Driving Range

Open to the public. Walking permitted. Golf lessons available.

Fees:

Weekday: 18-hole: $60 Cart: (N/A)
9-hole: (N/A) Cart: (N/A)
Weekend: 18-hole: $75 Cart: (N/A)
9-hole: (N/A) Cart: (N/A)

Located 15 minutes north of DFW Airport on FM 1171 in Flower Mound.

Tour 18 Golf Course

(7,033 yds) 817-430-2000

8718 Amen Corner
Flower Mound, TX 75028
Contact: Jim Wise
Description: Course features faithful re-creations of some of the most famous holes in American golf. Holes featured include Amen Corner and TPC 17 with island green. Opened in 1995, like successful Houston area layout with more elevation. **Par:** 72.
Rentals: Golf Carts, Golf Clubs, Driving Range

Open to the public. Golf lessons available. Mandatory carts.

Fees:

Weekday: 18-hole: $75 Cart: (N/A)
9-hole: (N/A) Cart: (N/A)
Weekend: 18-hole: $85 Cart: (N/A)
9-hole: (N/A) Cart: (N/A)

Take I-35E north to exit FM 1171 and drive 15 miles to Tour 18 entrance.

Floydada Country Club

(3,165 yds) 806-983-2769

Box 8
Floydada, TX 79235
Contact: James McNeil
Description: A nine-hole semiprivate course that was constructed in a canyon settting around a hill with a creek. Lots of deer, turkeys, and wildlife hang out on the course. **Par:** 36.
Rentals: Golf Carts, Golf Clubs, Driving Range

Open to the public. Walking permitted. Golf lessons available.

Fees:

Weekday: 18-hole: $12 Cart: $9
9-hole: (N/A) Cart: $4.50
Weekend: 18-hole: $18 Cart: $9
9-hole: (N/A) Cart: $4.50

Located south of town on Hwy 62.

Anderson Golf Course

(6,703 yds) 254-287-6921

Fort Hood Golf Facility
Bldg 5794
Fort Hood, TX 76544
Contact: Frank Jacobson
Description: This is the toughest Fort Hood course because it is long with lots of water, sand traps, and dogleg holes. Retired military, civilians pay higher green fees. The courses are four miles apart on the base. **Par:** 72.
Rentals: Golf Carts, Pull Carts, Driving Range

Open to military personnel and the public. Walking permitted. Golf lessons available.

Fees:

Weekday: 18-hole: $10 Cart: $7
9-hole: (N/A) Cart: (N/A)
Weekend: 18-hole: $15 Cart: $7
9-hole: (N/A) Cart: (N/A)

Located at East Gate at Fort Hood in Killeen.

Clear Creek Golf Course

(6,768 yds) 254-287-4130

Fort Hood Golf Facility
Bldg 52381
Fort Hood, TX 76544
Contact: Frank Jacobson
Description: Fort Hood allows civilians to play both courses for a slightly higher green fee. Clear Creek runs through the course with tight, hilly fairways and big greens. Food and pro shop. **Par:** 72.
Rentals: Golf Carts, Pull Carts, Golf Clubs, Driving Range

Open to military personnel and the public. Walking permitted. Golf lessons available.

Fees:

Weekday: 18-hole: $10 Cart: $7
9-hole: (N/A) Cart: (N/A)
Weekend: 18-hole: $15 Cart: $7
9-hole: (N/A) Cart: (N/A)

Located by West Gate; take Battalion Road through post to course at Clear Creek Road.

Fort Sam Houston Golf Course   (36 hs) 210-222-9386

Bldg 2901
Fort Sam Houston, TX 78234
Contact: Dick Bartel
LaLoma Grande Course Description:
A great 36-hole military course. The
LaLoma Grande Course was the site of
the 1956 Texas Open won by Gene
Littler with a 276 score, the highest
local winning score since World War II.
Course is mean. **Par:** 72 (6,470 yards).

Salado Course Description: The
Salado Course is a newer, very pretty
18-hole course. The front nine goes
around a lake. The back nine drops
down to a valley created by Salado
Creek. Beautiful new clubhouse opened
in June 1994. **Par:** 72 (6,755 yards).

Rentals: Golf Carts, Pull Carts, Golf
Clubs, Driving Range
Members and guests only. Golf lessons
available. Walking permitted.

Fees:

Weekday: 18-hole: $16 Cart: $8
9-hole: (N/A) Cart: $4
Weekend: 18-hole: $18 Cart: $8
9-hole: (N/A) Cart: $4

Located in San Antonio off Harry
Wurzbach Road.

Fort Stockton Golf Club   (6,655 yds) 915-336-2050

N. Highway 285 & Airport Road
Fort Stockton, TX 79735
Contact: Bill Marrow
Description: There are nine water
hazards in front of the greens on this
18-hole public course. The bentgrass
greens are multi-tiered and easy to
three-putt. Home course of PGA pro
Blaine McCallister. **Par:** 72.
Rentals: Golf Carts, Pull Carts, Driving
Range

Open to the public. Walking permitted.

Fees:

Weekday: 18-hole: $10 Cart: $8
9-hole: (N/A) Cart: $4
Weekend: 18-hole: $15 Cart: $8
9-hole: (N/A) Cart: $4

Located on Hwy 285 northwest of
town.

Carswell Golf Club

(6,568 yds) 817-738-8402

6520 White Settlement Road
Fort Worth, TX 76114
Contact: Stack Bowers
Description: Ben Hogan consulted in
the design of a golf course on a base
where he was stationed during World
War II. It is now a public course with a
beautiful clubhouse. **Par:** 71.
Rentals: Golf Carts, Pull Carts, Golf
Clubs, Driving Range

Open to the public. Walking permitted.
Golf lessons available.

Fees:

Weekday: 18-hole: $14 Cart: $10
9-hole: (N/A) Cart: (N/A)
Weekend: 18-hole: $20 Cart: $10
9-hole: (N/A) Cart: (N/A)

Located north of I-30 off Roaring
Springs Road in west Fort Worth.

Casino Beach Par-3

(1,110 yds) 817-237-3695

7464 Jacksboro Hwy
Fort Worth, TX 76114
Contact: Steve Champion
Description: Nice short game warmup
for golfers with three par-4 holes, the
longest being 232 yards. Practice range
has been in area for three decades with
nine-hole par-3 course added in 1987.
Trees, water make it tough. **Par:** 30.
Rentals: Pull Carts, Driving Range
Open to the public. Walking permitted.
Golf lessons available.

Fees:

Weekday: 18-hole: $6 Cart: (N/A)
9-hole: (N/A) Cart: $1
Weekend: 18-hole: $7.50 Cart: (N/A)
9-hole: (N/A) Cart: $1

Take I-30 to Loop 820 West. Exit
Jacksboro Hwy West, go left on access
road.

Colonial Country Club

(7,096 yds) 817-927-4243

3735 Country Club Drive
Fort Worth, TX 76109
Contact: Dow Finsterwald Jr.
Description: Colonial is one of the
most famous golf courses in Texas and
the annual site of the PGA's MasterCard
Colonial. There is a Ben Hogan museum
in the clubhouse. **Par:** 70.
Rentals: Golf Carts, Driving Range
Members and guests only. Golf lessons
available. Walking permitted.

Fees:

Weekday: 18-hole: $50 Cart: $15
9-hole: (N/A) Cart: $7.50
Weekend: 18-hole: $75 Cart: $15
9-hole: (N/A) Cart: $7.50

Located south of I-30 off University to
Country Club Drive.

Diamond Oaks Country Club   (6,941 yds) 817-834-6261

5821 Diamond Oaks Drive
Fort Worth, TX 76117
Contact: Dan Gibler
Description: A smart, challenging golf course with huge oak trees and not many bunkers on flat fairways of an old cattle ranch. Nice private clubhouse. **Par:** 70.
Rentals: Golf Carts, Driving Range

Members and guests only. Golf lessons available. Walking permitted.

Fees:

Weekday: 18-hole: $25 Cart: $18
9-hole: (N/A) Cart: $9
Weekend: 18-hole: $35 Cart: $18
9-hole: (N/A) Cart: $9

> Located northeast of Fort Worth off Hwy 377 south of Loop 820.

Eagle Mountain Country Club   (6,518 yds) 817-236-3400

7200 Golf Club Drive
Fort Worth, TX 76179
Contact: Steve Townsend
Description: A semiprivate golf course with a hilly back nine that has lots of out-of-bounds. Good golfers often have to hit layup tee shots. **Par:** 72.
Rentals: Golf Carts, Pull Carts, Golf Clubs, Driving Range
Open to the public. Walking permitted. Golf lessons available.

Fees:

Weekday: 18-hole: $15 Cart: $9
9-hole: $14 Cart: $4.50
Weekend: 18-hole: $22 Cart: $9
9-hole: $17 Cart: $4.50

> Located 4½ miles north of 820 off Boat Club Drive (FM 1220) off Hwy 199.

Fossil Creek Golf Club   (6,895 yds) 817-847-1900

3401 Club Gate Drive
Fort Worth, TX 76137
Contact: Robert Larkin
Description: A perfect Arnold Palmer go-for-broke public course where golfers can try to make eagles over par-5 water hazards. Plenty of trees and traps. **Par:** 72.
Rentals: Golf Carts, Golf Clubs, Driving Range

Open to the public. Golf lessons available. Mandatory carts.

Fees:

Weekday: 18-hole: $55 Cart: (N/A)
9-hole: (N/A) Cart: (N/A)
Weekend: 18-hole: $70 Cart: (N/A)
9-hole: (N/A) Cart: (N/A)

> Located one mile north of I-35W/Loop 820 intersection. Take Western Center exit off I-35W.

Glen Garden Golf & Country Club (6,166 yds) 817-535-7582

2916 Glen Garden Drive
Fort Worth, TX 76119
Contact: Alan Courtney
Description: The golf course where
Ben Hogan and Byron Nelson caddied
and took up golf. A semiprivate club
and former home of the LPGA's Sandra
Palmer. **Par:** 71.
Rentals: Golf Carts, Pull Carts, Driving
Range

Open to the public. Walking permitted.
Golf lessons available.

Fees:

Weekday: 18-hole: $25 Cart: $9
9-hole: (N/A) Cart: $4.50
Weekend: 18-hole: $35 Cart: $9
9-hole: (N/A) Cart: $4.50

Located off U.S. 287 south, exit
Wichita St., and south to Glen Garden.

Ideal Golf Ranch (1,759 yds) 817-572-7312

5151 Mansfield Hwy.
Fort Worth, TX 76119
Contact: Golf Shop
Description: Solid par-3 course for
those looking to strengthen their short
game. Ideal Golf has seven par 3 holes
with two medium length par 4s. Good
for beginners or those looking to brush
the rust off their game. **Par:** 29.

Fees:

Weekday: 9-hole: $7 Cart: (N/A)
Weekend: 9-hole: $7 Cart: (N/A)

Located on Mansfield Highway, just
inside Loop 820 on the southeast
corner of the intersection.

Meadowbrook Municipal Golf Course (6,416 yds) 817-457-4616

1815 Jensen Road
Fort Worth, TX 76112
Contact: Gary McMillon
Description: An excellent 18-hole
public course that is only 6,416 yards
but is tight and very hilly. Six holes
have water hazards that easily grab
errant golf balls. **Par:** 71.
Rentals: Golf Carts, Pull Carts, Golf
Clubs

Open to the public. Walking permitted.
Golf lessons available.

Fees:

Weekday: 18-hole: $11 Cart: $8.65
9-hole: (N/A) Cart: $4.85
Weekend: 18-hole: $13 Cart: $8.65
9-hole: (N/A) Cart: $4.85

Located south of I-30 off Loop 820 to
Jenson Road.

Mira Vista Country Club   (6,844 yds) 817-294-6600

6600 Mira Vista Blvd.
Fort Worth, TX 76132
Contact: Lindy Miller
Description: One of the smartest and most challenging golf courses in Texas. Tee shots must be straight and irons on line to hit the greens. Clubhouse has great view. **Par:** 71.
Rentals: Golf Carts, Golf Clubs, Driving Range

Members and guests only. Golf lessons available. Walking permitted.

Fees:

Weekday: 18-hole: $60 Cart: $12
9-hole: (N/A) Cart: $5.50
Weekend: 18-hole: $60 Cart: $12
9-hole: (N/A) Cart: $5.50

Located south of I-20 off Bryant Ervin Road.

Pecan Valley Golf Course   (36 hs) 817-249-1845

6400 Pecan Valley Drive
P.O. Box 26632
Fort Worth, TX 76126
Contact: Greg Scott
Hills Course Description: The Hills Course is the newer, shorter, and prettier layout in this very good 36-hole public layout. Great views of Benbrook Lake from some holes. Watch out for trees, traps, and turf triple play. **Par:** 70 (6,470 yards).

River Course Description: A 36-hole public golf complex. The River Course was redesigned to make it play tougher. The easy par-5 second hole was

converted to a par 4. The 18th hole is a go-for-broke par 5 over a water hazard. **Par:** 72 (6,579 yards).
Rentals: Golf Carts, Pull Carts, Golf Clubs, Driving Range
Open to the public. Walking permitted. Golf lessons available.

Fees:

Weekday: 18-hole: $11 Cart: $8
9-hole: (N/A) Cart: (N/A)
Weekend: 18-hole: $13 Cart: $8
9-hole: (N/A) Cart: (N/A)

Take I-20 west, exit 429B (Winscott Plover Road) to FM 1042.

Ridglea Country Club (36 hs) 817-732-8111

3700 Bernie Anderson Drive
Fort Worth, TX 76116
Contact: Keith Davidson
South Course Description: The South Course is more of a championship layout which is most popular with men and low handicappers. Good change of pace for 36-hole private club complex. Players can enjoy best of both courses. Food and drinks available at both courses. **Par:** 72 (7,192 yards).

North Course Description: The North Course is shorter but tighter than the South Course. It has tougher greens and hills. North clubhouse is the main clubhouse with restaurants, locker room, and pool. **Par:** 71 (6,975 yards).
Rentals: Golf Carts, Driving Range
Members and guests only. Golf lessons available. Walking permitted.

Fees:

Weekday: 18-hole: $40 Cart: $9
9-hole: (N/A) Cart: (N/A)
Weekend: 18-hole: $85 Cart: $9
9-hole: (N/A) Cart: (N/A)

Located off Camp Bowie.

River Crest Country Club (6,246 yds) 817-738-9221

1501 Western
Fort Worth, TX 76107
Contact: Mac Spikes
Description: One of the oldest golf courses in Texas, built in 1911. New routing causes lots of out-of-bounds. Club and course were redone in 1996 in celebration of 85 years. Clubhouse has restaurant, lockers, pool, tennis courts, and pro shop. **Par:** 70.
Rentals: Golf Carts, Driving Range

Members and guests only. Golf lessons available. Walking permitted.

Fees:

Weekday: 18-hole: $35 Cart: $10
9-hole: (N/A) Cart: (N/A)
Weekend: 18-hole: $60 Cart: $10
9-hole: (N/A) Cart: (N/A)

Located off I-30 exit Ashland north to club.

Rockwood Golf Course   (27 hs) 817-624-1771

1851 Jacksboro Hwy
Fort Worth, TX 76114
Contact: Ray Lopez
Description: A 27-hole public course.
Most golfers play the Red and White
nines as an 18-hole round. The Blue
nine at 3,600 yards is very long and
tough. **Par:** 71.
Rentals: Golf Carts, Pull Carts, Golf
Clubs, Driving Range

Open to the public. Walking permitted.
Golf lessons available.

Fees:

Weekday: 18-hole: $12.00 Cart:
$19.50 9-hole: (N/A) Cart: $10.80
Weekend: 18-hole: $16.00 Cart:
$19.50 9-hole: (N/A) Cart: $10.80

Located off Jacksboro Hwy turn left on
Rockwood Parkway in north Ft Worth.

Shady Oaks Country Club   (6,975 yds) 817-732-3333

320 Roaring Springs Road
Fort Worth, TX 76114
Contact: Mike Wright
Description: Ben Hogan's home course.
Hogan liked to hit balls on vacant holes
but never played. Members can also play
a nine-hole par-3 course. **Par:** 71.
Rentals: Golf Carts, Golf Clubs, Driving
Range
Members and guests only. Golf lessons
available. Walking permitted.

Fees:

Weekday: 18-hole: $50 Cart: $10
9-hole: (N/A) Cart: $5
Weekend: 18-hole: $60 Cart: $10
9-hole: (N/A) Cart: $5

From downtown, take I-30 west to
Roaring Springs Road and go north.
Club is on the left.

Southern Oaks Golf Course   (7,300 yds) 817-426-2400

Fort Worth, TX 76028
Contact: Golf Shop
Description: New design from PGA
golfer Mark Brooks opened in late April
and features a long, challenging course in
southwest Tarrant County near Burleson.
Plenty of trees along with water hazards
and undulating greens. **Par:** 72.

Fees:

Weekday: 18-hole: $60 w/ cart 9-hole:
(N/A)
Weekend: 18-hole: $70 w/ cart
9-hole: (N/A)

Call for directions

Sycamore Creek Golf Course   (3,070 yds) 817-535-7241

401 Martin Luther King
Fort Worth, TX 76104
Contact: Ira Meachem
Description: Reopened in January 1994. It was an executive course and is now a great nine-hole course with double tees to make an 18-hole round different from a nine-hole trip. **Par:** 35.
Rentals: Golf Carts, Pull Carts, Golf Clubs

Open to the public. Walking permitted.

Fees:

Weekday: 18-hole: $21 Cart: $10
9-hole: (N/A) Cart: $5
Weekend: 18-hole: $26 Cart: $10
9-hole: (N/A) Cart: $5

Take I-30 east to Beach St. exit, then south on Vickery.

Timber-View Golf Club   (6,395 yds) 817-478-3601

4508 E. Enon
Fort Worth, TX 76140
Contact: Tommy Fouts
Description: A short 18-hole public course with no bunkers, small greens, and flat fairways. A great course for newcomers and kids to get started. Senior discounts. **Par:** 72.
Rentals: Golf Carts, Pull Carts, Golf Clubs

Open to the public. Walking permitted. Golf lessons available.

Fees:

Weekday: 18-hole: $7 Cart: $8 9-hole: $5 Cart: $4
Weekend: 18-hole: $10 Cart: $8
9-hole: $7 Cart: $5

Located south of Loop 820 to Anglin Road.

Woodhaven Country Club   (6,506 yds) 817-457-2143

913 Country Club Lane
Fort Worth, TX 76112
Contact: Michael Harrison
Description: A very interesting 18-hole course with lots of hills, water, and tough greens. Great layout by Leon Howard has hosted three LPGA Tour events. **Par:** 71.
Rentals: Golf Carts, Golf Clubs, Driving Range

Members and guests only. Golf lessons available. Walking permitted.

Fees:

Weekday: 18-hole: $15 Cart: $10
9-hole: (N/A) Cart: $6
Weekend: 18-hole: $25 Cart: $10
9-hole: (N/A) Cart: $6

Located north of I-30; exit Bridgewood north, turn left on Bridge.

Z-Boaz Golf Course   (6,033 yds) 817-738-6287

3240 Lackland
Fort Worth, TX 76116
Contact: Greg Scott
Description: The most fun public
course in Fort Worth. Z-Boaz is just
over 6,000 yards from the white tees.
However, there are lots of trees,
requiring good tee shots. **Par:** 70.
Rentals: Golf Carts, Pull Carts, Golf
Clubs

Open to the public. Walking permitted.
Golf lessons available.

Fees:

Weekday: 18-hole: $10 Cart: $8
9-hole: (N/A) Cart: $4.50
Weekend: 18-hole: $12 Cart: $8
9-hole: (N/A) Cart: $4.50

Located south of I-30 exit 8A.

Oak Grove Golf Club   (3,545 yds) 409-828-9907

Franklin, TX 77857
Contact: Golf Shop
Description: Good nine-hole test in
tree-lined Brazos Valley surroundings.
Course features trees on most holes,
some water, and tricky greens. **Par:** 35.
Rentals: Golf Carts
Private but does allow some outside
play.

Fees:

Weekday: 18-hole: (N/A) Cart: (N/A)
9-hole: $7 Cart: $10
Weekend: 18-hole: (N/A) Cart: (N/A)
9-hole: $10 Cart: $10

Take Hwy 6 through Herne and go west
on Franklin cut-off. Course is one mile
west of town.

Dogwood Trails Golf Course   (3,300 yds) 903-876-4336

P.O. Box 1105
Frankston, TX 75763
Contact: Tom Lutz
Description: This nine-hole semiprivate
course is located in the piney woods,
which means very tight fairways. The
course is reasonably long and has water
and trees. **Par:** 36.
Rentals: Golf Carts
Open to the public. Walking permitted.

Fees:

Weekday: 18-hole: $8 Cart: $8 9-hole:
(N/A) Cart: (N/A)
Weekend: 18-hole: $8 Cart: $8 9-hole:
(N/A) Cart: (N/A)

Located six miles south of town on Hwy
155.

Lady Bird Johnson Golf Course   (6,432 yds) 800-950-8147

Highway 16 South
LBJ State Park
Fredericksburg, TX 78624
Contact: Russell Parsons
Description: One of the prettiest 18-hole public courses in Texas. Thanks to trees and hills, it is a classic Hill Country golf course with a flatter back nine. Worth any drive. **Par:** 72.
Rentals: Golf Carts, Pull Carts, Golf Clubs, Driving Range

Open to the public. Walking permitted. Golf lessons available.

Fees:

Weekday: 18-hole: $11 Cart: $7
9-hole: $6 Cart: $3.50
Weekend: 18-hole: $17.50 Cart: $7
9-hole: $7 Cart: $3.50

Located south of town on Hwy 16 at LBJ State Park.

Freeport Community Golf Course   (6,556 yds) 409-233-8311

830 Slaughter Road
Freeport, TX 77541
Contact: Larry Shaw
Description: A river runs behind this 18-hole public course, creating a lot of water hazards. There are elevated tees and greens and large sand traps. Pro shop and food. **Par:** 71.
Rentals: Golf Carts, Pull Carts, Golf Clubs, Driving Range

Open to the public. Walking permitted. Golf lessons available.

Fees:

Weekday: 18-hole: $10 Cart: $8
9-hole: (N/A) Cart: $4.50
Weekend: 18-hole: $13 Cart: $8
9-hole: (N/A) Cart: $4.50

Located south of Houston on Hwy 288.

Friendswood Country Club   (6,721 yds) 281-492-4653

No. 3 Country Club Drive
Friendswood, TX 77546
Contact: Bob Kirkpatrick
Description: A nice 18-hole public course which is laid out on a housing development that causes out-of-bounds. Water, mainly manmade lakes and natural creeks, can be a factor. **Par:** 72.
Rentals: Golf Carts, Pull Carts, Golf Clubs, Driving Range

Open to the public. Walking permitted. Golf lessons available.

Fees:

Weekday: 18-hole: $13 Cart: $9
9-hole: $10 Cart: $5
Weekend: 18-hole: $17 Cart: $9
9-hole: $10 Cart: $5

Take I-45 south of Houston, then west on Hwy 528.

Friona Country Club

(3,206 yds) 806-247-3125

1505 W. 5th St.
Friona, TX 79035
Contact: Board of Directors
Description: A nine-hole course that is short with flat fairways, trees, nice greens, some water, and grass bunkers. Clubhouse has a restaurant, locker room, and pro shop. **Par:** 36.
Rentals: Golf Carts

Members and guests only. Walking permitted.

Fees:

Weekday: 18-hole: $10.60 Cart: $14
9-hole: (N/A) Cart: $7
Weekend: 18-hole: $20.50 Cart: $14
9-hole: (N/A) Cart: $7

Located west on Hwy 60 to W. 5th St.

Plantation Resort Golf Club

(6,382 yds) 972-335-4653

4701 Plantation Lane
Frisco, TX 75035
Contact: Perry Arthur
Description: A very interesting 18-hole public course in the Dallas area. Two par-4 holes under 300 yards require irons off the tee to avoid the water in front of the green. Nice club in booming small city. **Par:** 72.
Rentals: Golf Carts, Golf Clubs, Driving Range

Open to the public. Golf lessons available. Mandatory carts.

Fees:

Weekday: 18-hole: $42 Cart: (N/A)
9-hole: (N/A) Cart: (N/A)
Weekend: 18-hole: $57 Cart: (N/A)
9-hole: (N/A) Cart: (N/A)

Located north of Hwy 121, three miles east of Hwy 289, look for signs.

Stonebriar Country Club

(7,064 yds) 972-625-8916

5050 Country Club Drive
Frisco, TX 75034
Contact: Bill Andre
Description: Former site of J.C. Penney LPGA Skins game. Course is long and very tight. Clubhouse is luxury at its finest with meeting rooms, lockers, food, and pro shop. **Par:** 72.
Rentals: Golf Carts, Golf Clubs, Driving Range

Members and guests only. Golf lessons available. Walking permitted.

Fees:

Weekday: 18-hole: $60 Cart: $11
9-hole: (N/A) Cart: $6
Weekend: 18-hole: $80 Cart: $11
9-hole: (N/A) Cart: $6

Located on Hwy 121 one block north of J.C. Penney headquarters.

Weston Lakes Country Club   (7,083 yds) 281-346-1227

32611 FM 1093 Road
Fulshear, TX 77441
Contact: Patrick Fitzpatrick
Description: Even low handicap golfers can shoot a high score on this very long 18-hole private course. Every hole has out-of-bounds, water is on 12 holes, and there are 76 sand traps.
Out-of-town golfers welcome. **Par:** 72.
Rentals: Golf Carts, Golf Clubs, Driving Range

Members and guests only. Golf lessons available. Mandatory carts.

Fees:

Weekday: 18-hole: $30 Cart: $12
9-hole: (N/A) Cart: $5.50
Weekend: 18-hole: $40 Cart: $12
9-hole: (N/A) Cart: $5.50

Located 15 miles west of Hwy 6 on FM 1903.

Gainesville Municipal Golf Course   (6,546 yds) 940-665-2161

200 S. Rusk Drive
Gainesville, TX 76240
Contact: Butch Links
Description: A nice 18-hole public course with a creek, flat wide fairways, par 3s with water, and a few traps. There is a pro shop in the clubhouse. **Par:** 71.
Rentals: Golf Carts, Golf Clubs, Driving Range

Open to the public. Walking permitted. Golf lessons available.

Fees:

Weekday: 18-hole: $11 Cart: $8
9-hole: (N/A) Cart: $3.50
Weekend: 18-hole: $14 Cart: $8
9-hole: (N/A) Cart: $3.50

Located west of I-35 on Hwy 82 near local Gainesville airport.

Galveston Country Club   (6,347 yds) 409-740-6476

14288 Stewart Road
Galveston, TX 77550
Contact: Bruce Rodysill
Description: Salt water runs around 16 holes on this 18-hole private course. The wind is a major factor plus lots of sand traps. Oldest club in Texas; moved three times due to hurricanes. **Par:** 72.
Rentals: Golf Carts, Pull Carts, Golf Clubs, Driving Range

Members and guests only. Golf lessons available. Walking permitted.

Fees:

Weekday: 18-hole: $60 Cart: $10
9-hole: (N/A) Cart: $5.03
Weekend: 18-hole: $70 Cart: $10
9-hole: (N/A) Cart: $5.03

Take I-45 south to 61st Street exit. Go right to Seawall Blvd, then west to 12-Mile Road. Turn right to club entrance.

Galveston Municipal Golf Course   (6,738 yds) 409-744-2366

1700 Sydnor Lane
Galveston, TX 77553
Contact: Joe Russo
Description: Great public course swirling around Syndor Bayou with water hazards on 14 holes. No tee times required during weekdays. Clubhouse has pro shop and snack bar. **Par:** 72.
Rentals: Golf Carts, Pull Carts, Golf Clubs, Driving Range

Open to the public. Walking permitted. Golf lessons available.

Fees:

Weekday: 18-hole: $18 Cart: $10
9-hole: $15 Cart: $9
Weekend: 18-hole: $25 Cart: $10
9-hole: $20 Cart: $9

Located near airport off Stewart Road to Sydnor.

Mustang Creek Country Club   (6,418 yds) 512-771-2424

Highway 59 County Road 202
Ganado, TX 77962
Contact: James Duncan
Description: A recently expanded 18-hole public course with some trouble due to scattered trees. The course is flat with a creek. No sand traps. Food and drinks. **Par:** 72.
Rentals: Golf Carts, Driving Range
Open to the public. Walking permitted.

Fees:

Weekday: 18-hole: $10 Cart: $8
9-hole: (N/A) Cart: $4
Weekend: 18-hole: $12 Cart: $8
9-hole: (N/A) Cart: $4

Located on the south side of Hwy 59.

Eastern Hills Country Club   (6,331 yds) 972-278-3051

3000 Country Club Drive
Garland, TX 75043
Contact: Brad McCollum
Description: A mid-length private 18-hole course with one hole protected by a huge pond. Designed in the 1950s by Ralph Plummer as a classic test of golf. Nice clubhouse. **Par:** 70.
Rentals: Golf Carts, Golf Clubs, Driving Range
Members and guests only. Golf lessons available. Walking permitted.

Fees:

Weekday: 18-hole: $30 Cart: $11.50
9-hole: (N/A) Cart: $4.50
Weekend: 18-hole: $40 Cart: $11.50
9-hole: (N/A) Cart: $4.50

Located east of I-635, exit Centerville Road, past Jupiter to Country Club Drive.

Firewheel Golf Park · (36 hs) 972-205-2795

600 W. Blackburn Road
Garland, TX 75044
Contact: Don Kennedy
Old Course Description: The best 36-hole public course in the Dallas area. Both courses have been the site of the Nitro Texas State Open and have hosted PGA Tour qualifying events. The Old Course is long and traditionally great. **Par:** 72 (7,054 yards).

Lakes Course Description: The Lakes Course is younger and shorter than the Old Course but just as tough with more water and trees. Clubhouse has a snack bar, pro shop, and pavillion. **Par:** 71 (6,626 yards).

Rentals: Golf Carts, Pull Carts, Golf Clubs, Driving Range
Open to the public. Walking permitted. Golf lessons available.

Fees:

Weekday: 18-hole: $18 Cart: $10
9-hole: (N/A) Cart: $4.75
Weekend: 18-hole: $26 Cart: $10
9-hole: (N/A) Cart: $4.75

> Located east of U.S. 75 to Arapaho and Garland Road.

Oakridge Country Club · (6,516 yds) 972-530-8004

2800 Diamond Oaks Drive
Garland, TX 75044
Contact: David Sanchez
Description: Wide fairways, but the 16th and 18th holes are tough enough to blow up a scorecard. Clubhouse has restaurant, pro shop, swimming pool, and tennis court. **Par:** 71.
Rentals: Golf Carts, Golf Clubs, Driving Range

Members and guests only. Golf lessons available. Walking permitted.

Fees:

Weekday: 18-hole: $38 Cart: $11.50
9-hole: (N/A) Cart: (N/A)
Weekend: 18-hole: $50 Cart: $11.50
9-hole: (N/A) Cart: (N/A)

> Located north of I-635 and east of Jupiter Road.

Up to Par Driving Range & Course   (876 yds) 972-530-0585

3015 N. Shiloh Road
Garland, TX 75045
Contact: Jeff Liesenselt
Description: A nice nine-hole par-3
course that is a pitch and putt with the
longest hole 122 yards and the shortest
60 yards. There are four ponds on the
course. **Par:** 27.
Rentals: Club Rentals, Driving Range

Open to the public. Walking permitted.
Golf lessons available.

Fees:

Weekday: 18-hole: $7 Cart: (N/A)
9-hole: $7 Cart: (N/A)
Weekend: 18-hole: $10 Cart: (N/A)
9-hole: $7 Cart: (N/A)

Located on the corner of Shiloh and
Belt Line.

Gatesville Country Club   (7,000 yds) 254-865-6917

Straws Mills Road
Gatesville, TX 76538
Contact: Fred Rhea
Description: A very nice, short 18-hole
private course with open fairways and
no sand traps. Eagles are possible on
the short par 5s. There is water on
eight holes. **Par:** 72.
Rentals: Golf Carts
Members and guests only. Golf lessons
available. Walking permitted.

Fees:

Weekday: 18-hole: $8.66 Cart: $6
9-hole: $6 Cart: $4
Weekend: 18-hole: $13 Cart: $6
9-hole: $8 Cart: $4

Located on Straw Mills Road, off Hwy
36 south of town.

Mesquite Country Club   (6,132 yds) 512-786-4721

P.O. Box 1629
George West, TX 78022
Contact: Wes Landreth
Description: This nine-hole semiprivate
course has extremely tight fairways with
lots of mesquite trees, out-of-bounds
over a fence, four water hazards, and
mid-width greens. **Par:** 35.
Rentals: Golf Carts, Pull Carts

Open to the public. Walking permitted.

Fees:

Weekday: 18-hole: $10 Cart: $7
9-hole: (N/A) Cart: $3.50
Weekend: 18-hole: $10 Cart: $7
9-hole: (N/A) Cart: $3.50

Located south of Three Rivers on Hwy
281, just north of George West.

Berry Creek Country Club — (6,648 yds) 512-930-4615

30500 Berry Creek Drive
Georgetown, TX 78628
Contact: Mike Grindle
Description: Holes eight and nine on this 18-hole private course are cut into a stone quarry. Slicers tend to find out-of-bounds a lot. A hilly course in a very scenic location. **Par:** 72.
Rentals: Golf Carts, Golf Clubs, Driving Range

Members and guests only. Golf lessons available. Walking permitted.

Fees:

Weekday: 18-hole: $45 Cart: $11
9-hole: $12.50 Cart: $5
Weekend: 18-hole: $55 Cart: $11
9-hole: $17.50 Cart: $5

Located off I-35 on exit 266 west.

Georgetown Country Club — (5,471 yds) 512-930-4577

1500 Country Club Drive
Georgetown, TX 78628
Contact: Dave Preston
Description: In order to shoot a good score on this very short 18-hole private course, a golfer must keep the ball in play because a river runs through 11 holes. Food and drinks. **Par:** 70.
Rentals: Golf Carts, Pull Carts

Members and guests only. Golf lessons available. Walking permitted.

Fees:

Weekday: 18-hole: $19 Cart: $7.50
9-hole: (N/A) Cart: $4
Weekend: 18-hole: $25 Cart: $7.50
9-hole: (N/A) Cart: $4

Located off I-35. West on Country Club Drive.

Kurth-Landrum Golf Course — (2,800 yds) 512-863-6511

Southwestern University
Southwest Blvd.
Georgetown, TX 78626
Contact: Pat Souright
Description: Lots of golfers may shoot their best nine-hole score on this short nine-hole public course. Not much water, wide fairways, little trouble, and flat greens at college site. **Par:** 34.
Rentals: Golf Carts, Pull Carts
Open to the public. Walking permitted.

Fees:

Weekday: 18-hole: $8.50 Cart: $8
9-hole: $6.50 Cart: $3.50
Weekend: 18-hole: $10.50 Cart: $8
9-hole: $7 Cart: $3.50

Located on east side of I-35 at College exit.

Legacy Hills Golf Club   (7,088 yds) 512-864-1222

301 Del Webb Blvd.
Georgetown, TX 78628
Contact: Susie Davis
Description: Not what you would expect from a retirement village course. Public layout designed by professional golfer Billy Casper and architect Greg Nash. Great Hill Country view with water, trees, and limestone. **Par:** 72.
Rentals: Golf Carts, Golf Clubs, Driving Range

Open to the public. Golf lessons available.

Fees:

Weekday: 18-hole: $45 Cart: (N/A)
9-hole: (N/A) Cart: (N/A)
Weekend: 18-hole: $50 Cart: (N/A)
9-hole: (N/A) Cart: (N/A)

Located five miles west of I-35 at FM 2338 (Lake Georgetown exit).

Giddings Country Club   (6,300 yds) 409-542-3777

Highway 290
Giddings, TX 78942
Contact: Randy Bishop
Description: A simple nine-hole semiprivate course that is fine with some trees, only two water hazards, and flat fairways with out-of-bounds. Mid-length course. Food and drinks. **Par:** 36.

Rentals: Golf Carts, Pull Carts, Golf Clubs, Driving Range
Open to the public. Walking permitted.

Fees:

Weekday: 18-hole: $7.50 Cart: $7
9-hole: (N/A) Cart: $3.50
Weekend: 18-hole: $10 Cart: $7
9-hole: (N/A) Cart: $3.50

Located on Hwy 290.

Gilmer Country Club   (6,072 yds) 903-734-4125

Highway 155
Gilmer, TX 75644
Contact: Pro Shop
Description: A short nine-hole private course with small greens, no sand traps, and water. Fairways are tight and some are slightly uphill. Club has great East Texas location with charm. **Par:** 35.
Rentals: Golf Carts, Golf Clubs, Driving Range

Members and guests only. Walking permitted.

Fees:

Weekday: 18-hole: $8 Cart: $7.50
9-hole: (N/A) Cart: (N/A)
Weekend: 18-hole: $16 Cart: $7.50
9-hole: (N/A) Cart: (N/A)

Located south of town on Hwy 155.

Gladewater Country Club   (6,100 yds) 903-845-4566

CR 3107
P.O. Box 66
Gladewater, TX 75647
Contact: Fay Mackey
Description: Golfers need to be very
accurate in approaching three of the
greens on this nine-hole public course
because they are on the bottom of a
hill. A creek runs through the course.
Par: 36.

Rentals: Golf Carts, Pull Carts
Open to the public. Walking permitted.

Fees:

Weekday: 18-hole: $8.20 Cart: $9
9-hole: (N/A) Cart: $3.63
Weekend: 18-hole: $11.20 Cart: $9
9-hole: (N/A) Cart: $3.63

Located south of town off Hwy 271.

Squaw Valley Golf Course   (6,749 yds) 254-897-7956

HCR 51-45-B
Glen Rose, TX 76043
Contact: Johnny Pilcher
Description: A great course for golf
outings open to the public. Clubhouse is
set in old dinosaur location with history,
charm, and golfing style. **Par:** 72.
Rentals: Golf Carts, Driving Range
Open to the public. Walking permitted.
Golf lessons available.

Fees:

Weekday: 18-hole: $31 Cart: (N/A)
9-hole: $12 Cart: $4
Weekend: 18-hole: $36 Cart: (N/A)
9-hole: $15 Cart: $4

Located off Hwy 67 on Hwy 144
southwest of Fort Worth.

Goldthwaite Municipal Golf Course (6,175 yds) 915-938-5652

State Highway 16
Goldthwaite, TX 76844
Contact: Bill Bowen
Description: The name of this
nine-hole public course was changed
from Mills County to Goldthwaite Muni.
It is a short, open golf course with no
sand traps and big greens. **Par:** 36.
Rentals: Golf Carts, Driving Range
Open to the public. Walking permitted.
Golf lessons available.

Fees:

Weekday: 18-hole: $8 Cart: $13.50
9-hole: (N/A) Cart: $7.50
Weekend: 18-hole: $11 Cart: $13.50
9-hole: (N/A) Cart: $7.50

Located three miles south of town on
Hwy 16.

Goliad County Recreational Assn.　(6,300 yds)　512-645-8478

1103 W. Fannin
Goliad, TX 77963
Contact: Mickey Sullivan
Description: Good nine-hole test in scenic surroundings. Course was opened in 1970s and features water on three holes, some trees, and some undulated greens. It may look easier than it really is. **Par:** 72.

Fees:

Weekday: 9-hole: $7 Cart: $13
Weekend: 9-hole $8 Cart: $13

Follow Fannin west of town; course is located two miles outside of town.

Independence Golf Course　(3,234 yds)　830-672-9926

P.O. Box 198
Gonzales, TX 78629
Contact: Bill Ploetz
Description: This nine-hole public course was constructed inside the loop of the Guadalupe River, but the river doesn't often come into play. Small greens and only one trap. **Par:** 35.
Rentals: Golf Carts, Pull Carts, Golf Clubs

Open to the public. Walking permitted.

Fees:

Weekday: 18-hole: $6 Cart: $6.50
9-hole: (N/A) Cart: $3.50
Weekend: 18-hole: $8 Cart: $6.50
9-hole: (N/A) Cart: $3.50

Located 14 miles south of I-10 on Hwy 183.

Cliffs Country Club　(6,800 yds)　940-779-4040

Star Route Box 19
Graford, TX 76045
Contact: Glenn Sockwell
Description: A very dramatic 18-hole golf course constructed on the hills overlooking Possum Kingdom Lake. Tough shots over valley or water. A new inn and clubhouse welcome golfers. **Par:** 71.
Rentals: Golf Carts, Golf Clubs, Driving Range

Open to the public. Golf lessons available. Mandatory carts.

Fees:

Weekday: 18-hole: $45 Cart: $12
9-hole: (N/A) Cart: (N/A)
Weekend: 18-hole: $55 Cart: $12
9-hole: (N/A) Cart: (N/A)

Located on Hwy 180 west to Hwy 16 7½ miles north.

Graham Country Club   (3,216 yds) 940-549-7721

Fort Belknap Road
Graham, TX 76450
Contact: J.R. Bohn
Description: To shoot a good round on this nine-hole semiprivate course, good golfers must play great on the last four holes, which are long and tight. Food, drinks, and a pro shop. **Par:** 36.
Rentals: Golf Carts, Pull Carts, Driving Range

Open to the public. Walking permitted. Golf lessons available.

Fees:

Weekday: 18-hole: $15 Cart: $10
9-hole: (N/A) Cart: $5
Weekend: 18-hole: $25 Cart: $10
9-hole: (N/A) Cart: $5

Located on Fort Belknap Road.

DeCordova Bend Country Club   (6,700 yds) 817-326-4505

5301 Country Club Circle
Granbury, TX 76048
Contact: Bill Richards
Description: A short 18-hole private course that is fun because of the pretty layout and scenery. Clubhouse overlooks a lake and has good pro shop. **Par:** 70.
Rentals: Golf Carts, Pull Carts, Golf Clubs, Driving Range

Members and guests only. Golf lessons available. Walking permitted.

Fees:

Weekday: 18-hole: $30 Cart: (N/A)
9-hole: (N/A) Cart: (N/A)
Weekend: 18-hole: $50 Cart: (N/A)
9-hole: (N/A) Cart: (N/A)

Located off Hwy 377 south to Hwy 167.

Granbury Country Club   (6,108 yds) 817-573-9912

Highway 377 East
Granbury, TX 76048
Contact: Mac McKinney
Description: A semiprivate nine-hole golf course that has flat, wide fairways, only one sand trap, and two water hazards. Clubhouse has a swimming pool and pro shop. **Par:** 36.
Rentals: Golf Carts, Pull Carts, Driving Range

Open to the public. Walking permitted.

Fees:

Weekday: 18-hole: $16 Cart: $6.50
9-hole: $6.50 Cart: $4
Weekend: 18-hole: $18 Cart: $6.50
9-hole: $11 Cart: $4

Located on Hwy 377.

Hidden Oaks Golf Course   (6,443 yds) 817-279-1078

2701 Hideaway Bay Court
Granbury, TX 76049
Contact: Tony Martinez
Description: Challenging new 18-hole daily fee course in golf-rich area. Scenic Lake Granbury comes into course property but not into play. Dozens of trees, bunkers, and bermuda greens. **Par:** 72.
Rentals: Golf Carts, Golf Clubs, Driving Range

Open to the public.

Fees:

Weekday: 18-hole: $29.50 w/ cart
9-hole: (N/A) Cart: (N/A)
Weekend: 18-hole: $35 w/ cart
9-hole: (N/A) Cart: (N/A)

Take Hwy 377 from Fort Worth, go west on Peck Rd., left on Old Granbury Rd. and follow signs to course.

Nutcracker Golf Club   (6,700 yds) 817-579-1811

9500 Orchard Drive
Granbury, TX 76049
Contact: Robbie Loving
Description: Senior golfers really enjoy playing this good 18-hole semiprivate course because they can reach the greens in regulation if they hit good shots. Out-of-town golfers welcome. Large bentgrass greens. **Par:** 36.
Rentals: Golf Carts, Driving Range

Members and guests only. Walking permitted.

Fees:

Weekday: 18-hole: $25 Cart: $8
9-hole: (N/A) Cart: (N/A)
Weekend: 18-hole: $25 Cart: $8
9-hole: (N/A) Cart: (N/A)

Located 40 minutes west of Fort Worth on Hwy 377.

Pecan Plantation Country Club   (6,832 yds) 817-573-2641

8650 Westover Court
Granbury, TX 76049
Contact: Jake Bechtold
Description: One of the original courses in Granbury, designed by noted architect Leon Howard in thick pecan grove, hence the name. **Par:** 72.
Rentals: Golf Carts, Pull Carts, Golf Clubs, Driving Range

Members and guests only. Golf lessons available. Walking permitted.

Fees:

Weekday: 18-hole: $25 Cart: $9
9-hole: (N/A) Cart: (N/A)
Weekend: 18-hole: $35 Cart: $9
9-hole: (N/A) Cart: (N/A)

Located on Hwy 377 40 minutes west of Fort Worth.

Fun City Golf Center

(3,205 yds) 972-262-0022

3990 Westcliff Road
Grand Prairie, TX 75051
Contact: Kathy Krabbenschmidt
Description: A new nine-hole par-3
course with an 18-hole executive course
that was finished in the fall of 1997.
The par 3s have water hazards. There is
a snack bar and pro shop. **Par:** 27.
Rentals: Club Rentals, Driving Range
Open to the public. Walking permitted.
Golf lessons available.

Fees:

Weekday: 18-hole: $7 Cart: (N/A)
9-hole: $5 Cart: (N/A)
Weekend: 18-hole: $10 Cart: (N/A)
9-hole: $10 Cart: (N/A)

Located off I-20 on FM 1382 to course
on left.

Grand Prairie Municipal Golf Course

(27 hs) 972-263-0661

3202 SE 14th St.
Grand Prairie, TX 75051
Contact: Jan Smith
Description: A 27-hole public course.
Playing 18 holes on either the Red,
White, or Blue nines is a mid-length
round. Clubhouse has a snack bar and
pro shop. **Par:** 72.
Rentals: Golf Carts, Golf Clubs, Driving
Range

Open to the public. Walking permitted.
Golf lessons available.

Fees:

Weekday: 18-hole: $16 Cart: $11.50
9-hole: (N/A) Cart: $4.87
Weekend: 18-hole: $18 Cart: $11.50
9-hole: (N/A) Cart: $4.87

Located off Mountain Creek Lake on
FM 1382.

Great Southwest Golf Club

(6,771 yds) 972-647-0116

612 Ave. J East
Grand Prairie, TX 75050
Contact: Kevin Semtner
Description: Ben Crenshaw won his
Texas state amateur title on this course
designed by Byron Nelson. It's a tight
course with water and trees. Recently
remodeled. **Par:** 71.
Rentals: Golf Carts, Driving Range

Members and guests only. Golf lessons
available. Walking permitted.

Fees:

Weekday: 18-hole: $45 Cart: $13
9-hole: (N/A) Cart: $5
Weekend: 18-hole: $60 Cart: $13
9-hole: (N/A) Cart: $5

Located two blocks north of I-30 and
one block east of Hwy 360.

I-Care Fitness Center & Golf Course (1,011 yds) 972-264-2510

242 Idlewild
Grand Prairie, TX 75051
Contact: Bob Coe
Description: A nice par-3 course that is part of an excellent fitness center. The clubhouse has a good short game practice area for those who don't have much time. **Par:** 27.
Open to the public. Walking permitted.

Fees:

Weekday: 18-hole: $5.39 Cart: (N/A)
9-hole: (N/A) Cart: (N/A)
Weekend: 18-hole: $5.39 Cart: (N/A)
9-hole: (N/A) Cart: (N/A)

Located just east of downtown Grand Prairie on Idlewild

Riverside Golf Club (7,025 yds) 817-640-7800

3000 Riverside Parkway
Grand Prairie, TX 75050
Contact: Bill Whitmore
Description: A long and tough public course with water hazards on nearly every hole. The 438-yard, par-4 ninth hole is very difficult. Clubhouse, pro shop, and food. **Par:** 72.
Rentals: Golf Carts, Golf Clubs, Driving Range

Open to the public. Walking permitted. Golf lessons available.

Fees:

Weekday: 18-hole: $48 Cart: (N/A)
9-hole: (N/A) Cart: (N/A)
Weekend: 18-hole: $53 Cart: (N/A)
9-hole: (N/A) Cart: (N/A)

Located on Hwy 360 south of DFW Airport.

Sunset Golf Center (3,503 yds) 972-331-8057

4906 E. Main St.
Grand Prairie, TX 75050
Contact: Bob Mims
Description: A nice nine-hole course with a large driving range facility and small clubhouse. The public course itself is a lot of fun. **Par:** 36.
Rentals: Golf Carts, Pull Carts, Golf Clubs, Driving Range
Open to the public. Walking permitted. Golf lessons available.

Fees:

Weekday: 18-hole: $10 Cart: $9
9-hole: $7 Cart: $8
Weekend: 18-hole: $14 Cart: $9
9-hole: $9 Cart: $8

Located two blocks west of Loop 12 on the east side of Grand Prairie on East Main.

Tangleridge Golf Club   (6,835 yds) 972-299-6837

818 Tangleridge Drive
Grand Prairie, TX 75052
Contact: Mark Viskoski
Description: Course has beautiful, rolling hills with views of Joe Pool Lake from some holes. Outstanding mounding on some holes and perfect landscaping. Considered by some as best new public course in area. **Par:** 72.
Rentals: Golf Carts, Golf Clubs, Driving Range

Open to the public. Walking permitted. Golf lessons available.

Fees:

Weekday: 18-hole: $35 Cart: $11
9-hole: (N/A) Cart: (N/A)
Weekend: 18-hole: $45 Cart: $11
9-hole: (N/A) Cart: (N/A)

Take I-35 south to Hwy 67 and go south eight miles, past I-20 and then right on Lakeridge Parkway. Club is on the left.

Woodcrest Country Club   (6,437 yds) 972-264-6161

3502 Country Club Drive
Grand Prairie, TX 75052
Contact: John Shelly
Description: A short but challenging 18-hole semiprivate club. A creek runs around the course, forcing go-for-broke shots. Clubhouse has restaurant and pro shop. **Par:** 72.
Rentals: Golf Carts, Golf Clubs, Driving Range

Members and guests only. Golf lessons available. Walking permitted.

Fees:

Weekday: 18-hole: $25 Cart: $10
9-hole: (N/A) Cart: $6.47
Weekend: 18-hole: $35 Cart: $10
9-hole: (N/A) Cart: $6.47

Located in southeast Grand Prairie near FM 1382 north of I-20.

Grapevine Municipal Golf Course   (6,953 yds) 817-481-0421

3800 Fairway Drive
Grapevine, TX 76051
Contact: Sid McClesky
Description: A Byron Nelson-designed smart 18-hole public course. The back nine is hilly with trees near Grapevine dam. Good find. **Par:** 72.
Rentals: Golf Carts, Pull Carts, Golf Clubs, Driving Range
Open to the public. Walking permitted. Golf lessons available.

Fees:

Weekday: 18-hole: $17 Cart: $10
9-hole: (N/A) Cart: $4.50
Weekend: 18-hole: $20 Cart: $10
9-hole: (N/A) Cart: $4.50

Located north of DFW Airport and east of Lake Grapevine. North of Hwy 121 off Hwy 26 next to Grapevine dam.

Hartline Golf Center   (964 yds) 903-555-PUTT

South Service Road I-30
Greenville, TX 75402
Contact: Kenny Hartline
Description: Challenging par 3 to go
along with driving range. Course
features four lakes, which come into
play for crooked shots. Greens average
4,500 square feet, with plenty of wedge
and putting practice. **Par:** 27.
Rentals: Pull Carts, Driving Range

Open to the public. Walking permitted.
Golf lessons available.

Fees:

Weekday: 18-hole: $5 Cart: (N/A)
9-hole: (N/A) Cart: (N/A)
Weekend: 18-hole: $5 Cart: (N/A)
9-hole: (N/A) Cart: (N/A)

Located at I-30 and Hwy 50, exit 101,
on south service road.

Oak Creek Country Club   (3,467 yds) 903-455-3971

FM 1570
Greenville, TX 75402
Contact: Andy Holder
Description: A classic rural Texas
nine-hole course that is 3,467 yards
with trees and water. Food, drinks, and
lockers in clubhouse. **Par:** 36.
Rentals: Golf Carts, Pull Carts, Golf
Clubs, Driving Range

Open to the public. Walking permitted.
Golf lessons available.

Fees:

Weekday: 18-hole: $15 Cart: $10
9-hole: $7.50 Cart: $14
Weekend: 18-hole: $25 Cart: $10
9-hole: $12.50 Cart: $14

Located 45 miles east of Dallas off I-30
to Hwy 34 and south to FM 1570.

Wright Park Municipal Golf Course (5,871 yds) 903-457-2996

4903 Moulton
Greenville, TX 75401
Contact: Bo Hartline
Description: Golfers playing this
nine-hole public course must be very
accurate off the tee thanks to water
hazards, out-of-bounds, and trees.
Clubhouse has nice pro shop. **Par:** 35.
Rentals: Golf Carts, Pull Carts, Golf
Clubs

Open to the public. Walking permitted.
Golf lessons available.

Fees:

Weekday: 18-hole: $8 Cart: $6.50
9-hole: (N/A) Cart: $3.25
Weekend: 18-hole: $12 Cart: $6.50
9-hole: (N/A) Cart: $3.25

From I-30, take exit 94B and go south
to Moulton (Hwy 69).

Port Groves Golf Club
(2,700 yds) 409-962-4030

5721 Monroe
Groves, TX 77619
Contact: Gary Freedman
Description: Two of the toughest par
3s in the piney woods are on this
nine-hole public course. Both require
tee shots over a pond to hit the small
greens. Double tees. Food and drink.
Par: 35.
Rentals: Golf Carts, Pull Carts, Golf
Clubs

Open to the public. Walking permitted.
Golf lessons available.

Fees:

Weekday: 18-hole: $6.50 Cart: $7.50
9-hole: $4 Cart: $3.50
Weekend: 18-hole: $7.75 Cart: $7.50
9-hole: $4 Cart: $3.50

Located north of Port Arthur in Groves
on Monroe Street.

Hillside Acres Country Club
(3,019 yds) 806-839-2188

Cotton Center Highway
Hale Center, TX 79041
Contact: Betty Black
Description: Plenty of wind with trees
and sand on some holes make this
9-hole course challenging. **Par:** 36.
Rentals: Golf Carts, Pull Carts
Open to the public. Walking permitted.

Fees:

Weekday: 18-hole: $6.25 Cart: $6.25
9-hole: (N/A) Cart: (N/A)
Weekend: 18-hole: $8.25 Cart: $6.25
9-hole: (N/A) Cart: (N/A)

Located two miles west of town on
Cotton Center Hwy (FM 1914).

Hallettsville Golf Course
(3,234 yds) 512-798-9908

P.O. Box 433
Hallettsville, TX 77964
Contact: Sandra Henneke
Description: In order to post a good
score on this short nine-hole public
course, a golfer must hit straight shots
off the tee and onto the small greens.
No traps. Drinks. **Par:** 35.
Rentals: Golf Carts, Pull Carts

Open to the public. Walking permitted.

Fees:

Weekday: 18-hole: $6 Cart: $7 9-hole:
(N/A) Cart: $4
Weekend: 18-hole: $8 Cart: $7 9-hole:
(N/A) Cart: $4

Located off Hwy 90 on City Park.

Perry Country Club

(6,082 yds) 254-386-3383

P.O. Box 711
Pottsville Road
Hamilton, TX 76531
Contact: Randy Gardner
Description: The clubhouse burned down in December 1993 and reopened in May 1994. This nine-hole semiprivate course has wide open fairways, small greens, no sand traps, and two water hazards. **Par:** 72.

Rentals: Golf Carts
Open to the public. Walking permitted.

Fees:

Weekday: 18-hole: $10 Cart: $8
9-hole: $8 Cart: $4
Weekend: 18-hole: $15 Cart: $8
9-hole: $10 Cart: $4

Located off Hwy 36.

Hamlin Golf Course

(3,600 yds) 915-576-3026

FM Road 2142
Hamlin, TX 79520
Contact: Golf Course
Description: Traditional small course layout with small greens, some trees, and overgrown rough. Course located next to dry lake bed. Not very crowded and open to all golfers. **Par:** 36.

Fees:

Weekday: 18-hole: $10 Cart: $12
Weekend: 18-hole $10 Cart: $12

Directions: 2 ½ miles west of Hamlin off FM 2142.

Lakeview Country Club

(6,750 yds) 254-698-4554

1901 Valley Oaks Drive
Harker Heights, TX 76548
Contact: Golf Shop
Description: A nine-hole semiprivate course that expanded to 18 holes in the fall of 1994. It is hilly with lots of trees but not much water. **Par:** 72.
Rentals: Golf Carts, Pull Carts
Open to the public. Walking permitted.
Golf lessons available.

Fees:

Weekday: 18-hole: $10 Cart: $8.50
9-hole: (N/A) Cart: $4.25
Weekend: 18-hole: $12.50 Cart: $8.50 9-hole: (N/A) Cart: $4.25

Located off Hwy 190 west, exit FM 2410 south to Cedar Knob.

Cottonwood Creek Golf Course   (1,245 yds) 956-428-0766

1001 S. Ed Carey Drive
Harlingen, TX 78552
Contact: Rosie Dominguez
Description: Golfers in Harlingen can
become great short game players
thanks to this par-3 course. This one is
a perfect practice facility because of
shots over water. Pro shop. **Par:** 27.
Rentals: Golf Carts, Pull Carts, Golf
Clubs, Driving Range

Open to the public. Walking permitted.
Golf lessons available.

Fees:

Weekday: 18-hole: $8 Cart: $8 9-hole:
$5 Cart: $5
Weekend: 18-hole: $8 Cart: $8 9-hole:
$5 Cart: $5

Located south of town on Hwy 77.

Harlingen Country Club   (6,541 yds) 956-412-4100

5500 El Camino
Harlingen, TX 78550
Contact: Buddy Kalencki
Description: Lots of palm trees make
this 18-hole private course play tight.
There are 14 water hazards around flat
fairways on this mid-length course.
Food, drinks, and pro shop. **Par:** 72.
Rentals: Golf Carts, Golf Clubs, Driving
Range

Members and guests only. Golf lessons
available. Walking permitted.

Fees:

Weekday: 18-hole: $37.54 Cart: (N/A)
9-hole: (N/A) Cart: $4
Weekend: 18-hole: $42.90 Cart: (N/A)
9-hole: (N/A) Cart: $4

Located west on Stuart Place Road.

Sunshine Country Club Estates   (3,100 yds) 956-425-1420

7000 Michigan Drive
Harlingen, TX 78550
Contact: Golf Shop
Description: A private par-3 course
that is part of a real estate
development. It is narrow with
out-of-bounds, lakes, and holes ranging
from 80 yards to 161. Carts only for
disabled. **Par:** 27
Rentals: Pull Carts

Members and guests only. Walking
permitted.

Fees:

Weekday: 18-hole: $5.50 Cart: (N/A)
9-hole: $4 Cart: (N/A)
Weekend: 18-hole: $5.50 Cart: (N/A)
9-hole: $4 Cart: (N/A)

Located off Hwy 77 north.

Tony Butler Municipal Golf Course (6,320 yds) 956-423-9913

2640 South M St.
Harlingen, TX 78550
Contact: Richard Flores
Description: A 27-hole public facility.
The 18-hole course is mid-length.
Clubhouse has snack bar and pro shop.
Nine-hole course is also challenging.
Par: 71.
Rentals: Golf Carts, Pull Carts, Golf
Clubs, Driving Range

Open to the public. Walking permitted.
Golf lessons available.

Fees:

Weekday: 18-hole: $10 Cart: $9
9-hole: $8 Cart: $10
Weekend: 18-hole: $10 Cart: $9
9-hole: $8 Cart: $10

Located off Hwy 83 M Street exit onto
Victor Park.

Treasure Hills Country Club (6,960 yds) 956-428-0351

3009 N. Augusta National Drive
Harlingen, TX 78550
Contact: K.C. Lauber
Description: A very long Robert Trent
Jones-designed course that has hills,
traps, out-of-bounds, and water in front
of par 3s. New clubhouse. **Par:** 72.
Rentals: Golf Carts, Golf Clubs, Driving
Range

Open to the public. Walking permitted.
Golf lessons available.

Fees:

Weekday: 18-hole: $16.23 Cart: $10
9-hole: $10.83 Cart: $5
Weekend: 18-hole: $21.65 Cart: $10
9-hole: $10.83 Cart: $5

Located off Treasure Hills to Cypress
Gardens.

Whispering Winds Golf Course (1,300 yds) 956-423-2010

2524 W. Spur 54
Harlingen, TX 78550
Contact: Lanell Penrod
Description: Recreational nine-hole
par-3 golf course, however, being
1,300 yards long, it can be reasonably
challenging. Teeing off is first
come/first serve. **Par:** 27.
Rentals: Golf Carts, Pull Carts, Golf
Clubs, Driving Range

Open to the public. Walking permitted.
Golf lessons available.

Fees:

Weekday: 18-hole: $8 Cart: $12
9-hole: $5 Cart: $7.50
Weekend: 18-hole: $8 Cart: $12
9-hole: $5 Cart: $7.50

Located off of West Spur 54.

Haskell Country Club

(5,852 yds) 940-864-3400

Route 1, Box 190
Haskell, TX 79521
Contact: Tim Johnson
Description: Slicers and hookers can easily hit a ball into water on this nine-hole semiprivate course. The club added water hazards left and right on eight holes. Elevated bentgrass greens. Food and drinks. **Par:** 36.
Rentals: Golf Carts, Pull Carts, Driving Range

Open to the public. Walking permitted. Golf lessons available.

Fees:

Weekday: 18-hole: $10 Cart: $5
9-hole: $5 Cart: $2.50
Weekend: 18-hole: $10 Cart: $5
9-hole: $5 Cart: $2.50

Located east of Hwy 227 and Hwy 380 intersection.

Willow Springs Golf Course

(6,158 yds) 817-439-4653

1714 Avondale-Haslet Road
Haslet, TX 76052
Contact: Kurt Hoffman
Description: One of the shortest 18-hole public courses in Texas, resulting in a fast 18-hole round and hopefully lower score. Restaurant and pro shop. **Par:** 72.
Rentals: Golf Carts, Pull Carts, Driving Range

Open to the public. Walking permitted.

Fees:

Weekday: 18-hole: $11 Cart: $8
9-hole: $8 Cart: $4
Weekend: 18-hole: $14 Cart: $8
9-hole: $10 Cart: $4

Located north of Fort Worth off I-35W to Hwy 287.

Hearne Municipal Golf Course

(6,510 yds) 409-279-3112

405 Northwood
Hearne, TX 77889
Contact: Sam Paradowski
Description: The greens on this nine-hole public course are very small, elevated, and tough to hit. There are three par 5s designed in the 1930s. No traps but has a creek. **Par:** 37.
Rentals: Golf Carts, Pull Carts, Golf Clubs, Driving Range

Open to the public. Walking permitted.

Fees:

Weekday: 18-hole: $7 Cart: $7.50
9-hole: (N/A) Cart: $3.75
Weekend: 18-hole: $10 Cart: $7.50
9-hole: (N/A) Cart: $3.75

Located on Hwy 6 north of Bryan.

Oak Valley Driving Range & Par 3   (1,075 yds) 210-695-2606

18632 Bandera Road
Helotes, TX 78023
Contact: Adam Morales
Description: A neat lighted public
par-3 course with trees and water
behind some greens. The greens have
no traps but are undulating. Yardage
ranges from 85 to 150 yards. **Par:** 27.
Open to the public. Walking permitted.

Fees:

Weekday: 18-hole: $6 Cart: (N/A)
9-hole: $4 Cart: (N/A)
Weekend: 18-hole: $10 Cart: (N/A)
9-hole: $5 Cart: (N/A)

Located north of town on Bandera
Road.

Fox Creek Golf Course   (5,727 yds) 409-826-2131

FM 359
P.O. Box 128F
Hempstead, TX 77445
Contact: Steve Green
Description: Public 18-hole course in
scenic farm land of Hempstead.
Originally private but ran into money
troubles. **Par:** 70.
Rentals: Golf Carts, Pull Carts, Driving
Range
Open to the public. Walking permitted.
Golf lessons available.

Fees:

Weekday: 18-hole: $10 Cart: $8
9-hole: (N/A) Cart: (N/A)
Weekend: 18-hole: $15 Cart: $8
9-hole: (N/A) Cart: (N/A)

Located northwest of Houston along FM
359 seven miles south of Hwy 290 and
15 miles north of I-10.

Hempstead Golf Course   (6,575 yds) 409-826-3212

P.O. Box 186
Hempstead, TX 77445
Contact: Jack Manak
Description: Shooting a good score on
this nine-hole public course is possible
thanks to wide fairways and good-sized
greens. There is water on four holes but
few traps. Food and pro shop. **Par:** 36.
Rentals: Golf Carts, Pull Carts, Golf
Clubs, Driving Range

Open to the public. Walking permitted.
Golf lessons available.

Fees:

Weekday: 18-hole: $5 Cart: $12
9-hole: (N/A) Cart: $5
Weekend: 18-hole: $10 Cart: $12
9-hole: (N/A) Cart: $5

Located northwest of Houston on Hwy
290.

Crepe Myrtle Creek Golf Course   (5,000 yds) 903-657-3325

514 W. Fordall
Henderson, TX 75652
Contact: Larry Sims
Description: Short, scenic East Texas public course just outside Henderson. Big hitters can rack up a low score with just one par 5 and several short par 4s. Short game is critical here with several water hazards over creek. **Par:** 66.
Rentals: Golf Carts

Open to the public.

Fees:

Weekday: 18-hole: $8.50 Cart: $13
9-hole: (N/A) Cart: (N/A)
Weekend: 18-hole: $13 Cart: $12
9-hole: (N/A) Cart: (N/A)

Take Fordall east off Hwy 43 in Henderson until you see the course.

Henderson Country Club   (4,719 yds) 903-657-6443

1095 Highway 45 East
Henderson, TX 75652
Contact: Randy Smith
Description: Ranked by the *Dallas Morning News* as one of the toughest nine-hole courses in Texas. A target course that often requires layup iron tee shots. Small greens. Food and drinks. **Par:** 35.
Rentals: Golf Carts, Pull Carts, Golf Clubs, Driving Range

Members and guests only. Golf lessons available. Walking permitted.

Fees:

Weekday: 18-hole: $15 Cart: $10
9-hole: (N/A) Cart: $5
Weekend: 18-hole: $20 Cart: $10
9-hole: (N/A) Cart: $5

Located on Hwy 43.

Clay County Country Club   (6,400 yds) 940-538-4339

P.O. Box 464
Henrietta, TX 76365
Contact: Jim Kennedy
Description: A semiprivate nine-hole course that is regular length with seven of the nine holes having water hazards. Out-of-bounds, large greens, and trees. Food and drinks. **Par:** 36.
Rentals: Golf Carts, Pull Carts, Golf Clubs

Open to the public. Walking permitted.

Fees:

Weekday: 18-hole: $6.50 Cart: $7.50
9-hole: (N/A) Cart: $4
Weekend: 18-hole: $7.50 Cart: $7.50
9-hole: (N/A) Cart: $4

Located east of town on Business 287.

Pitman Municipal Golf Course   (7,103 yds) 806-363-7139

P.O. Box 1982
Hereford, TX 79045
Contact: Cal Garrett
Description: A very long 18-hole public course that has a creek on 11 holes, 400 trees, no sand traps, and small bentgrass greens. Wide fairways are hilly. Pro shop only. **Par:** 71.
Rentals: Golf Carts, Pull Carts, Golf Clubs, Driving Range

Open to the public. Walking permitted. Golf lessons available.

Fees:

Weekday: 18-hole: $6 Cart: $7.27
9-hole: (N/A) Cart: $3.64
Weekend: 18-hole: $10 Cart: $7.27
9-hole: (N/A) Cart: $3.64

Located on U.S. 60 off Amarillo Hwy.

Bluebonnet Country Club   (4,800 yds) 254-796-4122

Fairy Road
Hico, TX 76457
Contact: Lester Simpson
Description: A semiprivate rural Texas nine-hole course that is open to anybody who wants to play. Nice bentgrass greens, grass bunkers, hilly fairways, and five water hazards. **Par:** 36.
Rentals: Golf Carts

Open to the public. Walking permitted.

Fees:

Weekday: 18-hole: $9 Cart: $7 9-hole: (N/A) Cart: $3.50
Weekend: 18-hole: $12 Cart: $7
9-hole: (N/A) Cart: $3.50

Located two miles east of Hwy 281.

Hillsboro Country Club   (5,808 yds) 254-582-8211

P.O. Box 455
Hillsboro, TX 76645
Contact: Bill Mass
Description: A short semiprivate nine-hole course that really plays longer because the course is hilly. There are special lower green fees on Wednesdays and Thursdays. **Par:** 36.
Rentals: Golf Carts, Golf Clubs, Driving Range

Open to the public. Walking permitted.

Fees:

Weekday: 18-hole: $7.50 Cart: $8
9-hole: (N/A) Cart: $4
Weekend: 18-hole: $12.50 Cart: $8
9-hole: (N/A) Cart: $4

Located off I-35 to FM 286 to Country Club Drive.

Hilltop Lakes Resort   (6,300 yds) 409-855-2100

P.O. Box 42A
Hilltop Lakes, TX 77871
Contact: Darrell Heflin
Description: An 18-hole private course that has lots of yaupon trees and ponds on the back nine. It is a very tight course but not real long. Food, drinks, and pro shop. **Par:** 72.
Rentals: Golf Carts, Pull Carts, Golf Clubs, Driving Range

Members and guests only. Golf lessons available. Walking permitted.

Fees:

Weekday: 18-hole: $15 Cart: $17
9-hole: (N/A) Cart: $4.50
Weekend: 18-hole: $18 Cart: $17
9-hole: (N/A) Cart: $4.50

> Located nine miles west of town on Hwy 3.

Houston Oaks Golf Club   (36 hs) 800-86-LINKS

Route 2, Box 206
Hockley, TX 77447
Contact: Todd Harbour
Oaks Course Description: The Oaks Course is very tight with 14 holes covered by water hazards. Oak trees guard the greens. Both courses are open to employees of Tennaco Gas Corp. **Par:** 72 (6,600 yards.)

Links Course Description: A 36-hole semiprivate course. The Links Course rolls around a lake in the middle of the land. It's not long and the fairways are wide open. Water hazards are not that

threatening. Good club. **Par:** 71 (6,778 yards).
Rentals: Golf Carts, Golf Clubs, Driving Range
Members and guests only. Golf lessons available. Walking permitted.

Fees:

Weekday: 18-hole: $32/37 Cart: (N/A) 9-hole: (N/A) Cart: $5
Weekend: 18-hole: $52/57 Cart: (N/A) 9-hole: (N/A) Cart: $5

> Take Hwy 290 north to Hagen Road, east six miles, then right on Magnolia.

Hondo Golf Course   (6,004 yds) 830-426-2331

P.O. Box 609
Hondo, TX 78861
Contact: Brett Hutto
Description: This nine-hole public course has flat, narrow fairways and small, undulating greens that are very well trapped. No water. Double tees. **Par:** 36.
Rentals: Golf Carts, Golf Clubs, Driving Range

Open to the public. Walking permitted. Golf lessons available.

Fees:

Weekday: 18-hole: $9.50 Cart: $7
9-hole: $5 Cart: $3.50
Weekend: 18-hole: $11.50 Cart: $7
9-hole: $6 Cart: $3.50

Located at the intersection of Hwy 90 and Hwy 173.

Horseshoe Bay Resort & Club   (54 hs) 830-598-2511

P.O. Box 7766
Horseshoe Bay, TX 78654
Contact: Trey Franklin
Ram Rock Course Description: A 54-hole resort that has three outstanding Robert Trent Jones Sr.-designed courses. The Ram Rock Course is considered to be the most difficult course in Texas. Long, tight, hilly, and well-bunkered. **Par:** 71 (6,946 yards).

Slick Rock Course Description: The Slick Rock course is the easiest Trent Jones course, but it is not that easy. It is a tight course that is flatter than Ram Rock but has nine water hazards. Open only to guests of resort. Great golf. **Par:** 72 (6,834 yards).

Apple Rock Course Description: The Apple Rock Course is the newest Trent Jones course. It is just as hilly as Ram Rock, but the 11th and 12th holes go down to Lake LBJ. Lots of balls in the water. **Par:** 72 (6,999 yards).
Rentals: Golf Carts, Golf Clubs, Driving Range
Members and guests only. Golf lessons available. Mandatory carts.

Fees:

Weekday: 18-hole: $75 Cart: $20
9-hole: (N/A) Cart: $7.50
Weekend: 18-hole: $85 Cart: $20
9-hole: (N/A) Cart: $7.50

Located on Hwy 71 west of Austin.

Bay Oaks Country Club (7,011 yds) 281-488-8753

14545 Bay Oaks Blvd.
Houston, TX 77059
Contact: Ken McDonald
Description: An excellent 18-hole
private course with lots of trees, water,
and undulating greens. Clubhouse is a
perfect private facility. **Par:** 72.
Rentals: Golf Carts, Golf Clubs, Driving
Range
Members and guests only. Walking
permitted.

Fees:

Weekday: 18-hole: $50 Cart: $11
9-hole: (N/A) Cart: (N/A)
Weekend: 18-hole: $50 Cart: $11
9-hole: (N/A) Cart: (N/A)

Located south of Houston off I-45 to
Clear Lake City exit to Hwy 3.

Bear Creek Golf World (54 hs) 281-859-8188

16001 Clay Road and Highway 6
Houston, TX 77084
Contact: Mike Torres
Challenger Course Description: The
Challenger Course looks like it is easy,
but it's not. It has the longest par 5 of
all 54 holes, eight par 3s, and water on
ten holes. It is short but tough. Food,
drinks, and pro shop. **Par:** 66 (5,295
yards).
Rentals: Golf Carts, Pull Carts, Golf
Clubs, Driving Range
Open to the public. Walking permitted.
Golf lessons available.

Masters Course Description: The
Masters Course is long but very fair
because of a traditional design. The
shortest par 4 is 393 yards. The rest
are more than 400 yards. Front nine is
tight. USGA held the national Public
Links here. **Par:** 72 (7,048 yards).
Presidents Course Description:
Considered to be a very good public
complex in Texas with 54 holes that are
a wide variety. The Presidents Course is
flat and wide open with few traps and
only three water hazards. **Par:** 72
(6,562 yards).

Fees:

Weekday: 18-hole: $17 Cart: $11
9-hole: (N/A) Cart: (N/A)
Weekend: 18-hole: $20 Cart: $11
9-hole: (N/A) Cart: (N/A)

Fees:

Weekday: 18-hole: $42 Cart: (N/A)
9-hole: (N/A) Cart: (N/A)
Weekend: 18-hole: $56 Cart: (N/A)
9-hole: (N/A) Cart: (N/A)

Located west on Hwy 6 East.

Brae-Burn Country Club (6,808 yds) 713-774-8788

8101 Bissonnet
Houston, TX 77074
Contact: Breene Cantwell
Description: Lots of water will cause penalty strokes on this 18-hole classic private course. The greens are big and small, and the fairways narrow. Recently remodeled. Great history in club. **Par:** 72.
Rentals: Golf Carts, Golf Clubs, Driving Range

Members and guests only. Golf lessons available. Walking permitted.

Fees:

Weekday: 18-hole: $40 Cart: $11
9-hole: (N/A) Cart: $5
Weekend: 18-hole: $60 Cart: $11
9-hole: (N/A) Cart: $5

Located off Hwy 59 at Bisssonet Exit

Brock Park Municipal Golf Course (6,487 yds) 281-458-1350

8201 John Ralston Road
Houston, TX 77044
Contact: Robert Olson
Description: This 18-hole public course is not real long but is very tight. Fairways lined with pine trees and water hazards on twelve holes. Small greens and traps. **Par:** 72.
Rentals: Golf Carts, Pull Carts, Golf Clubs, Driving Range

Open to the public. Walking permitted. Golf lessons available.

Fees:

Weekday: 18-hole: $8.50 Cart: $8
9-hole: (N/A) Cart: $4.42
Weekend: 18-hole: $11.50 Cart: $8
9-hole: (N/A) Cart: $4.42

Located off Hwy 90 at John Ralston Road.

Champions Golf Club

(36 hs) 281-444-6449

13722 Champions Drive
Houston, TX 77069
Contact: Tad Weeks
Cypress Creek Course Description:
One of the most famous golf courses in
Texas. The Cypress Creek Course was
the site of the 1967 Ryder Cup, 1969
U.S. Open, 1993 U.S. Amateur, and
1997, '99 PGA Tour Championship.
Pure, classic golf at its best. **Par:** 71
(7,147 yards).

Jackrabbit Course Description: The
Jackrabbit Course is almost as great as
the Cypress Creek Course. It is just as
long and tight. Pure golf at its finest for
those who love the game at its best.
Par: 72 (7,115 yards).

Rentals: Golf Carts, Driving Range
Members and guests only. Golf lessons
available. Walking permitted.

Fees:

Weekday: 18-hole: $40 Cart: $21
9-hole: (N/A) Cart: $5
Weekend: 18-hole: $50 Cart: $21
9-hole: (N/A) Cart: $5

Located west of I-45 off FM 1960. Take
Champions Drive north to club
entrance.

Clear Creek Golf Course

(6,758 yds) 281-738-8000

3902 Fellows Road
Houston, TX 77047
Contact: Carey Swanson
Description: This 18-hole public
course looks easy but plays tougher
because of long holes, rolling hills, and
water. Lack of trees makes it look easy.
Food. **Par:** 72.
Rentals: Golf Carts, Pull Carts, Golf
Clubs, Driving Range

Open to the public. Walking permitted.
Golf lessons available.

Fees:

Weekday: 18-hole: $20 Cart: $9
9-hole: (N/A) Cart: $7
Weekend: 18-hole: $30 Cart: $9
9-hole: (N/A) Cart: $7

Located off Hwy 288 to Beltway and
Tom Bass Park.

Clear Lake Golf Course

(6,757 yds) 713-488-0252

1202 Reseda Drive
Houston, TX 77062
Contact: Jerry Honza
Description: Built in 1964 to provide golf fun for NASA folks. Clubhouse has a snack bar, bar, meeting room, and pro shop. Plenty of water. **Par:** 72.
Rentals: Golf Carts, Pull Carts, Golf Clubs, Driving Range

Open to the public. Walking permitted. Golf lessons available.

Fees:

Weekday: 18-hole: $18.50 Cart: $12
9-hole: $10 Cart: $7
Weekend: 18-hole: $27 Cart: $12
9-hole: $12.50 Cart: $7

Located 20 miles south of Houston on I-45; east on El Dorado to Diana Lane.

Glenbrook Golf Course

(6,427 yds) 713-649-8089

8205 N. Bayou
Houston, TX 77017
Contact: Paul Donnelly
Description: A bayou comes into play on nine holes of this 18-hole public course that also has narrow and wide fairways to large greens with sand traps. **Par:** 71.
Rentals: Golf Carts, Pull Carts, Golf Clubs

Open to the public. Walking permitted. Golf lessons available.

Fees:

Weekday: 18-hole: $10 Cart: $8.66
9-hole: (N/A) Cart: $5.68
Weekend: 18-hole: $13 Cart: $8.66
9-hole: (N/A) Cart: $5.68

Located in southeast Houston off I-45.

Gus Wortham Park Golf Course

(6,234 yds) 713-921-3227

7000 N. Capital
Houston, TX 77011
Contact: Paul Reed
Description: Shooting a good score on this 18-hole public course is possible. It doesn't have much water or traps and there are few hills, wide fairways, and medium-size greens. **Par:** 72.
Rentals: Golf Carts, Pull Carts, Golf Clubs, Driving Range

Open to the public. Walking permitted. Golf lessons available.

Fees:

Weekday: 18-hole: $10 Cart: $8.50
9-hole: (N/A) Cart: $4.25
Weekend: 18-hole: $13 Cart: $8.50
9-hole: (N/A) Cart: $4.25

Located in southeast Houston at Wayside and Lawndale.

Hearthstone Country Club   (27 hs) 281-463-2204

7615 Ameswood
Houston, TX 77095
Contact: Darren Busker
Description: A 27-hole private course.
The Wolf Corner nine is the easiest of
the three nines as it is short and wide.
The Horsepen and Jackrabbit nines
make the good 18, being long and
narrow. **Par:** 71 (6,547 yards).
Rentals: Golf Carts, Golf Clubs, Driving
Range

Members and guests only. Golf lessons
available. Walking permitted.

Fees:

Weekday: 18-hole: $40 Cart: (N/A)
9-hole: (N/A) Cart: $4.50
Weekend: 18-hole: $50 Cart: (N/A)
9-hole: (N/A) Cart: $4.50

> Go east on FM 529 off Hwy 6 in west
> Houston to Hearthstone subdivision.

Hermann Park Golf Course   (5,965 yds) 713-526-0077

6201 Golf Course Drive
Houston, TX 77030
Contact: David Henning
Description: Golfers in Houston can
post great scores on this redesigned
18-hole public course because it is
short with wide fairways, not much
water, and small greens. **Par:** 71.
Rentals: Golf Carts, Pull Carts, Golf
Clubs, Driving Range

Open to the public. Walking permitted.
Golf lessons available.

Fees:

Weekday: 18-hole: $12 Cart: $8.30
9-hole: (N/A) Cart: (N/A)
Weekend: 18-hole: $15 Cart: $8.30
9-hole: (N/A) Cart: (N/A)

> Located in Hermann Park in south
> central Houston.

Herron Lakes Golf Club   (6,400 yds) 281-894-0621

7910 N. Sam Houston Parkway
Houston, TX 77064
Contact: Ed Shinn
Description: Newly opened public
course at site of former driving range.
Water on every hole but no sand traps.
Carts mandatory on weekends. Very
tight driving fairways. **Par:** 72.
Rentals: Golf Carts, Driving Range
Open to the public. Walking permitted.
Golf lessons available.

Fees:

Weekday: 18-hole: $20 Cart: $18
9-hole: (N/A) Cart: (N/A)
Weekend: 18-hole: $30 Cart: $22
9-hole: (N/A) Cart: (N/A)

> Located on Sam Houston Pkwy across
> Hwy 249 from race track.

ston Public Library

;HTS LIBRARY

:omer Name: Morice, Fabian
:omer ID: **********5636

s that you checked out

⊤¡Buen viaje, beb├®!
33477465939556
Monday, January 31, 2022

Animales a jugar
33477464477195
Monday, January 31, 2022

El peque├▒o ping├╝ino
33477466448540
Monday, January 31, 2022

Little elephants = Los elefantitos
33477488718744
Monday, January 31, 2022

Nieve
33477465867107
Monday, January 31, 2022

The Texas golf guide
R0118874442
Monday, January 31, 2022

items: 6
unt balance: $0.00
'2022 3:27 PM
cked out: 10
due: 0
requests: 13
ly for pickup: 0

k you for using the Houston Public Library.

(7,023 yds) 713-465-8381

ers and guests only. Golf lessons
ible. Walking permitted.

kday: 18-hole: $60 Cart: $22
e: (N/A) Cart: (N/A)
kend: 18-hole: $85 Cart: $22
e: (N/A) Cart: (N/A)

ated in west Houston between
morial Drive and Woodway.

(3,232 yds) 281-933-2300

to the public. Walking permitted.
lessons available.

kday: 18-hole: $10.83 Cart: $12
e: (N/A) Cart: $5
kend: 18-hole: $16.24 Cart: $12
e: (N/A) Cart: $5

ated off Hwy 59 south to Beltway 8
Ruffino Road.

(27 hs) 281-448-0239

bers and guests only. Golf lessons
able. Walking permitted.

kday: 18-hole: $20 Cart: $9
le: (N/A) Cart: $5.50
kend: 18-hole: $30 Cart: $9
le: (N/A) Cart: $5.50

cated northwest of downtown
uston on Antoine

Jersey Meadow Golf Course   (27 hs) 713-896-0900

8502 Rio Grande
Houston, TX 77040
Contact: Darryl Henning
Description: A great 27-hole public course. The Red and White nines have water on 15 holes, huge three-putt greens, and traps. The Blue nine opened in 1992 with water on seven holes. **Par:** 71 (6,495 yards).
Rentals: Golf Carts, Pull Carts, Golf Clubs, Driving Range

Open to the public. Walking permitted. Golf lessons available.

Fees:

Weekday: 18-hole: $30 Cart: (N/A)
9-hole: (N/A) Cart: (N/A)
Weekend: 18-hole: $42 Cart: (N/A)
9-hole: (N/A) Cart: (N/A)

Located on Hwy 290 north.

Lakeside Country Club   (6,983 yds) 281-497-2228

100 Wilcrest Drive
Houston, TX 77042
Contact: Gary Ray
Description: Even though this 18-hole private course is somewhat long, posting a good score is tougher thanks to undulating greens with traps, and tight fairways. **Par:** 72.
Rentals: Golf Carts, Driving Range

Members and guests only. Golf lessons available. Walking permitted.

Fees:

Weekday: 18-hole: $55 Cart: $11
9-hole: (N/A) Cart: $8
Weekend: 18-hole: $75 Cart: $11
9-hole: (N/A) Cart: $8

Located three miles north of Westheimer.

Lochinvar Golf Club   (6,479 yds) 281-821-0220

2000 Farrell Road
Houston, TX 77073
Contact: Brian Smith
Description: A Jack Nicklaus-designed 18-hole private course that only allows men to play. Fairly long with bentgrass greens and wide fairways. It is extremely exclusive. **Par:** 72.
Rentals: Golf Clubs, Driving Range
Members and guests only. Golf lessons available. Walking permitted.

Fees:

Weekday: 18-hole: $50 Cart: $10
9-hole: (N/A) Cart: (N/A)
Weekend: 18-hole: $85 Cart: $10
9-hole: (N/A) Cart: (N/A)

Located in north Houston. Take I-45 to Rankin Road, turn right to Hardy Toll Road, left to Farrell, and right to club.

✓ Melrose Golf Course & Driving Range (1,811 yds) 281-847-1214

401 Canino Road
Houston, TX 77076
Contact: Joan Dement
Description: Perhaps the only 18-hole par-3 course that is a pitch and putt with four lakes and small greens. The longest hole is 150 yards and most are under 100 yards. **Par:** 54.
Rentals: Golf Clubs, Driving Range

Open to the public. Walking permitted. Golf lessons available.

Fees:

Weekday: 18-hole: $10 Cart: (N/A)
9-hole: (N/A) Cart: (N/A)
Weekend: 18-hole: $12 Cart: (N/A)
9-hole: (N/A) Cart: (N/A)

Located east of I-45 north on Canino Road.

Memorial Park Golf Course (7,267 yds) 713-862-4033

6501 Memorial Drive
Houston, TX 77007
Contact: Brent Blackburn
Description: This great 18-hole public course was often the site of the PGA Tour's Houston Open. It is extremely long with lots of trees, large three-putt greens, and water. Great site. **Par:** 72.
Rentals: Golf Carts, Pull Carts, Golf Clubs, Driving Range

Open to the public. Walking permitted. Golf lessons available.

Fees:

Weekday: 18-hole: $22.50 Cart: $15
9-hole: (N/A) Cart: $3.50
Weekend: 18-hole: $32 Cart: $15
9-hole: (N/A) Cart: $3.50

Located off I-10 at Westcott.

Northgate Country Club (6,540 yds) 281-440-5302

17110 Northgate Forest Drive
Houston, TX 77068
Contact: David Esch
Description: A strong 18-hole private target course with small greens protected by mounds and traps. The greens are elevated and undulating. Water on 14 holes. Food, drinks, tennis, and pool. **Par:** 70.

Rentals: Golf Carts, Golf Clubs, Driving Range
Members and guests only. Golf lessons available. Walking permitted.

Fees:

Weekday: 18-hole: $40 Cart: $22
9-hole: (N/A) Cart: $6
Weekend: 18-hole: $50 Cart: $22
9-hole: (N/A) Cart: $6

Located off FM 1960 west of I-45.

✓ Pasadena Municipal Golf Course (6,750 yds) 281-481-0834

1000 Duffer Lane
Houston, TX 77034
Contact: Jon Cutshall
Description: Hitting the greens in regulation on this 18-hole public course can be difficult because the greens are very small with lots of traps. Lots of water. **Par:** 72.
Rentals: Golf Carts, Pull Carts, Golf Clubs, Driving Range

Open to the public. Walking permitted. Golf lessons available.

Fees:

Weekday: 18-hole: $7.05 Cart: $7.78 9-hole: (N/A) Cart: $4.90
Weekend: 18-hole: $10.05 Cart: $7.78 9-hole: (N/A) Cart: $4.90

Located south of town off I-45 to Hwy 3.

Pine Crest Golf Club (6,927 yds) 713-462-4914

3080 Gessner
Houston, TX 77080
Contact: Steve Bratcher
Description: With 13 lakes and 72 sand traps, this 18-hole semiprivate course is rather tough with large undulating greens. Carts are mandatory on weekends. All golfers welcome. Restaurant and pro shop. **Par:** 72.
Rentals: Golf Carts, Golf Clubs, Driving Range

Open to the public. Walking permitted. Golf lessons available.

Fees:

Weekday: 18-hole: $30 Cart: (N/A) 9-hole: (N/A) Cart: $8.50
Weekend: 18-hole: $45 Cart: (N/A) 9-hole: (N/A) Cart: (N/A)

Located 20 minutes from downtown. Take I-10 west to Gessner and go north for five miles; club is on the right.

Pine Forest Country Club (27 hs) 281-463-1234

18003 Clay Road
Houston, TX 77084
Contact: Charlie Epps
Description: An 18-hole private course that added a third nine called the White nine. Most members play the Green and Gold nines with water on every hole. The White nine has severe cross wind and ditches. **Par:** 72 (6,831 yards).
Rentals: Golf Carts, Golf Clubs, Driving Range

Members and guests only. Golf lessons available. Walking permitted.

Fees:

Weekday: 18-hole: $35 Cart: $20 9-hole: $15 Cart: $6
Weekend: 18-hole: $45 Cart: $20 9-hole: $21 Cart: $6

Located north of Hwy 6, 6 miles west of I-10, right on Clay Rd.

River Oaks Country Club

(6,828 yds) 713-529-4321

1600 River Oaks Blvd.
Houston, TX 77019
Contact: Dick Harmon
Description: With extremely large undulating greens on this 18-hole private course, golfers frequently three-putt for bogies, double bogies, and worse. A moss-draped course located in posh section of Houston.
Par: 72.
Rentals: Golf Carts, Driving Range

Members and guests only. Golf lessons available. Walking permitted.

Fees:

Weekday: 18-hole: $75 Cart: $11
9-hole: (N/A) Cart: $4.50
Weekend: 18-hole: $75 Cart: $11
9-hole: (N/A) Cart: $4.50

Located at Westheimer and River Oaks Blvd. in southwest Houston.

Sharpstown Golf Course

(6,655 yds) 713-988-2099

6600 Harbor Town Drive
Houston, TX 77036
Contact: Doug Randall
Description: Lee Trevino won his first tournament, the 1965 Texas State Open, on this wide open 18-hole public course. With large greens, even Trevino made three-putts. Food. **Par:** 70.
Rentals: Golf Carts, Pull Carts, Golf Clubs

Open to the public. Walking permitted.

Fees:

Weekday: 18-hole: $10.50 Cart: $8.50 9-hole: (N/A) Cart: $3.75
Weekend: 18-hole: $13.50 Cart: $8.50 9-hole: (N/A) Cart: $3.75

Located in southwest Houston.

Texaco Country Club

(6,300 yds) 713-453-7501

12800 Texaco Road
Houston, TX 77013
Contact: Lonnie Dunn
Description: Out-of-town golfers or members of other country clubs are welcome. The course is a lot of fun to play. **Par:** 72.
Rentals: Golf Carts, Pull Carts, Golf Clubs
Members and guests only. Walking permitted.

Fees:

Weekday: 18-hole: $12 Cart: $14
9-hole: $12 Cart: $8
Weekend: 18-hole: $18 Cart: $14
9-hole: $18 Cart: $8

Located two miles north of I-10, east on Federal Road.

Texas Par Golf Academy   (3,036 yds) 281-493-3276

4035 S. Highway 6
Houston, TX 77082
Contact: Ruben Lopaz
Description: One of the most difficult nine-hole public par-3 courses in the state with holes ranging from 126 yards to 226 yards with water and sand traps. Great lessons. **Par:** 27.
Rentals: Golf Carts, Pull Carts, Golf Clubs, Driving Range

Open to the public. Walking permitted. Golf lessons available.

Fees:

Weekday: 18-hole: $10.75 Cart: $7.50 9-hole: $7 Cart: $3.75
Weekend: 18-hole: $10.75 Cart: $7.50 9-hole: $7.50 Cart: $3.75

Located south of Westheimer on Hwy 6.

Westwood Country Club   (6,989 yds) 713-774-3011

8888 Country Creek Drive
Houston, TX 77036
Contact: Scott Olsen
Description: A traditional style 18-hole private course constructed in 1928. It has well-trapped, large undulating greens, water on seven holes on the front nine, and is a long course. **Par:** 72.
Rentals: Golf Carts, Golf Clubs, Driving Range

Members and guests only. Golf lessons available. Walking permitted.

Fees:

Weekday: 18-hole: $50 Cart: $11 9-hole: (N/A) Cart: $7.39
Weekend: 18-hole: $75 Cart: $11 9-hole: (N/A) Cart: $7.39

Located southwest on Hwy 59 on Bissonnet exit.

World Houston Golf Club   (6,617 yds) 281-449-8384

4000 Greens Road
Houston, TX 77032
Contact: Matt Landreau
Description: The fairways on this 18-hole public course are flat with not a lot of trees. However, there is water on twelve holes and the greens are very small and elevated. **Par:** 72.
Rentals: Golf Carts, Pull Carts, Golf Clubs, Driving Range

Open to the public. Walking permitted. Golf lessons available.

Fees:

Weekday: 18-hole: $22 Cart: NA 9-hole: $8 Cart: $4
Weekend: 18-hole: $31 Cart: NA 9-hole: $10 Cart: $4

Located west of Hwy 59 on Greens Road next to George Bush IAH Airport.

Lake Houston Golf Club   (6,940 yds) 281-324-1841

27350 Afton Way
Huffman, TX 77336
Contact: Jim Belcher
Description: This 18-hole public
course is reasonably long with not much
water. But the narrow fairways are
protected by big pine trees and the very
large greens may be automatic
three-putts. **Par:** 72.
Rentals: Golf Carts, Pull Carts, Golf
Clubs, Driving Range

Open to the public. Walking permitted.
Golf lessons available.

Fees:

Weekday: 18-hole: $21 Cart: (N/A)
9-hole: (N/A) Cart: (N/A)
Weekend: 18-hole: $26 Cart: (N/A)
9-hole: (N/A) Cart: (N/A)

Located off FM 2100 north on FM
1960.

El Dorado Country Club   (7,118 yds) 281-458-1010

7900 Old North Belt Drive
Humble, TX 77338
Contact: Mike Shoelen
Description: An extremely long
18-hole private course that has little
water but lots of trees on narrow
fairways and traps protecting three-putt
greens. Food and drinks. **Par:** 72.
Rentals: Golf Carts, Golf Clubs, Driving
Range

Members and guests only. Golf lessons
available. Walking permitted.

Fees:

Weekday: 18-hole: $25 Cart: $10
9-hole: $15 Cart: $6
Weekend: 18-hole: $35 Cart: $10
9-hole: $20 Cart: $6

Located north of Houston off Hwy 59
and North Belt Line Drive.

Tour 18 Golf Course   (6,807 yds) 281-540-1818

3102 FM 1960 East
Humble, TX 77338
Contact: Greg Saul
Description: The most unique 18-hole
public course in Texas. Every hole is
designed like a great PGA Tour hole,
including Augusta National, Doral, TPC
Sawgrass, Harbour Town, and Colonial.
Mandatory carts, huge clubhouse. A
must-play course **Par:** 72.
Rentals: Golf Carts, Driving Range

Open to the public. Golf lessons
available. Mandatory carts.

Fees:

Weekday: 18-hole: $65 Cart: (N/A)
9-hole: $37.50 Cart: (N/A)
Weekend: 18-hole: $75 Cart: (N/A)
9-hole: $47.50 Cart: (N/A)

Located north of Houston. Take Hwy 59
north to FM 1960. Club is ½ mile east.

Walden on Lake Houston C.C.　　(6,781 yds)　281-852-3467

18100 Walden Forest Drive
Humble, TX 77346
Contact: Jimmy Odell
Description: A tough target golf
course. Scenic lakeside views.
Clubhouse has restaurant, bar, lockers,
showers, meeting room, tennis courts,
and pro shop. **Par:** 72.
Rentals: Golf Carts, Pull Carts, Golf
Clubs, Driving Range

Members and guests only. Golf lessons
available. Walking permitted.

Fees:

Weekday: 18-hole: $30 Cart: $10
9-hole: (N/A) Cart: (N/A)
Weekend: 18-hole: $40 Cart: $10
9-hole: (N/A) Cart: (N/A)

> From downtown Houston, take Hwy 59
> north to FM 1960 east.

Country Campus Golf Course　　(6,150 yds)　409-291-0008

Route 13, Box 832
Huntsville, TX 77340
Contact: Bill Kacatik
Description: A rolling nine-hole public
course constructed on the land that was
the old Sam Houston College. Course is
short with trees, ditches, and small
greens. **Par:** 35.
Rentals: Golf Carts, Pull Carts, Golf
Clubs

Open to the public. Walking permitted.

Fees:

Weekday: 18-hole: $9 Cart: $8 9-hole:
(N/A) Cart: $3.50
Weekend: 18-hole: $10.50 Cart: $8
9-hole: (N/A) Cart: $3.50

> Located off I-45 north to Hwy 19.

Elkins Lake Country Club　　(6,640 yds)　409-295-4312

282 Elkins Lake Road
Huntsville, TX 77340
Contact: Ray Sarno
Description: Penalty strokes are quite
common on this 18-hole private course
thanks to out-of-bounds, seven water
holes, and big trees that knock balls out
of bounds and into the water. Food and
drinks. **Par:** 72.
Rentals: Golf Carts, Driving Range

Members and guests only. Golf lessons
available. Walking permitted.

Fees:

Weekday: 18-hole: $20 Cart: $9
9-hole: (N/A) Cart: $4.50
Weekend: 18-hole: $25 Cart: $9
9-hole: (N/A) Cart: $4.50

> Located south of town off I-45.

Outlaw Gap Golf Course   (1,706 yds) 409-295-5525

Route 4, Box 1365
Huntsville, TX 77340
Contact: Raymond Outlaw
Description: A rather difficult
nine-hole public par-3 course. The
course has lots of trees and water, and
some holes go uphill or downhill. The
holes range from 99 yards to 205
yards. **Par:** 27.
Open to the public. Walking permitted.

Fees:

Weekday: 18-hole: $6 Cart: (N/A)
9-hole: $3 Cart: (N/A)
Weekend: 18-hole: $8 Cart: (N/A)
9-hole: $4 Cart: (N/A)

Located on U.S. 75 two miles south of
Huntsville.

Waterwood National Resort & C.C. (6,807 yds) 409-891-5050

One Waterwood Drive
Huntsville, TX 77340-9612
Contact: Eddie Dey
Description: Pete Dye designed this
hard 18-hole semiprivate course that is
open to the public and resort guests.
The course is hilly with holes on Lake
Livingston. A tough target course with
small greens and traps. **Par:** 71.
Rentals: Golf Carts, Golf Clubs, Driving
Range

Open to the public. Walking permitted.
Golf lessons available.

Fees:

Weekday: 18-hole: $27.50 Cart: $10
9-hole: (N/A) Cart: $4.50
Weekend: 18-hole: $40 Cart: $10
9-hole: (N/A) Cart: $4.50

Take I-45 north to Hwy 190 in
Huntsville. Go east 18 miles to
Waterwood Parkway, turn left, and go
eight miles to club.

Island Oaks Golf Club   (3,553 yds) 806-892-2839

County Road 33
Idalou, TX 79329
Contact: Golf Shop
Description: Typical West Texas layout
with small, changing greens and plenty
of wind. Not many trees or water but
can be tough if you can't find the
fairways. Can be played as 18-hole
layout with different tees. **Par:** 36.
Rentals: Golf Carts

Open to the public.

Fees:

Weekday: 18-hole: (N/A) Cart: (N/A)
9-hole: $11 Cart: $10
Weekend: 18-hole: (N/A) Cart: (N/A)
9-hole: $15 Cart: $10

Located two miles east of Idalou on
County Road 33.

Iraan Country Club

(3,335 yds) 915-639-8892

P.O. Box 356
Iraan, TX 79744
Contact: Club Manager
Description: A typical rural West Texas nine-hole public course. It is a flat course, but wind is a major factor. The course is reasonably long with some trees. **Par:** 36.
Open to the public. Walking permitted.

Fees:

Weekday: 18-hole: $4 Cart: (N/A)
9-hole: (N/A) Cart: (N/A)
Weekend: 18-hole: $6 Cart: (N/A)
9-hole: (N/A) Cart: (N/A)

Located off Hwy 349.

Four Seasons Resort and Club

(36 hs) 972-717-2530

4150 N. MacArthur Blvd.
Irving, TX 75038
Contact: Paul Earnest
Cottonwood Valley Course
Description: Cottonwood Valley is a members course and part of the Four Seasons complex. The first two rounds of the GTE Byron Nelson Classic are played here. The first green is shaped like the state of Texas. **Par:** 70 (6,846 yards).
Rentals: Golf Carts, Golf Clubs, Driving Range
Members and guests only. Golf lessons available. Mandatory carts.

Fees:

Weekday: 18-hole: $60 Cart: (N/A)
9-hole: (N/A) Cart: (N/A)
Weekend: 18-hole: $80 Cart: (N/A)
9-hole: (N/A) Cart: (N/A)

TPC Course Description: Site of GTE Byron Nelson Classic. A great resort hotel to go with a great tournament course which is played by resort guests the rest of the year. A really fun course to play with double greens on holes five through nine. **Par:** 70 (6,916 yards).
Contact: Jamie Elliott
Rentals: Golf Carts, Golf Clubs, Driving Range
Members and resort guests only. Golf lessons available. Mandatory carts.

Fees:

Weekday: 18-hole: $105 Cart: (N/A)
9-hole: (N/A) Cart: (N/A)
Weekend: 18-hole: $140 Cart: (N/A)
9-hole: (N/A) Cart: (N/A)

Located on North MacArthur between Hwy 114 and Hwy 183, and across from Northlake College. Take MacArthur exit to course.

Hackberry Creek Country Club   (7,013 yds) 972-869-9364

1901 Royal Lane
Irving, TX 75063
Contact: Bob Burns
Description: A strong 18-hole private club. The course rolls up and down hills and across water hazards. A perfect private clubhouse. **Par:** 72.
Rentals: Golf Carts, Golf Clubs, Driving Range

Members and guests only. Golf lessons available. Walking permitted.

Fees:

Weekday: 18-hole: $45 Cart: $10
9-hole: (N/A) Cart: $5
Weekend: 18-hole: $75 Cart: $10
9-hole: (N/A) Cart: $5

Located east of Hwy 114. Exit off Valley View, turn left on Royal Lane.

Las Colinas Country Club   (6,809 yds) 972-541-1141

4900 N. O'Connor Road
Irving, TX 75062
Contact: Robert Singletary
Description: Development of the club in 1964 launched the start of the most famous part of Irving. The expansive club has a restaurant, bar, lockers, showers, tennis courts, and meeting rooms. Site of Senior PGA event in 1999. **Par:** 71.
Rentals: Golf Carts, Pull Carts, Golf Clubs, Driving Range

Members and guests only. Golf lessons available. Walking permitted.

Fees:

Weekday: 18-hole: $50 Cart: $10
9-hole: (N/A) Cart: (N/A)
Weekend: 18-hole: $75 Cart: $10
9-hole: (N/A) Cart: (N/A)

Located west of Hwy 114.

Twin Wells Municipal Golf Course   (6,606 yds) 972-438-4340

2000 E. Shady Grove
Irving, TX 75060
Contact: Rich Richeson
Description: The only public course in Irving. Twin Wells is a simple golf course with some water, undulation, and not many trees. Clubhouse has a snack bar and pro shop. **Par:** 72.
Rentals: Golf Carts, Pull Carts, Golf Clubs, Driving Range

Open to the public. Walking permitted. Golf lessons available.

Fees:

Weekday: 18-hole: $17.32 Cart: $12
9-hole: (N/A) Cart: (N/A)
Weekend: 18-hole: $26 Cart: $12
9-hole: (N/A) Cart: (N/A)

Located east of Loop 12 on Shady Grove Road.

Jacksboro Golf & Country Club   (3,397 yds) 940-567-3726

309 N. 8th St.
Jacksboro, TX 76458
Contact: James Gammon
Description: A nine-hole semiprivate
course that was remodeled in 1993.
The tees were extended and the greens
expanded. Trees are the main factor.
Par: 35.
Rentals: Golf Carts, Pull Carts, Golf
Clubs, Driving Range

Open to the public. Walking permitted.
Golf lessons available.

Fees:

Weekday: 18-hole: $14 Cart: $8
9-hole: (N/A) Cart: $3.25
Weekend: 18-hole: $18 Cart: $8
9-hole: (N/A) Cart: $3.25

Located 1½ miles north of town on
Hwy 148.

Cherokee Country Club   (6,208 yds) 903-586-2141

P.O. Box 1069
Henderson Highway
Jacksonville, TX 75766
Contact: Tom Campbell
Description: Nine of the 18 holes have
lots of pine trees that make the holes
tough. The other nine holes have trees
but are more open. **Par:** 71.
Rentals: Golf Carts, Golf Clubs, Driving
Range

Open to the public. Walking permitted.
Golf lessons available.

Fees:

Weekday: 18-hole: $16 Cart: $10
9-hole: (N/A) Cart: $4.25
Weekend: 18-hole: $22 Cart: $10
9-hole: (N/A) Cart: $4.25

Located four miles north of town on
Hwy 79 east.

Jasper Country Club   (6,397 yds) 409-384-4342

P.O. Box 477
Jasper, TX 75951
Contact: Golf Shop
Description: Out-of-town golfers are
welcome to play this nine-hole private
course. It has small greens, narrow
fairways lined with pine trees, and two
water hazards. Food. **Par:** 36.
Rentals: Golf Carts, Golf Clubs, Driving
Range

Members and guests only. Golf lessons
available. Walking permitted.

Fees:

Weekday: 18-hole: $21.25 Cart: $8
9-hole: (N/A) Cart: $4
Weekend: 18-hole: $21.25 Cart: $8
9-hole: (N/A) Cart: $4

Located north of town on Hwy 96.

Rusty Rail Country Club   (6,144 yds) 903-665-7245

113 W. Lafayette
Jefferson, TX 75657
Contact: Frank Kresh
Description: A typical piney woods nine-hole semiprivate golf course with a lot of trees and a creek on six holes. No sand traps. The par-4 first hole is a par 5 on the next nine. **Par:** 35.
Rentals: Golf Carts, Pull Carts, Golf Clubs, Driving Range

Members and guests only. Walking permitted.

Fees:

Weekday: 18-hole: $7.60 Cart: $6
9-hole: (N/A) Cart: $3.20
Weekend: 18-hole: $11.60 Cart: $7
9-hole: (N/A) Cart: $3.20

Located north of town on Hwy 59.

Mountain Valley Country Club   (6,542 yds) 817-295-7126

Lakeside Drive
Joshua, TX 76058
Contact: Mike Petrovich
Description: An 18-hole private course that is tougher than it looks because the doglegs go around trees, demanding perfectly placed tee shots. Clubhouse has restaurant, lockers, and pro shop. **Par:** 71.
Rentals: Golf Carts, Golf Clubs, Driving Range

Members and guests only. Walking permitted.

Fees:

Weekday: 18-hole: $18 Cart: $9
9-hole: $10 Cart: $3.75
Weekend: 18-hole: $25 Cart: $9
9-hole: $12.50 Cart: $3.75

Located on Hwy 174 north.

Junction Golf Club   (2,800 yds) 915-446-2968

FM 2169 West
Junction, TX 76849
Contact: John Rimes
Description: This nine-hole public course is very short, but with water on eight holes, rolling fairways, and small greens, it can play rather tough. **Par:** 35.
Rentals: Golf Carts, Pull Carts, Driving Range

Open to the public. Walking permitted.

Fees:

Weekday: 18-hole: $10 Cart: $8
9-hole: (N/A) Cart: $3.98
Weekend: 18-hole: $12 Cart: $14
9-hole: (N/A) Cart: $3.98

Located off I-10 west on FM 2169.

Club at Cinco Ranch   (7,014 yds) 281-395-4653

25030 Cinco Ranch Blvd.
Katy, TX 77450
Contact: Layne Ricks
Description: Great daily-fee course located in booming housing development. Course features plenty of water and sand and more than 200 trees. Wind can also be a factor. Expansive clubhouse, friendly staff and well-stocked pro shop. **Par:** 72.
Rentals: Golf Carts, Golf Clubs, Driving Range

Open to the public. Golf lessons available. Mandatory carts.

Fees:

Weekday: 18-hole: $40 Cart: (N/A)
9-hole: (N/A) Cart: (N/A)
Weekend: 18-hole: $50 Cart: (N/A)
9-hole: (N/A) Cart: (N/A)

Take Grand Ave. (Hwy 99) exit off I-10 west to Cinco Ranch subdivision.

Club at Falcon Point   (6,771 yds) 281-392-7888

24503 Falcon Point Drive
Katy, TX 77494
Contact: David Goldblum
Description: Target golf 18-hole course. Wind can be tough here. Clubhouse recently remodeled with restaurant, bar, lockers, pro shop, meeting rooms, and tennis courts. **Par:** 72.
Rentals: Golf Carts, Golf Clubs, Driving Range

Members and guests only. Golf lessons available. Walking permitted.

Fees:

Weekday: 18-hole: $35 Cart: $22
9-hole: (N/A) Cart: (N/A)
Weekend: 18-hole: $45 Cart: $22
9-hole: (N/A) Cart: (N/A)

Located off I-10 west to exit 742; turn left.

Green Meadows Golf Club   (5,440 yds) 281-391-3670

6138 Franz Road
Katy, TX 77493
Contact: Mike McRoberts
Description: One of the shortest 18-hole public courses in Texas. The course is flat with some trees, no sand traps, water on nine holes, and small greens. Snack bar. **Par:** 70.
Rentals: Golf Carts, Pull Carts, Golf Clubs

Open to the public. Walking permitted. Golf lessons available.

Fees:

Weekday: 18-hole: $14 Cart: $17.30
9-hole: $9.20 Cart: $9.30
Weekend: 18-hole: $20.60 Cart: $17.30 9-hole: $11.85 Cart: $9.30

Located west of Houston off I-10.

Willow Fork Country Club   (6,853 yds) 281-579-6262

21055 Westheimer Parkway
Katy, TX 77450
Contact: Duane Criswell
Description: A very strong 18-hole private course. Clubhouse has restaurant, lockers, showers, meeting rooms, tennis courts, and pro shop. **Par:** 72.
Rentals: Golf Carts, Golf Clubs, Driving Range

Members and guests only. Golf lessons available. Walking permitted.

Fees:

Weekday: 18-hole: $52 Cart: (N/A)
9-hole: (N/A) Cart: (N/A)
Weekend: 18-hole: $62 Cart: (N/A)
9-hole: (N/A) Cart: (N/A)

Take I-10 west to Fry Road. Turn left on Westheimer Parkway.

Cedar Creek Country Club   (6,723 yds) 903-498-8419

Route 1, Box 136
Kemp, TX 75143
Contact: Dale Folmar
Description: A magnificent golf course next to Cedar Creek Lake southeast of Dallas. The course is long and tight. Clubhouse has nice private club facilities. **Par:** 72.
Rentals: Golf Carts, Driving Range

Members and guests only. Walking permitted.

Fees:

Weekday: 18-hole: $20 Cart: $15.50
9-hole: (N/A) Cart: (N/A)
Weekend: 18-hole: $25 Cart: $15.50
9-hole: (N/A) Cart: (N/A)

Located four miles south of Kemp on Hwy 175.

Kings Creek Golf Club   (6,750 yds) 903-498-8888

P.O. Box 529
Kemp, TX 75143
Contact: Doug Smith
Description: A solid public golf course with overnight accommodations upstairs in the clubhouse. Good lakeside views and a steady wind are enough to battle any golfer. **Par:** 71.
Rentals: Golf Carts, Pull Carts, Golf Clubs, Driving Range

Open to the public. Walking permitted. Golf lessons available.

Fees:

Weekday: 18-hole: $10 Cart: $8
9-hole: (N/A) Cart: (N/A)
Weekend: 18-hole: $20 Cart: $8
9-hole: (N/A) Cart: (N/A)

Located on Hwy 175 southeast of Dallas.

Karnes County Country Club   (6,500 yds) 830-583-3200

Highway 181 South
Kenedy, TX 78119
Contact: Fernando De Leon
Description: There is a lake in the middle of this nine-hole public course. Some of the holes are open while others are tight with trees. All greens are small. **Par:** 36.
Rentals: Golf Carts, Pull Carts, Golf Clubs

Open to the public. Walking permitted.

Fees:

Weekday: 18-hole: $10.50 Cart: $7.50 9-hole: (N/A) Cart: $3.23
Weekend: 18-hole: $12.50 Cart: $7.50 9-hole: (N/A) Cart: $3.23

Located on Hwy 181 southeast of San Antonio.

Winkler County Golf Course   (4,929 yds) 915-586-9243

1010 Tascola
Kermit, TX 79745
Contact: Bob Stangby
Description: This nine-hole public course is getting tougher because trees and water hazards were added to the layout. It was reasonably tough already thanks to elevated bentgrass greens. **Par:** 36.
Rentals: Golf Carts, Driving Range

Open to the public. Walking permitted. Golf lessons available.

Fees:

Weekday: 18-hole: $10 Cart: $7 9-hole: (N/A) Cart: $3.50
Weekend: 18-hole: $10 Cart: $7 9-hole: (N/A) Cart: $3.50

Located west of town on Hwy 302.

Riverhill Country Club   (6,855 yds) 830-792-1143

100 Riverhill Club Lane
Kerrville, TX 78028
Contact: Mark Fuller
Description: Byron Nelson designed the course and he and his wife, Peggy, travel here a lot to play golf. Club has 18 cabins for rent and visitors may play the course. Classic Hill Country links. **Par:** 72.
Rentals: Golf Carts, Golf Clubs, Driving Range

Members and guests only. Walking permitted.

Fees:

Weekday: 18-hole: $50 Cart: $9 9-hole: (N/A) Cart: $6
Weekend: 18-hole: $75 Cart: $9 9-hole: (N/A) Cart: $6

Located off Loop 173, two miles east on Hwy 39 to Riverhill Club Lane.

Scott Schreiner Municipal G. C.   (6,544 yds) 830-257-4982

One Country Club Drive
Kerrville, TX 78028
Contact: Guy Cullins
Description: There is water on several holes of this 18-hole public course. A lake dominates some holes. The fairways are wide open. Not many sand traps. **Par:** 72.
Rentals: Golf Carts, Pull Carts, Golf Clubs

Open to the public. Walking permitted. Golf lessons available.

Fees:

Weekday: 18-hole: $8.50 Cart: $6.65 9-hole: (N/A) Cart: $3.23
Weekend: 18-hole: $11.50 Cart: $6.65 9-hole: (N/A) Cart: $3.23

Located in town on Hwy 16 near the high school football field.

Roy H. Laird Country Club   (3,117 yds) 903-984-3155

P.O. Box 956
Kilgore, TX 75662
Contact: Randy Pate
Description: A nine-hole private course that is very tight with trees and four holes on a creek. The greens are elevated. One of the nicer nine-hole courses in East Texas. **Par:** 36.
Rentals: Golf Carts, Golf Clubs, Driving Range

Members and guests only. Golf lessons available. Walking permitted.

Fees:

Weekday: 18-hole: $16.24 Cart: $18.94 9-hole: $10.83 Cart: $7.50
Weekend: 18-hole: $21.65 Cart: $18.95 9-hole: $12.65 Cart: $7.50

Located off Hwy 259 on Houston St.

Killeen Municipal Golf Course   (7,000 yds) 254-699-6034

406 S. Roy Reynolds Drive
Killeen, TX 76543
Contact: Greg Antunes
Description: An interesting 18-hole public course with a long, par-37 front nine with rolling hills and trees. The par-35 back nine is flat and shorter. Snacks. **Par:** 72.
Rentals: Golf Carts, Pull Carts, Golf Clubs, Driving Range

Open to the public. Walking permitted. Golf lessons available.

Fees:

Weekday: 18-hole: $8.50 Cart: $10.83 9-hole: (N/A) Cart: $4
Weekend: 18-hole: $11 Cart: $10.83 9-hole: (N/A) Cart: $4

Located next to Killeen Airport.

Packsaddle Golf Club

(7,133 yds) 915-388-3863

Skyline Drive
Kingsland, TX 78639
Contact: Bill Roberts
Description: Shooting a good score is quite common on this 18-hole semiprivate course. It is a wide open course with no sand traps, not much rough, and average-sized greens. **Par:** 72.
Rentals: Golf Carts, Pull Carts, Golf Clubs, Driving Range

Open to the public. Walking permitted. Golf lessons available.

Fees:

Weekday: 18-hole: $13 Cart: $10
9-hole: $5.50 Cart: $5.50
Weekend: 18-hole: $20 Cart: $10
9-hole: $6.75 Cart: $5.50

Located at corner of Skyline and Euell Moore.

L.E. Ramey Golf Course

(6,995 yds) 512-592-1101

FM 3320
Kingsville, TX 78363
Contact: Frank Monsevain
Description: The greens on this 18-hole public course are so large a three-putt is common. The fairways are wide with trees, water on nine holes, and 17 sand traps. Pretty, tropical South Texas setting. **Par:** 72.
Rentals: Golf Carts, Pull Carts, Golf Clubs, Driving Range

Open to the public. Walking permitted. Golf lessons available.

Fees:

Weekday: 18-hole: $8 Cart: $7.50
9-hole: $5 Cart: $5
Weekend: 18-hole: $10 Cart: $7.50
9-hole: $5.50 Cart: $5

Located on FM 3320 near Texas A&M-A&I campus.

Deerwood Golf Club

(7,108 yds) 281-360-1065

1717 Forest Garden Drive
Kingwood, TX 77345
Contact: Robby Ware
Description: This very long 18-hole private course is constructed through a pine forest with large greens protected by deep sand traps. Final scenes of movie *Tin Cup* filmed at fourth hole. **Par:** 72.
Rentals: Golf Carts, Golf Clubs, Driving Range

Members and guests only. Golf lessons available. Walking permitted.

Fees:

Weekday: 18-hole: $40 Cart: $22
9-hole: (N/A) Cart: (N/A)
Weekend: 18-hole: $55 Cart: $22
9-hole: (N/A) Cart: (N/A)

Located off Kingwood Drive via Highway 59 northeast of Houston.

Kingwood Country Club   (72 hs) 281-358-2171

1700 Lake Kingwood Trail
Kingwood, TX 77339
Contact: DarenWhitney
Forest Course Description: Kingwood Country Club is Texas' largest country club. New Forest Course opened in late 1996 to make it a 72-hole complex. Beautiful setting. **Par:** 72 (7,092 yds).
Rentals: Golf Carts, Golf Clubs, Driving Range
Members and guests only. Golf lessons available. Walking permitted.

Fees:

Weekday: 18-hole: $85 Cart: $13.50
9-hole: (N/A) Cart: $5
Weekend: 18-hole: $100 Cart: $13.50
9-hole: (N/A) Cart: $5

Island Course Description: The 578-yard par-5 18th hole on the Island Course is considered one of the most difficult holes in Texas. Golfers must hit over water to reach the fairway and more water to an island green. Great views! **Par:** 72 (7,309 yards).
Rentals: Golf Carts, Golf Clubs, Driving Range
Members and guests only. Golf lessons available. Walking permitted.

Fees:

Weekday: 18-hole: $55 Cart: $10
9-hole: (N/A) Cart: $5
Weekend: 18-hole: $65 Cart: $12
9-hole: (N/A) Cart: $5

Lakes Course Description: The Lakes Course is the second shortest course at Kingwood, but it is 7,089 yards long with the front nine having three par 3s and three par 5s. There are long par 4s, trees, and water on the backside. **Par:** 72 (7,089 yards).
Rentals: Golf Carts, Golf Clubs, Driving Range
Members and guests only. Golf lessons available. Walking permitted.

Fees:

Weekday: 18-hole: $40 Cart: $10
9-hole: (N/A) Cart: $5
Weekend: 18-hole: $55 Cart: $12
9-hole: (N/A) Cart: $5

Marsh Course Description: The Marsh Course is the shortest of the four courses at 6,935 yards, and is the most scenic. It has layup holes that make it a target course. Four great courses. **Par:** 72 (6,935 yards).
Rentals: Golf Carts, Golf Clubs, Driving Range
Members and guests only. Golf lessons available. Walking permitted.

Fees:

Weekday: 18-hole: $40 Cart: $10
9-hole: (N/A) Cart: $5
Weekend: 18-hole: $55 Cart: $12
9-hole: (N/A) Cart: $5

Located north of Houston off Hwy 59 to Kingwood Road.

Kingwood Cove Golf Club

(6,732 yds) 281-358-1155

805 Hamblen Road
Kingwood, TX 77339
Contact: Chris Lauterbach
Description: A strong 18-hole private course with tight tree-lined fairways with water on seven holes and traps. Clubhouse has an overnight facility with restaurant and meeting room. **Par:** 71.
Rentals: Golf Carts, Pull Carts, Golf Clubs, Driving Range

Open to the public. Walking permitted. Golf lessons available.

Fees:

Weekday: 18-hole: $25 Cart: (N/A)
9-hole: (N/A) Cart: $4.50
Weekend: 18-hole: $35 Cart: (N/A)
9-hole: (N/A) Cart: $4.50

Located off Hwy 59 and Kingwood Drive.

Knox City Country Club

(3,360 yds) 940-658-3911

P.O. Box 734
Knox City, TX 79529
Contact: Sam Boom
Description: A nice nine-hole public course that has open fairways, bentgrass greens, and a par 4 that is a par 5 the second time around. No traps. Food, pool, and 19th hole. **Par:** 35.

Open to the public. Walking permitted.

Fees:

Weekday: 18-hole: $10 Cart: $10
9-hole: $5 Cart: (N/A)
Weekend: 18-hole: $10 Cart: $10
9-hole: $5 Cart: (N/A)

Located on Hwy 6 south of town.

Bar-K Par 3

(2,774 yds) 512-267-1226

FM 1431
Lago Vista, TX 78645
Contact: Jess Aldridge
Description: Very scenic par-3 course on side of cliff overlooking Lake Travis and Lago Vista. Practice will help your game if you don't get caught daydreaming. Holes range from 60 to 243 yards over water. **Par:** 27.
Rentals: Pull Carts
Open to the public. Walking permitted.

Fees:

Weekday: 18-hole: $5.41 Cart: $7.58
9-hole: (N/A) Cart: (N/A)
Weekend: 18-hole: $8.06 Cart: $7.58
9-hole: (N/A) Cart: (N/A)

Located off FM 1431 across from Lohman's Crossing and Lago Vista Resort.

Lago Vista Country Club   (36 hs) 512-267-1685

P.O. Box 4500
Lago Vista, TX 78645
Contact: Jeff Thomasson
Highland Lakes Course Description:
Orville Moody used to live near this hilly
18-hole public course. With bentgrass
greens and 93 sand traps, it is a neat,
pretty course. **Par:** 72 (6,529 yards).

Lago Vista Course Description: This
18-hole public course is next to
Highland Lakes and is part of a resort
concept. Course is hilly with water and
traps. Bentgrass greens and spectacular
views make this a compelling package.
Par: 72 (6,550 yards).

Rentals: Golf Carts, Golf Clubs, Driving
Range
Open to the public. Walking permitted.
Golf lessons available.

Fees:

Weekday: 18-hole: $25 Cart: (N/A)
9-hole: $5 Cart: $5
Weekend: 18-hole: $35 Cart: (N/A)
9-hole: $5 Cart: $5

Located 15 miles northwest of Austin
along Lake Travis. Take Lohman's
Crossing off FM 1431.

Frisch Auf Valley Country Club   (2,985 yds) 409-968-6113

575 Country Club Drive
La Grange, TX 78945
Contact: Margret Burton
Description: This nine-hole semiprivate
course is somewhat simple with double
tees, wide open fairways, only two
water hazards, elevated greens, and a
hill on the first hole. **Par:** 36.
Rentals: Golf Carts, Pull Carts, Golf
Clubs

Open to the public. Walking permitted.

Fees:

Weekday: 18-hole: $12 Cart: $8
9-hole: (N/A) Cart: $5
Weekend: 18-hole: $14 Cart: $8
9-hole: (N/A) Cart: $5

Located north of I-10 on Hwy 71.

Riverside Country Club   (6,556 yds) 409-798-9141

P.O. Box 158
Lake Jackson, TX 77566
Contact: Jim Brisbin
Description: Golfers who hit the greens in regulation on this 18-hole private course have good birdie putts thanks to small greens. Only seven holes with water and trees. **Par:** 72.
Rentals: Golf Carts, Pull Carts, Golf Clubs, Driving Range

Members and guests only. Golf lessons available. Walking permitted.

Fees:

Weekday: 18-hole: $25 Cart: $8
9-hole: (N/A) Cart: $5
Weekend: 18-hole: $30 Cart: $8
9-hole: (N/A) Cart: $5

Located off FM 2004 west to Hwy 332.

Lake Kiowa Country Club   (6,621 yds) 940-668-7394

903 Kiowa Drive
Lake Kiowa, TX 76240
Contact: Brown McCrory
Description: A strong 18-hole private course surrounded by Lake Kiowa. Every hole has out-of-bounds. Bentgrass greens. Club has a 19th hole and pro shop. **Par:** 72.
Rentals: Golf Carts, Driving Range

Members and guests only. Golf lessons available. Walking permitted.

Fees:

Weekday: 18-hole: $20 Cart: $16
9-hole: (N/A) Cart: $8
Weekend: 18-hole: $26 Cart: $16
9-hole: (N/A) Cart: $8

Located seven miles southeast of Gainesville on FM 902.

Hills Of Lakeway   (6,949 yds) 512-261-7272

26 Club Estates Parkway
Lakeway, TX 78738
Contact: Glenn Lee
Description: This Jack Nicklaus-designed 18-hole private course is one of the best in Texas. The 173-yard par-3 seventh hole is memorable as tee shot goes over a waterfall. The course is hilly, tight, and pretty. Site of Nike Tour event. **Par:** 72.
Rentals: Golf Carts, Driving Range

Members and guests only. Golf lessons available. Walking permitted.

Fees:

Weekday: 18-hole: $110 Cart: (N/A)
9-hole: (N/A) Cart: (N/A)
Weekend: 18-hole: $150 Cart: (N/A)
9-hole: (N/A) Cart: (N/A)

Located on RR 620 on Lake Travis, approximately 20 miles west of Austin.

Lakeview Country Club   (6,227 yds) 409-935-6811

1219 Palm
P.O. Box 128
La Marque, TX 77568
Contact: Greg Mazzantini
Description: A links-style 18-hole private course that welcomes out-of-town golfers. It has long par 5s and par 4s, small greens, no traps, and wide fairways. Food and drinks. **Par:** 72.
Rentals: Golf Carts, Driving Range

Members and guests only. Walking permitted.

Fees:

Weekday: 18-hole: $8 Cart: $7.50
9-hole: (N/A) Cart: $3.75
Weekend: 18-hole: $10 Cart: $7.50
9-hole: (N/A) Cart: $3.75

Located south of Houston off I-45.

Lamesa Country Club   (3,308 yds) 806-872-2608

P.O. Box 380
Lamesa, TX 79331
Contact: Jay Plunkett
Description: A creek runs through three holes of this nine-hole private course. The fairways are wide and no traps protect the bentgrass greens. Restaurant, bar, and pro shop. **Par:** 36.
Rentals: Golf Carts, Golf Clubs, Driving Range

Members and guests only. Golf lessons available. Walking permitted.

Fees:

Weekday: 18-hole: $10 Cart: $6.20
9-hole: (N/A) Cart: $3
Weekend: 18-hole: $15 Cart: $8.25
9-hole: (N/A) Cart: $3

Located south of town on Hwy 87.

Plains Fairway Public Golf Course   (3,000 yds) 806-872-8100

201 S. 5th Ave.
Lamesa, TX 79331
Contact: Ron Scott
Description: A short but challenging nine-hole course where tee times are not needed. First come/first serve. Clubhouse has a pro shop and meeting room. **Par:** 35.
Rentals: Golf Carts, Pull Carts, Golf Clubs

Open to the public. Walking permitted. Golf lessons available.

Fees:

Weekday: 18-hole: $8 Cart: $12.90
9-hole: $8 Cart: $12
Weekend: 18-hole: $12.90 Cart: $12.90 9-hole: $12.90 Cart: $12

Located west of Lamesa off Hwy 180 to 5th Avenue.

Hancock Park Golf Course

(6,029 yds) 512-556-3202

Highway 281 South
Lampasas, TX 76550
Contact: Van Berry
Description: A high quality 18-hole public course that has water hazards on five of the first nine holes. No sand traps and very small greens. The course is flat and wide open. Food. **Par:** 72.
Rentals: Golf Carts

Open to the public. Walking permitted.

Fees:

Weekday: 18-hole: $12.50 Cart: $7.50 9-hole: (N/A) Cart: $3.75
Weekend: 18-hole: $17.50 Cart: $7.50 9-hole: (N/A) Cart: $3.75

Located on Hwy 281 South.

Country View Golf Club

(6,609 yds) 972-227-0995

240 W. Beltline Road
Lancaster, TX 75146
Contact: David Royar
Description: One of the best public courses south of downtown Dallas. Wide fairways that set up the need for good approach shots to elevated greens. Clubhouse has a pro shop. **Par:** 72.
Rentals: Golf Carts, Pull Carts, Golf Clubs, Driving Range

Open to the public. Walking permitted. Golf lessons available.

Fees:

Weekday: 18-hole: $12 Cart: $9 9-hole: (N/A) Cart: (N/A)
Weekend: 18-hole: $17 Cart: $9 9-hole: (N/A) Cart: (N/A)

Located on Belt Line Rd. west of I-35E.

Bay Forest Golf Course

(6,756 yds) 281-471-4653

201 Bay Forest Drive
La Porte, TX 77571
Contact: Alex Osmond
Description: With water on 16 holes, it is easy to lose golf balls on this 18-hole public course. The fairways are tight with large greens well protected by traps. **Par:** 72.
Rentals: Golf Carts, Pull Carts, Golf Clubs, Driving Range

Open to the public. Walking permitted. Golf lessons available.

Fees:

Weekday: 18-hole: $23 Cart: $8 9-hole: (N/A) Cart: $5
Weekend: 18-hole: $29 Cart: $8 9-hole: (N/A) Cart: $5

Located near Fairmont Parkway and Hwy 146.

Casa Blanca Golf Course   (7,100 yds) 956-791-7262

311 S. Dakota
Laredo, TX 78041
Contact: Balt Ramos
Description: This 18-hole public course was recently renovated to put more water hazards on the course and make the course longer. It was already plenty long. Good pro shop and clubhouse. **Par:** 72.
Rentals: Golf Carts, Pull Carts, Golf Clubs

Open to the public. Walking permitted. Golf lessons available.

Fees:

Weekday: 18-hole: $10.10 Cart: $7.50 9-hole: $6 Cart: (N/A)
Weekend: 18-hole: $12 Cart: $7.50 9-hole: $6 Cart: (N/A)

> Located on Hwy 59 off Dakota in Laredo

Laredo Country Club   (7,125 yds) 956-727-0183

1450 Country Club Drive
Laredo, TX 78041
Contact: Todd Zunker
Description: Out-of-town members of private clubs are welcome at this 18-hole private course. It is 7,125 yards long with lots of hills, traps, water on 11 holes, and three-putt greens. Food. **Par:** 72.
Rentals: Golf Carts, Golf Clubs, Driving Range

Members and guests only. Golf lessons available. Walking permitted.

Fees:

Weekday: 18-hole: $60 Cart: $10 9-hole: (N/A) Cart: $4.25
Weekend: 18-hole: $75 Cart: $10 9-hole: (N/A) Cart: $4.25

> Located off I-35. Exit at Delmar to Plantation subdivision.

Leaning Pine Golf Course   (3,181 yds) 956-298-5451

SSRG Golf Course Blvd.
Bldg 494
Laughlin AFB, TX 78843-5000
Contact: Roy Goodwin
Description: A military nine-hole course that is semiprivate. The pines do not lean on the course, but the course is long and has four water holes and traps. New double tees. **Par:** 36.
Rentals: Golf Carts, Pull Carts, Golf Clubs, Driving Range

Open to the public. Walking permitted. Golf lessons available.

Fees:

Weekday: 18-hole: $10 Cart: $6 9-hole: (N/A) Cart: $3.50
Weekend: 18-hole: $12 Cart: $6 9-hole: (N/A) Cart: $3.50

> Located east of Del Rio on Hwy 90.

Las Palomas Country Club (7,039 yds) 830-217-4653

120 Las Palomas Drive
La Vernia, TX 78121
Contact: Mike Wiggins
Description: Native wildlife, trees, and brush on this new semiprivate course make for a tough layout, especially from the back tees. **Par:** 72.
Rentals: Golf Carts, Driving Range
Open to the public. Walking permitted.
Golf lessons available.

Fees:

Weekday: 18-hole: $18 Cart: (N/A)
9-hole: (N/A) Cart: (N/A)
Weekend: 18-hole: $28 Cart: (N/A)
9-hole: (N/A) Cart: (N/A)

Located between San Antonio and Seguin off Hwy 87.

Beacon Lakes Golf Course (3,300 yds) 281-337-1459

801 FM 646
League City, TX 77539
Contact: Dean Wilson
Description: New course which opened in the summer of 1996 takes ample advantage of highly scenic surroundings. Tight course features plenty of trees, Southeast Texas moss and vines, and water on several holes.
Par: 36.

Rentals: Golf Carts, Driving Range
Open to the public. Walking permitted.

Fees:

Weekday: 18-hole: $15 Cart: $7
9-hole: (N/A) Cart: (N/A)
Weekend: 18-hole: $16 Cart: $7
9-hole: (N/A) Cart: (N/A)

Located near exit 645 off I-45.

South Shore Harbour Country Club (27 hs) 281-334-0521

4300 South Shore Blvd.
League City, TX 77573
Contact: Daren Heflin
Description: A 27-hole links-style resort course that is only open to members and hotel guests. There is water on 14 holes and 70 sand traps guarding the greens. Drinks. **Par:** 71 (6,663 yards).
Rentals: Golf Carts, Golf Clubs, Driving Range

Members and guests only. Golf lessons available. Walking permitted.

Fees:

Weekday: 18-hole: $40 Cart: $10
9-hole: (N/A) Cart: (N/A)
Weekend: 18-hole: $54 Cart: $10
9-hole: (N/A) Cart: (N/A)

Located south of Houston off I-45.

Crystal Falls Golf Course   (6,654 yds) 512-259-5855

P.O. Box 319
3400 Crystal Falls Parkway
Leander, TX 78641
Contact: Archer Logan
Description: An 18-hole city-owned
public course that has some of the best
views in the Hill Country. **Par:** 72.
Rentals: Golf Carts, Pull Carts, Golf
Clubs, Driving Range

Open to the public. Walking permitted.
Golf lessons available.

Fees:

Weekday: 18-hole: $23 Cart: (N/A)
9-hole: (N/A) Cart: (N/A)
Weekend: 18-hole: $32 Cart: (N/A)
9-hole: (N/A) Cart: (N/A)

Take Hwy 183 north from Austin; turn
left at the third light north of FM 1431.

Point Venture Country Club   (3,100 yds) 512-267-1151

422 Venture Blvd.
Leander, TX 78645
Contact: Dennis Allen
Description: Even though this
nine-hole public course is located next
to Lake Travis, there are no water
hazards. The fairways are tight and the
greens are large. Food. **Par:** 36.
Rentals: Golf Carts, Pull Carts, Golf
Clubs, Driving Range

Open to the public. Walking permitted.

Fees:

Weekday: 18-hole: $15 Cart: (N/A)
9-hole: $7 Cart: $4.50
Weekend: 18-hole: $18 Cart: (N/A)
9-hole: $9 Cart: $4.50

Located north of Cedar Park off FM
1431.

Levelland Country Club   (6,300 yds) 806-894-3288

908 College Ave.
Levelland, TX 79336
Contact: Chad Davis
Description: This nine-hole private
course has had its greens expanded
with more sand traps and bentgrass.
The course is tight and lined with trees.
Food, drinks, and pro shop. **Par:** 35.
Rentals: Golf Carts, Golf Clubs, Driving
Range

Members and guests only. Golf lessons
available. Walking permitted.

Fees:

Weekday: 18-hole: $13.47 Cart:
$8.62 9-hole: $7 Cart: $3.75
Weekend: 18-hole: $21.55 Cart:
$8.62 9-hole: $12 Cart: $3.75

Located off Brownfield Hwy.

Lake Park Golf Course (6,759 yds) 972-436-5332

6 Lake Park Road
Lewisville, TX 75057
Contact: Marty Coulson
Description: PGA superstar Lanny Wadkins is a part owner in this recently remodeled course just north of Dallas. A nine-hole par-29 executive course is fairly new. **Par:** 72.
Rentals: Golf Carts, Pull Carts, Golf Clubs, Driving Range

Open to the public. Walking permitted. Golf lessons available.

Fees:

Weekday: 18-hole: $17.70 Cart: $12.50 9-hole: (N/A) Cart: (N/A)
Weekend: 18-hole: $28 Cart: $12.50 9-hole: (N/A) Cart: (N/A)

Located east of I-35E; take Mill Road north to Park Road.

Magnolia Ridge Country Club (6,438 yds) 409-336-3551

100 Country Club Road
Liberty, TX 77575
Contact: Joey Stone
Description: This nine-hole private course is open to the public on Fridays. It has lots of trees, double tees, three water hazards, no sand traps, and tight fairways. Food. **Par:** 36.
Rentals: Golf Carts, Driving Range

Members and guests only. Walking permitted.

Fees:

Weekday: 18-hole: $8 Cart: $9 9-hole: (N/A) Cart: $4.50
Weekend: 18-hole: $11 Cart: $9 9-hole: (N/A) Cart: $4.50

Located off Hwy 90 on Old Beaumont Road.

Shallow Creek Country Club (6,527 yds) 903-984-5335

Route 3, Box 212B
Liberty City, TX 75647
Contact: Pro Shop
Description: A former nine-hole public course that added a second nine to make the 18-hole course very long. There is a 2,634-yard difference between the front and back tees. Very hilly. **Par:** 71.
Rentals: Golf Carts

Open to the public. Walking permitted.

Fees:

Weekday: 18-hole: $11 Cart: $9 9-hole: (N/A) Cart: $4.30
Weekend: 18-hole: $14 Cart: $9 9-hole: (N/A) Cart: $4.30

Located north of I-20 on Hwy 135.

Garden Valley Golf Resort

(36 hs) 903-882-6107

22049 FM 1995
Lindale, TX 75771
Contact: Donnie Baker
Hummingbird Course Description:
Golfers driving down I-20 have always
seen Garden Valley Resort. It is now a
36-hole public course. The
Hummingbird Course is the original
course that is hilly with lots of water
and traps. **Par:** 71 (6,446 yards).
Rentals: Golf Carts, Pull Carts, Golf
Clubs, Driving Range
Open to the public. Walking permitted.
Golf lessons available.

Fees:

Weekday: 18-hole: $26 Cart: (N/A)
9-hole: $7 Cart: $7
Weekend: 18-hole: $32 Cart: (N/A)
9-hole: $12 Cart: $7

Dogwood Course Description: When
the Japanese purchased Garden Valley,
they added a second 18-hole course
that is longer than the old course with
50 sand traps, bentgrass greens, and
water. Condos available for rent. Food
and drinks. **Par:** 72 (6,754 yards).
Rentals: Golf Carts, Golf Clubs, Driving
Range
Open to the public. Golf lessons
available. Mandatory carts.

Fees:

Weekday: 18-hole: $51 Cart: (N/A)
9-hole: $20 Cart: $7
Weekend: 18-hole: $62 Cart: (N/A)
9-hole: $20 Cart: $7

Located south of I-20 off Hwy 110,
northwest of Tyler.

Hide-A-Way-Lake Golf Course

(27 hs) 903-882-8511

302 Hide-A-Way-Lake
Lindale, TX 75771
Contact: Teresa Harrell
Description: People driving down I-20
can't help but see this 27-hole private
course on the north side of the road. It
has five par 3s and five par 5s with
water and small greens. **Par:** 72
(6,300 yards).
Rentals: Golf Carts, Pull Carts, Golf
Clubs, Driving Range

Members and guests only. Golf lessons
available. Walking permitted.

Fees:

Weekday: 18-hole: $22 Cart: $9
9-hole: (N/A) Cart: $4.50
Weekend: 18-hole: $27 Cart: $9
9-hole: (N/A) Cart: $4.50

From I-20, take FM 849 exit north.

Littlefield Country Club   (3,150 yds) 806-385-3309

P.O. Box 505
Littlefield, TX 79339
Contact: Greg Katerba
Description: A golfer can post his or her best nine-hole score on this public course. It is short and wide open with no out-of-bounds or water. Bentgrass greens. Food, drinks, and pro shop. **Par:** 36.
Rentals: Golf Carts, Pull Carts, Driving Range

Open to the public. Walking permitted. Golf lessons available.

Fees:

Weekday: 18-hole: $7 Cart: $7 9-hole: (N/A) Cart: $3.50
Weekend: 18-hole: $12 Cart: $7 9-hole: (N/A) Cart: $3.50

Located on Hwy 385 north of town.

Livingston Municipal Golf Course   (5,800 yds) 409-327-4901

Mathews Street
Livingston, TX 77351
Contact: Sonny Nash
Description: Posting a good score is normal on this nine-hole public course. It is short with wide fairways, only one water hole, small greens, and just five sand traps. **Par:** 35.
Open to the public. Walking permitted.

Fees:

Weekday: 18-hole: $10 Cart: $4
9-hole: (N/A) Cart: $3.25
Weekend: 18-hole: $15 Cart: $7.50
9-hole: (N/A) Cart: $3.25

Located on Mathews St. off Hwy 59.

Mill Ridge Golf Center   (3,000 yds) 409-327-3535

1501 Mill Ridge Drive
Livingston, TX 77351
Contact: Bobby Brame
Description: A nine-hole par-35 course that can be challenging, as it requires a good short game. Clubhouse has a pro shop. **Par:** 35.
Rentals: Golf Carts, Pull Carts, Golf Clubs, Driving Range

Open to the public. Walking permitted. Golf lessons available.

Fees:

Weekday: 18-hole: $15 Cart: $8
9-hole: $9 Cart: $5
Weekend: 18-hole: $22 Cart: $14
9-hole: $10 Cart: $6

Located on Hwy 59 loop just south of Hwy 190 intersection.

Llano Golf Club

(6,094 yds) 915-247-5100

301 N. Main
Llano, TX 78643
Contact: Golf Shop
Description: A former nine-hole public course converted to an 18-hole course in the fall of 1994. The old nine is flat with two holes along the Llano River. **Par:** 71.
Rentals: Golf Carts, Pull Carts, Golf Clubs

Open to the public. Walking permitted. Golf lessons available.

Fees:

Weekday: 18-hole: $10 Cart: $15
9-hole: (N/A) Cart: $7.50
Weekend: 18-hole: $15 Cart: $15
9-hole: (N/A) Cart: $7.50

Located off FM 152 near Robinson City Park.

Lockhart State Park Golf Course

(2,982 yds) 210-398-3479

FM 20 West
Box 69
Lockhart, TX 78644
Contact: Mike Mauser
Description: Good scores are normal on this nine-hole public course thanks to wide fairways, not many trees, large greens, and only two bunkers. Only three water hazards. **Par:** 35.
Rentals: Golf Carts, Pull Carts

Open to the public. Walking permitted.

Fees:

Weekday: 18-hole: $9.10 Cart: $9
9-hole: (N/A) Cart: $3.50
Weekend: 18-hole: $10 Cart: $14
9-hole: (N/A) Cart: $3.50

Located two miles from town on FM 20.

Alpine Country Club

(6,000 yds) 903-753-4515

2385 Smelley Road
Longview, TX 75605
Contact: Mike Wilson
Description: A unique 18-hole par-72 course that is constructed among hills and trees so the wind has little effect. The fairways are tight and there is a creek. **Par:** 72.
Rentals: Golf Carts, Pull Carts, Golf Clubs

Open to the public. Walking permitted.

Fees:

Weekday: 18-hole: $12 Cart: $8
9-hole: (N/A) Cart: $4
Weekend: 18-hole: $17 Cart: $8
9-hole: (N/A) Cart: $4

Located in town on Loop 281.

Longview Country Club (5,840 yds) 903-759-9251

2300 Highway 42
Longview, TX 75604
Contact: Buster Cupit
Description: A short 18-hole public course that has lots of ditches, traps, and one big hill. The greens are small but elevated. Clubhouse has large pro shop. Site of Oilman's Classic. **Par:** 70.
Rentals: Golf Carts, Pull Carts, Golf Clubs, Driving Range

Open to the public. Walking permitted. Golf lessons available.

Fees:

Weekday: 18-hole: $18 Cart: $15
9-hole: (N/A) Cart: $5
Weekend: 18-hole: $22 Cart: $15
9-hole: (N/A) Cart: $5

Located on Hwy 42 east of town.

Oak Forest Country Club (6,867 yds) 903-297-3448

601 Tomlinson Parkway
Longview, TX 75604
Contact: Kit Thomson
Description: A creek runs through the front nine with water hazards and out-of-bounds on the back nine. Greens are large with traps. Oak Forest has a health club. **Par:** 70.
Rentals: Golf Carts, Golf Clubs, Driving Range

Members and guests only. Golf lessons available. Walking permitted.

Fees:

Weekday: 18-hole: $20 Cart: $8.75
9-hole: $10 Cart: $4.50
Weekend: 18-hole: $25 Cart: $8.75
9-hole: $12.50 Cart: $4.50

Located off Loop 281 north on Bill Owens Parkway to Tomlinson.

Pinecrest Country Club (6,500 yds) 903-758-8000

214 Club Drive
Longview, TX 75606
Contact: Jack Goetz
Description: The nines were reversed, so golfers must deal with a tough nine at the start of a round. Very tight fairways, tough greens, and creeks. Clubhouse is very nice. **Par:** 70.
Rentals: Golf Carts, Pull Carts, Golf Clubs, Driving Range

Members and guests only. Golf lessons available. Walking permitted.

Fees:

Weekday: 18-hole: $25 Cart: $9
9-hole: (N/A) Cart: $5
Weekend: 18-hole: $35 Cart: $9
9-hole: (N/A) Cart: $5

Located off Hwy 149 north to Cotton Road.

Wood Hollow Golf Course   (6,106 yds) 903-663-4653

5121 McCann Road
Longview, TX 75605
Contact: Trey Griffith
Description: A nice 18-hole public course where golfers can shoot good scores thanks to wide fairways, no traps, and big greens. Club has a pro shop. **Par:** 70.
Rentals: Golf Carts, Pull Carts, Golf Clubs, Driving Range

Open to the public. Walking permitted. Golf lessons available.

Fees:

Weekday: 18-hole: $12 Cart: $8.50 9-hole: (N/A) Cart: $4
Weekend: 18-hole: $17 Cart: $8.50 9-hole: (N/A) Cart: $4

> Located north of Longview on north Loop 281 to McCann Road.

Lorenzo Country Club   (3,285 yds) 806-634-5787

Route 1, Box 230
Lorenzo, TX 79343
Contact: Bobby Sansom
Description: A 38-year-old nine-hole semiprivate course. Tall trees that are 40 years old make for tight but flat fairways. Bentgrass greens. Food, drinks, and pro shop. **Par:** 36.
Rentals: Golf Carts

Open to the public. Walking permitted. Golf lessons available.

Fees:

Weekday: 18-hole: $9 Cart: $9 9-hole: (N/A) Cart: $4.50
Weekend: 18-hole: $11 Cart: $9 9-hole: (N/A) Cart: $4.50

> Located off Hwy 82.

Elm Grove Golf Club   (6,401 yds) 806-799-7801

3202 Milwaukee Avenue
Lubbock, TX 79407
Contact: Jim Puckett
Description: Although this 18-hole public course is reasonably long, it has dry fairways to extend tee shots and no water hazards. Course has 2,000 trees. New clubhouse with style. **Par:** 71.
Rentals: Golf Carts, Pull Carts, Golf Clubs, Driving Range

Open to the public. Walking permitted. Golf lessons available.

Fees:

Weekday: 18-hole: $10 Cart: $9 9-hole: (N/A) Cart: $4.50
Weekend: 18-hole: $13 Cart: $9 9-hole: (N/A) Cart: $4.50

> Located west of town on 34th Street.

Hillcrest Country Club (6,862 yds) 806-765-5208

North University Road
Lubbock, TX 79408
Contact: Tommy Doland
Description: Strong golf course. Club has eight tennis courts, swimming pool and pool club, restaurant, bar, lockers, showers, meeting room, and good pro shop. **Par:** 72.
Rentals: Golf Carts, Pull Carts, Driving Range

Members and guests only. Golf lessons available. Walking permitted.

Fees:

Weekday: 18-hole: $35 Cart: $10
9-hole: (N/A) Cart: (N/A)
Weekend: 18-hole: $50 Cart: $10
9-hole: (N/A) Cart: (N/A)

Located four miles north of Lubbock on University Ave.

Lake Ridge Country Club (6,800 yds) 806-794-4444

8802 Vicksburg St.
Lubbock, TX 79424
Contact: Terry Dear
Description: The front nine and the back nine revolve around two different lakes with several tough holes. Club has food, drinks, tennis, and pro shop. **Par:** 72.
Rentals: Golf Carts, Golf Clubs, Driving Range

Members and guests only. Golf lessons available. Walking permitted.

Fees:

Weekday: 18-hole: $30 Cart: $10.25
9-hole: (N/A) Cart: $5
Weekend: 18-hole: $40 Cart: $10.25
9-hole: (N/A) Cart: $5

Southwest of city off Loop 289 to Slide Road.

Lubbock Country Club (6,991 yds) 806-763-1871

P.O. Box 1477
Lubbock, TX 79408
Contact: Mark Vinson
Description: An extremely tight course with lots of trees, long holes, wind, and a creek. Clubhouse has food, drinks, pool, tennis, and pro shop. **Par:** 72.
Rentals: Golf Carts, Driving Range
Members and guests only. Golf lessons available. Walking permitted.

Fees:

Weekday: 18-hole: $55 Cart: $10
9-hole: (N/A) Cart: $5
Weekend: 18-hole: $65 Cart: $10
9-hole: (N/A) Cart: $5

Located south of Lubbock Airport; exit Vucca Lane off I-27.

Meadowbrook Municipal Golf Course   (36 hs) 806-765-6679

601 E. Municipal Drive
Lubbock, TX 79403
Contact: Brian Cook
Canyon Course Description: The Canyon Course is the newer, longer, and tougher part of this 36-hole complex. Built on scenic West Texas land, the two courses offer a stern public golf test. **Par:** 71 (6,700 yards).

Creek Course Description: The Creek Course, the first 18, is short but challenging. Clubhouse has restaurant, pro shop, and meeting room. **Par:** 71

(6,400 yards).
Rentals: Golf Carts, Pull Carts, Driving Range
Open to the public. Walking permitted. Golf lessons available.

Fees:

Weekday: 18-hole: $21.58 Cart: (N/A) 9-hole: (N/A) Cart: (N/A)
Weekend: 18-hole: $29.18 Cart: (N/A) 9-hole: (N/A) Cart: (N/A)

½ mile east of I-27 on Municipal Drive.

Pine Valley Golf Course   (4,486 yds) 806-748-1448

11010 Indiana Ave.
Lubbock, TX 79423
Contact: Walter Denzer
Description: A unique 18-hole public course. The front nine is a par-3 nine with water on all holes and elevated tees and greens. The back nine is regular length. **Par:** 63.
Rentals: Golf Carts, Pull Carts, Golf Clubs, Driving Range

Open to the public. Walking permitted. Golf lessons available.

Fees:

Weekday: 18-hole: $9 Cart: $8 9-hole: $6.50 Cart: $5
Weekend: 18-hole: $12 Cart: $8 9-hole: (N/A) Cart: (N/A)

Located south of Loop 289.

Shadow Hills Golf Course   (6,777 yds) 806-793-9700

6002 3rd St.
Lubbock, TX 79499
Contact: Golf Shop
Description: An 18-hole public course that underwent a lot of renovation to make it tougher. Trees and water hazards were added to make the wide, flat fairways tough. **Par:** 72.
Rentals: Golf Carts, Pull Carts, Golf Clubs, Driving Range

Open to the public. Walking permitted. Golf lessons available.

Fees:

Weekday: 18-hole: $14 Cart: $7 9-hole: (N/A) Cart: $4
Weekend: 18-hole: $17.25 Cart: $9 9-hole: (N/A) Cart: $4

Located west of Loop 289 on 3rd St.

Treasure Island Golf Center   (3,205 yds) 806-795-9311

501 Frankford Road
Lubbock, TX 79416
Contact: Sam Garcia
Description: A very popular 18-hole course in the Panhandle. It has 17 par 3s and one narrow par 4. Lighted course with two lakes. The holes range from 78 to 180 yards with a 240-yard par 4. **Par:** 55.
Rentals: Golf Carts, Pull Carts, Golf Clubs, Driving Range

Open to the public. Walking permitted. Golf lessons available.

Fees:

Weekday: 18-hole: $8 Cart: $6 9-hole: (N/A) Cart: $3.50
Weekend: 18-hole: $9 Cart: $6 9-hole: (N/A) Cart: $3.50

Located on Loop 289.

Crown Colony Country Club   (6,674 yds) 409-637-8800

900 Crown Colony Drive
Lufkin, TX 75901
Contact: Bob Diamond
Description: Considered one of the best golf courses in Texas. Target golf holes make 6,674 yards play long. Great East Texas piney woods views with water traps and trouble. **Par:** 72.
Rentals: Golf Carts, Golf Clubs, Driving Range

Members and guests only. Walking permitted. Golf lessons available.

Fees:

Weekday: 18-hole: $110 Cart: (N/A) 9-hole: $75 Cart: $10
Weekend: 18-hole: $110 Cart: (N/A) 9-hole: $75 Cart: $10

Located on Hwy 59 south of Lufkin.

Lufkin Country Club   (6,347 yds) 409-639-3664

1624 Sayers St.
Lufkin, TX 75901
Contact: Board of Directors
Description: A pretty 18-hole private course with lots of pine and oak trees and a 16-acre lake. Good greens and lots of sand traps. Clubhouse has food, tennis, and pro shop. **Par:** 72.
Rentals: Golf Carts, Golf Clubs, Driving Range

Members and guests only. Walking permitted.

Fees:

Weekday: 18-hole: $20 Cart: $7.50 9-hole: (N/A) Cart: (N/A)
Weekend: 18-hole: $25 Cart: $7.50 9-hole: (N/A) Cart: (N/A)

Located off Loop 287 to Sayers St.

Luling Golf Club
(5,987 yds) 830-875-5114

1005 S. Magnola
Luling, TX 78648
Contact: Janice Baker
Description: The 480-yard par-4
seventh hole on this nine-hole public
course has the San Marcos River
running through it. It is a traditional
course with double tees and bunkers.
Par: 35.
Rentals: Golf Carts, Pull Carts

Open to the public. Walking permitted.

Fees:

Weekday: 18-hole: $8 Cart: $7.50
9-hole: (N/A) Cart: $3.50
Weekend: 18-hole: $10 Cart: $7.50
9-hole: (N/A) Cart: $3.50

Located on I-10 east of San Antonio at
Luling exit, head north to town & river.

Pinnacle Club
(6,605 yds) 903-451-9797

200 Pinnacle Club Drive
Mabank, TX 75147
Contact: Jeff Holt
Description: A tight 18-hole course
with lots of trees. First nine opened in
1986 and the second nine in 1990
when repurchased by a Canadian
company. **Par:** 71.
Rentals: Golf Carts, Golf Clubs, Driving
Range

Open to the public. Walking permitted.
Golf lessons available.

Fees:

Weekday: 18-hole: $24 Cart: $8
9-hole: (N/A) Cart: (N/A)
Weekend: 18-hole: $36.50 Cart: $8
9-hole: (N/A) Cart: (N/A)

Located off Hwy 198 between Mabank
and Malakoff.

Oak Ridge Country Club
(6,617 yds) 409-348-6264

FM 1452
Madisonville, TX 77864
Contact: Neil Berry
Description: Out-of-town golfers are
welcome to play this nine-hole private
course. It is short and hilly with lots of
trees. Water on one hole. Pro shop.
Par: 36.
Rentals: Golf Carts, Pull Carts, Golf
Clubs, Driving Range

Members and guests only. Walking
permitted.

Fees:

Weekday: 18-hole: $17 Cart: $8
9-hole: $15 Cart: $4
Weekend: 18-hole: $20 Cart: $8
9-hole: $15 Cart: $4

Located south of Hwy 21 on FM 1452.

Star Harbor Municipal Golf Course (4,746 yds) 903-489-0091

P.O. Drawer 949
Malakoff, TX 75148
Contact: Wyatt Parkins
Description: A very short nine-hole
public course that has wide fairways,
few trees, and no water hazards or
bunkers. The small greens are elevated,
demanding good approaches. **Par:** 34.
Rentals: Golf Carts, Golf Clubs

Open to the public. Walking permitted.

Fees:

Weekday: 18-hole: $10 Cart: (N/A)
9-hole: (N/A) Cart: (N/A)
Weekend: 18-hole: $12 Cart: (N/A)
9-hole: (N/A) Cart: (N/A)

Located on FM 3062 north of town.

Walnut Creek Country Club (36 hs) 817-473-6114

1151 Country Club Drive
Mansfield, TX 76063
Contact: Junior Salinas
Old Course Description: A 36-hole
private club with lots of dogleg holes
and trees. Club has restaurant, locker
rooms, pool, tennis, and pro shop. **Par:**
71 (6,600 yards).

New Course Description: A stern test
with 7,100 yards stretched over a par
70. Plenty of trees and traps. The creek
also gives plenty of trouble. **Par:** 70
(7,100 yards).

Rentals: Golf Carts, Golf Clubs, Driving
Range
Members and guests only. Golf lessons
available. Walking permitted.

Fees:

Weekday: 18-hole: $30 Cart: $9
9-hole: (N/A) Cart: $4.50
Weekend: 18-hole: $40 Cart: $9
9-hole: (N/A) Cart: $4.50

Located off Hwy 287.

Blue Lake Golf Club (2,376 yds) 830-598-5524

214 W. Blue Bonnet Road
Marble Falls, TX 78654
Contact: Roger Weathers
Description: A nine-hole semiprivate
course that has five par 3s, three par
4s, and one par 5. No water or sand
traps. The course is narrow and hilly.
Pro shop and deck. **Par:** 32.
Rentals: Golf Carts, Pull Carts, Golf
Clubs

Open to the public. Walking permitted.

Fees:

Weekday: 18-hole: $9 Cart: $7 9-hole:
$6 Cart: $4
Weekend: 18-hole: $11 Cart: $7
9-hole: $8 Cart: $4

Located off Hwy 71 to Blue Bonnet
Road.

Meadowlakes Country Club   (6,710 yds) 830-693-7826

220 Meadowlakes Drive
Marble Falls, TX 78654
Contact: Donnie Zavala
Description: The front nine of this
18-hole semiprivate course is in a pecan
orchard. The back nine starts with five
water holes. Large greens, plus
out-of-bounds. **Par:** 72.
Rentals: Golf Carts, Pull Carts, Golf
Clubs, Driving Range

Open to the public. Walking permitted.
Golf lessons available.

Fees:

Weekday: 18-hole: $16 Cart: $11
9-hole: (N/A) Cart: $5.50
Weekend: 18-hole: $25 Cart: $11
9-hole: (N/A) Cart: $5.50

Located on Hwy 281 over river to club.

Marfa Municipal Golf Course   (6,550 yds) 915-729-4043

P.O. Box 308
Marfa, TX 79843
Contact: Ernest Villarreal
Description: The rough on this
nine-hole public course is very rough.
Missing the wide fairways can cause a
tough shot. Elevated small greens and
no traps on four holes. **Par:** 36.
Rentals: Golf Carts, Pull Carts, Golf
Clubs, Driving Range

Open to the public. Walking permitted.

Fees:

Weekday: 18-hole: $6.38 Cart: $7.44
9-hole: (N/A) Cart: $3.19
Weekend: 18-hole: $8.50 Cart: $7.44
9-hole: (N/A) Cart: $3.19

Located on FM 1112 past the post
office.

Marlin Country Club   (3,600 yds) 254-803-6101

Route 1, Box 34
Marlin, TX 76661
Contact: Michael Stanfield
Description: The fairways on this
nine-hole private course slope toward
the lake the course runs around. Also,
out-of-bounds leave wild hitters in
trouble. Good clubhouse. **Par:** 36.
Rentals: Golf Carts, Driving Range

Members and guests only. Walking
permitted.

Fees:

Weekday: 18-hole: $12 Cart: $7.50
9-hole: (N/A) Cart: (N/A)
Weekend: 18-hole: $12 Cart: $7.50
9-hole: (N/A) Cart: (N/A)

Located two miles northwest of town.

Cypress Valley Country Club   (6,953 yds) 903-938-4941

P.O. Box 307
Marshall, TX 75671
Contact: Lou Dechert
Description: Golfers have a lot of fun on this 18-hole semiprivate course when they see a lot of friendly deer running out of the pine woods which guard the fairways. No sand traps. **Par:** 71.
Rentals: Golf Carts, Pull Carts

Open to the public. Walking permitted.

Fees:

Weekday: 18-hole: $12 Cart: $7.50
9-hole: (N/A) Cart: $3.75
Weekend: 18-hole: $15 Cart: $7.50
9-hole: (N/A) Cart: $3.75

Located off I-20 exit 628.

Marshall Lakeside Country Club   (6,257 yds) 903-938-4211

Highway 43
Marshall, TX 75671
Contact: Bud Gibbs
Description: Considered to be one of the best nine-hole courses in Texas, this private course was built in 1919 and has traditional style holes with fast greens, tall pines, and water. Food, drinks, tennis, and pool. **Par:** 36.
Rentals: Golf Carts, Driving Range

Members and guests only. Golf lessons available. Walking permitted.

Fees:

Weekday: 18-hole: $20 Cart: $10
9-hole: (N/A) Cart: (N/A)
Weekend: 18-hole: $20 Cart: $10
9-hole: (N/A) Cart: (N/A)

Located on Hwy 43 north of Marshall.

Oak Lawn Country Club   (2,994 yds) 903-935-7555

4307 Victory Drive
Marshall, TX 75670
Contact: Bob Collins
Description: This nine-hole semiprivate course is short, but all the par 3s are very hard. The par-3 fifth hole is 215 yards over water that will blow up a scorecard. **Par:** 36.
Rentals: Golf Carts
Open to the public. Walking permitted.

Fees:

Weekday: 18-hole: $10 Cart: $7
9-hole: (N/A) Cart: $3.25
Weekend: 18-hole: $15 Cart: $7
9-hole: (N/A) Cart: $3.25

Located on Hwy 80 East.

Battle Lake Golf Course

(6,601 yds) 254-876-2837

Battle Lake Road
Highway 6
Mart, TX 76664
Contact: Chuck Higgins
Description: A fun 18-hole course. Excellent pro shop with the best golf supplies in Central Texas. Clubhouse has a snack bar and peaceful Central Texas views. **Par:** 72.
Rentals: Golf Carts, Pull Carts, Golf Clubs

Open to the public. Walking permitted. Golf lessons available.

Fees:

Weekday: 18-hole: $8.75 Cart: $9.75
9-hole: (N/A) Cart: (N/A)
Weekend: 18-hole: $12 Cart: $9.75
9-hole: (N/A) Cart: (N/A)

Located on Hwy 6 east of Waco.

Comanche Creek Golf Course

(3,063 yds) 915-347-5798

Fort Mason Park
Mason, TX 76856
Contact: Bill Baze
Description: Scenic 9-hole public course located in pleasant parklike surroundings. Plenty of trees, ever-present winds, and sand. As name would suggest, water is also a problem for unwary golfers. **Par:** 36.
Rentals: Golf Carts, Pull Carts

Open to the public. Walking permitted.

Fees:

Weekday: 18-hole: $7 Cart: $12.70
9-hole: (N/A) Cart: $7.40
Weekend: 18-hole: $10 Cart: $12.70
9-hole: (N/A) Cart: $7.40

Located in Fort Mason Park near downtown.

McAllen Country Club

(6,400 yds) 956-631-1103

615 Wichita Ave.
McAllen, TX 78503
Contact: Neil Etter
Description: A short 18-hole private course that is real tight but doesn't have much water. There are lots of out-of-bounds and fairway traps, not to mention South Texas palms. Food, drinks, pro shop, and swimming pool. **Par:** 71.
Rentals: Golf Carts, Golf Clubs, Driving Range

Members and guests only. Golf lessons available. Walking permitted.

Fees:

Weekday: 18-hole: $25 Cart: $8
9-hole: (N/A) Cart: $5
Weekend: 18-hole: $40 Cart: $8
9-hole: (N/A) Cart: $5

Located on Wichita Ave. south of town.

Palm View Municipal Golf Course   (27 hs) 956-687-9591

2701 S. Ware Road
Box 1035
McAllen, TX 78503
Contact: Scott Henry
Description: A 27-hole public course.
Most golfers play the West and South
nines for 18 holes with water, not many
trees, and out-of-bounds. The East nine
has large, three-putt greens. **Par:** 72
(6,575 yards).
Rentals: Golf Carts, Pull Carts, Golf
Clubs, Driving Range

Open to the public. Walking permitted.
Golf lessons available.

Fees:

Weekday: 18-hole: $6 Cart: $8 9-hole:
$7.50 Cart: $3.50
Weekend: 18-hole: $10.25 Cart: $8
9-hole: $7.50 Cart: $3.50

Located south of Hwy 83.

McCamey Country Club   (6,200 yds) 915-652-8904

P.O. Box 1226
McCamey, TX 79752
Contact: Golf Shop
Description: Double tees make this
nine-hole private course great. Thick
rough and elevated tees make up the
difference of no water hazards.
Bentgrass greens. Out-of-town golfers
welcome. **Par:** 35.
Rentals: Driving Range

Members and guests only. Walking
permitted.

Fees:

Weekday: 18-hole: $8.50 Cart: $15
9-hole: $5 Cart: (N/A)
Weekend: 18-hole: $10.65 Cart: $15
9-hole: $5 Cart: (N/A)

Located on FM 1901.

Eldorado Country Club   (6,770 yds) 972-529-2770

2604 Country Club Drive
McKinney, TX 75070
Contact: Kevin Sledge
Description: A hilly golf course with
lots of trees and water. The bentgrass
greens are very fast to set up
three-putts. The par 3s are long.
Recently rebuilt clubhouse. **Par:** 72.
Rentals: Golf Carts, Golf Clubs, Driving
Range

Members and guests only. Golf lessons
available. Walking permitted.

Fees:

Weekday: 18-hole: $40 Cart: $11.30
9-hole: (N/A) Cart: $4.66
Weekend: 18-hole: $50 Cart: $11.30
9-hole: (N/A) Cart: $4.66

Located west of U.S. 75, exit Eldorado
Parkway in McKinney.

Hank Haney Golf Ranch

(3,300 yds) 972-529-2221

4101 Custer Road
McKinney, TX 75070
Contact: Hank Haney
Description: A nine-hole par-33 course
that is the only nine-hole course Pete
Dye designed. Good golfers can shoot
43 because it's so tough. Lots of
lessons are available. **Par:** 33.
Rentals: Golf Carts, Golf Clubs, Driving
Range

Open to the public. Walking permitted.
Golf lessons available.

Fees:

Weekday: 18-hole: $25 Cart: $11
9-hole: $15 Cart: $5.50
Weekend: 18-hole: $25 Cart: $11
9-hole: $15 Cart: $5.50

Located north of Hwy 121 on Custer
Road.

McKinney Country Club

(6,355 yds) 972-562-7731

1099 Country Club Road
McKinney, TX 75069
Contact: Dudley Wysong
Description: A private nine-hole course
built in 1927. Several holes sit on top
of a hill, with two holes over water and
only four sand traps on the course.
Par: 36.
Rentals: Golf Carts, Driving Range
Members and guests only. Golf lessons
available. Walking permitted.

Fees:

Weekday: 18-hole: $15 Cart: $9
9-hole: (N/A) Cart: $4.50
Weekend: 18-hole: $25 Cart: $9
9-hole: (N/A) Cart: $4.50

Located east of U.S. 75 off Stacy Road
and north to FM 1378.

McKinney Municipal Golf Course

(6,300 yds) 972-542-4523

3005 N. McDonald Street
McKinney, TX 75069
Contact: David Clark
Description: An upgraded city golf
course which recently opened nine more
holes in the spring of 1998. It is very
possible to lose a ball on this
interesting layout. Small greens and
long holes can cause a bogey. **Par:** 72
Rentals: Golf Carts, Pull Carts, Golf
Clubs, Driving Range

Open to the public. Walking permitted.
Golf lessons available.

Fees:

Weekday: 18-hole: $14.50 Cart: $8
9-hole: (N/A) Cart: $4
Weekend: 18-hole: $23.50 Cart: $8
9-hole: (N/A) Cart: $4

From U.S. 75 go east on Hwy 380 to
Hwy 5, then north approximately one
mile to course on the left.

Stonebridge Country Club   (7,235 yds) 972-380-1088

7703 Beacon Hill Road
Stonebridge Ranch
McKinney, TX 75070
Contact: Kent Wood
Description: The only Pete Dye 18-hole
golf course in the Dallas area and the
site of the 1994 NCAA championship.
Rated as one of the toughest courses in
Texas. Home of '98 U.S. Amateur
Champion Hank Kuehne. **Par:** 72.
Rentals: Golf Carts, Golf Clubs, Driving
Range

Members and guests only. Golf lessons
available. Walking permitted.

Fees:

Weekday: 18-hole: $55 Cart: $12
9-hole: (N/A) Cart: $6
Weekend: 18-hole: $65 Cart: $12
9-hole: (N/A) Cart: $6

Located west of U.S. 75 to Virginia
Parkway and south on Stonebridge.

Ranch Country Club   (6,535 yds) 972-529-5991

5901 Glen Oaks Drive
Stonebridge Ranch
McKinney, TX 75070
Contact: Bryan McMurray
Description: A very unique semiprivate
golf club with the most unusual par 3 in
Texas. The 156-yard 11th hole has 10
tees and combined greens. Part of
Stonebridge CC. **Par:** 72.
Rentals: Golf Carts, Golf Clubs, Driving
Range

Open to the public. Walking permitted.
Golf lessons available.

Fees:

Weekday: 18-hole: $45 Cart: $11.50
9-hole: (N/A) Cart: (N/A)
Weekend: 18-hole: $65 Cart: $11.50
9-hole: (N/A) Cart: (N/A)

Located west of U.S. 75 to Virginia
Parkway and south on East Ridge.

McLean Country Club   (3,325 yds) 806-779-8809

217 N. Main
McLean, TX 79057
Contact: Golf Shop
Description: Another typical West
Texas city layout. Originally founded by
local Lions Club for members and
townsfolk to play. Play still continues
with small greens, trees, one water
hazard, and ever-present wind. **Par:** 36.
Rentals: Golf Carts, Golf Clubs

Open to the public.

Fees:

Weekday: 18-hole: (N/A) Cart: (N/A)
9-hole: $7 Cart: $7
Weekend: 18-hole: (N/A) Cart: (N/A)
9-hole: $9 Cart: $7

Located on Main St. just west of town.
Visible from road.

Memphis Country Club   (2,734 yds) 806-259-3237

517 S. 10th St.
Memphis, TX 79425
Contact: Donnie Bridges
Description: Looking at the scorecard, golfers would think this short nine-hole private course would be easy. However, with all that strong wind, good scores don't always happen. **Par:** 34.
Rentals: Golf Carts, Golf Clubs, Driving Range

Members and guests only. Walking permitted.

Fees:

Weekday: 18-hole: $8 Cart: $8 9-hole: (N/A) Cart: (N/A)
Weekend: 18-hole: $10 Cart: $8 9-hole: (N/A) Cart: (N/A)

Located south of town on Hwy 256.

La Floresta Golf Course   956-565-6314

Route 1, Box 1600
Mercedes, TX 77785
Contact: Tommy Bixley
Description: A nine-hole public par-3 course that can be surprising. One hole is a hidden hole with the tee shot going over trees. The holes are between 100 yards and 166 yards. No water. **Par:** 27.
Rentals: Golf Clubs, Driving Range

Open to the public. Walking permitted.

Fees:

Weekday: 18-hole: $8 Cart: (N/A) 9-hole: $5 Cart: (N/A)
Weekend: 18-hole: $8 Cart: (N/A) 9-hole: $5 Cart: (N/A)

Located on Expressway 83.

Llano Grande Golf Course   (6,038 yds) 956-565-3351

P.O. Box 1002
Mercedes, TX 78570
Contact: John Aguillon
Description: A simple nine-hole public course with trees in a floodway, no sand traps, water on four holes, and flat greens. Clubhouse, food, and pro shop. **Par:** 36.
Rentals: Golf Carts, Pull Carts, Golf Clubs, Driving Range

Open to the public. Walking permitted.

Fees:

Weekday: 18-hole: $8.50 Cart: $6.90 9-hole: (N/A) Cart: $3.45
Weekend: 18-hole: $8.50 Cart: $6.90 9-hole: (N/A) Cart: $3.45

Located south of Hwy 83 on Mile Two-West.

Mid-Valley Golf Club

(7,114 yds) 956-565-3211

FM 491
Mercedes, TX 78570
Contact: Joe Powell
Description: Good, public course opened recently in Rio Grande Valley. Plenty of water for unwary golfers, some palm trees, and plenty of rough with heather around the course. **Par:** 72.
Rentals: Golf Carts, Pull Carts, Golf Clubs

Open to the public. Walking permitted.

Fees:

Weekday: 18-hole: $11 Cart: $8
9-hole: (N/A) Cart: $5
Weekend: 18-hole: $9 Cart: $8 9-hole: (N/A) Cart: $5

Located 2½ miles north on FM 491 in Mercedes.

Bosque Valley Golf Club

(6,108 yds) 254-435-2692

FM 1991
Meridian, TX 76665
Contact: Phil Guinn
Description: Golfers playing this nine-hole semiprivate course will experience all of golf with three par 3s, three par 4s, and three par 5s. Lots of trees and small greens. Food and drinks. **Par:** 36.
Rentals: Golf Carts, Pull Carts, Driving Range

Open to the public. Walking permitted. Golf lessons available.

Fees:

Weekday: 18-hole: $10 Cart: $7
9-hole: (N/A) Cart: $3.50
Weekend: 18-hole: $15 Cart: $7
9-hole: (N/A) Cart: $3.50

Located on FM 1991.

Merkel Country Club

(6,136 yds) 915-928-3193

200 Country Club Road
Merkel, TX 79536
Contact: George DiJulio
Description: A classic rural Texas nine-hole semiprivate course. Reasonable to play well because the course is rather short but windy. Clubhouse and pro shop. **Par:** 36.
Rentals: Golf Carts

Open to the public. Walking permitted.

Fees:

Weekday: 18-hole: $8 Cart: $7.50
9-hole: (N/A) Cart: (N/A)
Weekend: 18-hole: $12 Cart: $7.50
9-hole: (N/A) Cart: (N/A)

Located north of town on Hwy 126.

Mesquite Golf Club   (6,280 yds) 972-270-7457

825 N. Highway 67
Mesquite, TX 75150
Contact: Richard Beasley
Description: Excellent learning center and a golf course that will challenge a golfer to use the lessons. The clubhouse has a grill and pro shop. Lessons are well thought out. **Par:** 71.
Rentals: Golf Carts, Pull Carts, Golf Clubs, Driving Range

Open to the public. Walking permitted. Golf lessons available.

Fees:

Weekday: 18-hole: $15.09 Cart: $19.93 9-hole: (N/A) Cart: (N/A)
Weekend: 18-hole: $19.40 Cart: $19.93 9-hole: (N/A) Cart: (N/A)

Take Beltline exit from I-635 and loop around to westbound frontage road. Course is one mile off Beltline.

Town East Golf Center   (1,300 yds) 972-226-1959

3134 N. Beltline Road
Mesquite, TX 75182
Contact: Larry Billingsly
Description: A neat nine-hole executive course with six par 3s, two par 4s, and a par 5. Water hazards are on six holes. Small greens protected by sand traps. **Par:** 31.
Rentals: Golf Carts
Open to the public. Walking permitted.

Fees:

Weekday: 18-hole: $8 Cart: (N/A) 9-hole: (N/A) Cart: (N/A)
Weekend: 18-hole: $10 Cart: (N/A) 9-hole: (N/A) Cart: (N/A)

Located two miles south of I-30 on Beltline Road.

Olde Oaks Golf & Country Club   (6,400 yds) 254-562-2391

P.O. Box 88
Mexia, TX 76667
Contact: Paul Luna
Description: The fairways on this nine-hole semiprivate course are very rolling. The slope kicks tee shots into a lake the course plays around. Long par 4s and double tees. **Par:** 36.
Rentals: Golf Carts, Golf Clubs, Driving Range

Open to the public. Walking permitted. Golf lessons available.

Fees:

Weekday: 18-hole: $8.10 Cart: $7 9-hole: (N/A) Cart: $3
Weekend: 18-hole: $10 Cart: $7 9-hole: (N/A) Cart: $3

Located two miles south on Hwy 39.

Green Tree Country Club

(27 hs) 915-694-8413

4900 Green Tree Blvd.
Midland, TX 79707
Contact: Chris Carpenter
Description: A 27-hole private course
where members play any two nines to
post an 18-hole score. The North nine
is the longest nine, the West nine is the
shortest. An 18-hole round can be 73,
72, or 71. Neat golf. **Par:** 73.
Rentals: Golf Carts, Pull Carts, Golf
Clubs, Driving Range

Members and guests only. Golf lessons
available. Walking permitted.

Fees:

Weekday: 18-hole: $30 Cart: $9
9-hole: (N/A) Cart: $4.50
Weekend: 18-hole: $40 Cart: $9
9-hole: (N/A) Cart: $4.50

> Take Loop 250 to N. Midland Drive;
> turn north to course.

Hogan Park Golf Course

(27 hs) 915-685-7360

North Fairground Road
Midland, TX 79705
Contact: Greg Sikes
Description: A 27-hole public course
that is the most popular in Midland. It
is a hilly course with tough par 3s and
dangerous ponds. Food and drinks.
Par: 72.
Rentals: Golf Carts, Pull Carts, Golf
Clubs, Driving Range

Open to the public. Walking permitted.
Golf lessons available.

Fees:

Weekday: 18-hole: $9.50 Cart: $7.50
9-hole: (N/A) Cart: $4.25
Weekend: 18-hole: $14 Cart: $7.50
9-hole: (N/A) Cart: $4.25

> Located off Fairground Road northeast
> of town.

Midland Country Club

(7,300 yds) 915-683-3621

6101 N. Highway 349
Midland, TX 79705
Contact: Terry Lester
Description: One of the best West
Texas private courses with very thick
trees, lots of out-of-bounds, and water.
Outstanding clubhouse with great
facility. **Par:** 72.
Rentals: Golf Carts, Pull Carts, Golf
Clubs, Driving Range

Members and guests only. Golf lessons
available. Walking permitted.

Fees:

Weekday: 18-hole: $35 Cart: $9
9-hole: (N/A) Cart: $4
Weekend: 18-hole: $50 Cart: $9
9-hole: (N/A) Cart: $4

> Located 3½ miles north of the city on
> Lamesa Hwy.

Ranchland Hills Country Club   (6,560 yds) 915-683-2041

1600 E. Wadley Road
Midland, TX 79705
Contact: Bob Pritchett
Description: A traditional style par-70 course into the wind. Clubhouse has a restaurant, bar, lockers, pro shop, showers, meeting room, and tennis courts. **Par:** 70.
Rentals: Golf Carts, Pull Carts, Golf Clubs, Driving Range

Members and guests only. Golf lessons available. Walking permitted.

Fees:

Weekday: 18-hole: $27 Cart: (N/A)
9-hole: (N/A) Cart: (N/A)
Weekend: 18-hole: $38 Cart: (N/A)
9-hole: (N/A) Cart: (N/A)

Located ½ mile east of Lamesa Hwy.

Pecan Trails Golf Course   (5,000 yds) 972-723-1376

434 Edgefield Road
Midlothian, TX 76065
Contact: Mark Wells
Description: A fun par-33 nine-hole course. A new nine holes is currently planned to be much longer. **Par:** 33.
Rentals: Golf Carts, Golf Clubs, Driving Range
Open to the public. Walking permitted. Golf lessons available.

Fees:

Weekday: 18-hole: $8 Cart: $7 9-hole: $5 Cart: $5
Weekend: 18-hole: $11 Cart: $7
9-hole: $6 Cart: $5

Located on Hwy 67 north; take a right on Shiloh Road and left on Edgefield ½ mile later.

Mineola Country Club   (5,953 yds) 903-569-2472

225 Country Club Drive
Mineola, TX 75773
Contact: Donnie Duboise
Description: Golfers playing this nine-hole semiprivate course don't usually have flat lies on the fairways. They can easily pull shots into one of five creeks and miss small greens. Senior discounts. **Par:** 35.
Rentals: Golf Carts, Pull Carts

Open to the public. Walking permitted.

Fees:

Weekday: 18-hole: $10.50 Cart: $8
9-hole: (N/A) Cart: $3
Weekend: 18-hole: $16 Cart: $8
9-hole: (N/A) Cart: $3

Course is just off Hwy 80 in Mineola.

Holiday Hills Country Club   (6,200 yds) 940-325-8403

P.O. Box 68
Mineral Wells, TX 76068
Contact: Bill McGoha
Description: Golfers driving down Highway 180 will see this 18-hole semiprivate course and think it is easy because the holes look open. That's the front nine, but the back nine is tight and the course is hilly. **Par:** 71.
Rentals: Golf Carts, Pull Carts, Golf Clubs, Driving Range

Open to the public. Walking permitted.

Fees:

Weekday: 18-hole: $15 Cart: $7.50
9-hole: (N/A) Cart: $3.75
Weekend: 18-hole: $20 Cart: $7.50
9-hole: (N/A) Cart: $3.75

Located on Hwy 180 in Mineral Wells.

Club at Cimarron   (6,821 yds) 956-581-7408

1200 S. Sherry
Mission, TX 78572
Contact: Craig Wooly
Description: With water on 16 holes of this 18-hole private course, golfers can lose balls. The greens are elevated, large, and easy to three-putt. Top facilities in the Valley. **Par:** 72.
Rentals: Golf Carts, Golf Clubs, Driving Range

Members and guests only. Golf lessons available. Walking permitted.

Fees:

Weekday: 18-hole: $25 Cart: $20
9-hole: (N/A) Cart: $11
Weekend: 18-hole: $50 Cart: $20
9-hole: (N/A) Cart: $11

Located south of Hwy 83 on Hwy 494.

Martin's Valley Ranch Golf Course   (27 hs) 956-585-6330

7400 W. Expressway 83
Mission, TX 78572
Contact: Lori Gaffney
18-hole Course Description: A beautiful golf course in the Rio Grande Valley that allows quick 18-hole rounds. A simple clubhouse with a restaurant, bar, and pro shop. **Par:** 72 (6,695 yards).

9-hole Course Description: A nine-hole course was added to the original 18 holes in 1993. It is as challenging as the 18 hole course, being 3,428 yards and par 36. Located near the original 18 holes. **Par:** 36 (3,428 yards).
Rentals: Golf Carts, Pull Carts, Golf Clubs, Driving Range
Open to the public. Walking permitted. Golf lessons available.

Fees:

Weekday: 18-hole: $10.62 Cart: $6 9-hole: $6 Cart: $6
Weekend: 18-hole: $18.75 Cart: $6 9-hole: $6 Cart: $6

Located five miles west of Mission on Expressway 83.

Seven Oaks Resort   (6,089 yds) 956-581-6267

1300 Circle Drive
Mission, TX 78572
Contact: Mike Fernuik
Description: This 18-hole semiprivate course recently put in 50 new sand traps. The front nine has water on all holes. There is out-of-bounds on all 18 holes. Small greens. Food. **Par:** 70.
Rentals: Golf Clubs, Golf Carts, Driving Range

Open to the public. Walking permitted. Golf lessons available.

Fees:

Weekday: 18-hole: $13.50 Cart: $8.50 9-hole: $9.50 Cart: $5
Weekend: 18-hole: $13.50 Cart: $8.50 9-hole: $9.50 Cart: $5

Located off Los Ebanos Road.

Shary Municipal Golf Course   (6,025 yds) 956-580-8770

2201 Mayberry St.
Mission, TX 78572
Contact: Chencho Ramirez
Description: This 18-hole public
course has room for a new nine-hole
course. Right now the course is tight
with the 365-yard par-4 hole having
double greens. **Par:** 71.
Rentals: Golf Carts, Pull Carts, Golf
Clubs

Open to the public. Walking permitted.

Fees:

Weekday: 18-hole: $9.50 Cart: $7.50
9-hole: $7.50 Cart: $4
Weekend: 18-hole: $9.50 Cart: $7.50
9-hole: $7.50 Cart: $4

Located off Expressway 83 and Bryon
Road.

Quail Valley Golf Club   (36 hs) 281-437-8277

2880 La Quinta Road
P.O. Box 445
Missouri City, TX 77459
Contact: David Denz
La Quinta Course Description: A
36-hole private course with two good
18-hole courses and an 18-hole par-3
course. The La Quinta Course is
traditional with lots of water and trees.
Drinks. **Par:** 72 (6,816 yards).
Rentals: Golf Carts, Golf Clubs, Driving
Range
Members and guests only. Golf lessons
available. Walking permitted.

Fees:

Weekday: 18-hole: $75 Cart: $9
9-hole: $6 Cart: $5
Weekend: 18-hole: $75 Cart: $9
9-hole: $10 Cart: $5

El Dorado/Executive Course
Description: The El Dorado course is
rather tough with five par 3s with the
shortest hole 190 yards. The par 4s
play real long. The executive course is a
nine-hole par 3 and nine-hole par 32
with water. **Par:** 70 (6,680 yards).
Rentals: Golf Carts, Golf Clubs, Driving
Range
Members and guests only. Golf lessons
available. Walking permitted.

Fees:

Weekday: 18-hole: $30 Cart: $20
9-hole: $6 Cart: $5
Weekend: 18-hole: $45 Cart: $20
9-hole: $10 Cart: $5

Located south of Houston off Hwy 6.
Turn right on FM 1092 and follow the
signs to Quail Valley.

Willowisp Country Club (6,879 yds) 281-437-8210

14502 Fondren
P.O. Box 6
Missouri City, TX 77459
Contact: Randy Lewis
Description: An 18-hole private course
that has lots of trees along mid-width
fairways. The greens are huge with
many three-putts. Pool, food, and 19th
hole. **Par:** 71.
Rentals: Golf Carts, Golf Clubs, Driving
Range

Members and guests only. Golf lessons
available. Walking permitted.

Fees:

Weekday: 18-hole: $30 Cart: $15
9-hole: (N/A) Cart: $5
Weekend: 18-hole: $40 Cart: $15
9-hole: (N/A) Cart: $5

Located just south of Houston off Hwy
alternate 90.

Ward County Golf Course (6,669 yds) 915-943-5044

P.O. Box 1693
Monahans, TX 79756
Contact: Douglas J. Ward
Description: The area where LPGA
star Kathy Whitworth took up golf. The
18-hole public course is hilly with trees,
big water hazards, and sand traps.
Snack bar and drinks. **Par:** 72.
Rentals: Golf Carts, Pull Carts, Golf
Clubs, Driving Range

Open to the public. Walking permitted.
Golf lessons available.

Fees:

Weekday: 18-hole: $15 Cart: $8
9-hole: (N/A) Cart: $4
Weekend: 18-hole: $15 Cart: $8
9-hole: (N/A) Cart: $4

Located 1½ miles north of town on
Hwy 18.

April Sound Country Club (6,367 yds) 409-447-1700

1000 April Sound Blvd.
Montgomery, TX 77356
Contact: David Scott
Description: A short, narrow, and hilly
18-hole private course that has a
nine-hole executive course. Lots of
water along Lake Conroe, plus
out-of-bounds. Food, drinks, and tennis.
Par: 71.
Rentals: Golf Carts, Golf Clubs, Driving
Range

Members and guests only. Golf lessons
available. Mandatory carts.

Fees:

Weekday: 18-hole: $25 Cart: $10
9-hole: $20 Cart: $5
Weekend: 18-hole: $40 Cart: $10
9-hole: $20 Cart: $5

Located west of town on Hwy 105.

Bentwater Yacht & Country Club   (36 hs) 409-353-1912

800 Bentwater Drive
Montgomery, TX 77356
Contact: Brett Lossin
Miller Course Description: The original course at this spectacular 36-hole private course is tight with rolling hills, pine trees, and great Lake Conroe views. Some fairways are split.
Par: 72 (6,802 yards).

Weiskopf Course Description: The Weiskopf 18 is simply great golf in a great setting. The Lake Conroe site gives Bentwater the prettiest golf in the Conroe/Houston area. Bentgrass greens, split fairways, trees, and sand. It has it all. **Par:** 72 (6,902 yards).

Rentals: Golf Carts, Golf Clubs, Driving Range
Members and guests only. Golf lessons available. Walking permitted.

Fees:

Weekday: 18-hole: $40 Cart: $10
9-hole: $20 Cart: $5
Weekend: 18-hole: $60 Cart: $10
9-hole: $25 Cart: $5

> Located on FM 1097.

Del Lago Resort & Conference Center (6,633 yds) 409-582-6100

500 LaCosta Drive
Montgomery, TX 77356
Contact: Bobby Cleboski
Description: A reasonably long 18-hole public course with undulating fairways on the back nine. Water figures on several holes. All fairways are tight. Food, drinks, and pro shop.
Par: 71.
Rentals: Golf Carts, Golf Clubs, Driving Range

Open to the public. Walking permitted. Golf lessons available.

Fees:

Weekday: 18-hole: $45 Cart: $10
9-hole: (N/A) Cart: (N/A)
Weekend: 18-hole: $55 Cart: $10
9-hole: (N/A) Cart: (N/A)

> Located off I-45 to Hwy 105.

Walden On Lake Conroe Golf & C.C. (6,765 yds) 409-448-4668

13101 Walden Road
Montgomery, TX 77356
Contact: Ron Coville
Description: A very difficult Von Hagge/Devlin course with lots of holes on Lake Conroe. Plenty of great private club golf in a super setting. **Par:** 72.
Rentals: Golf Carts, Golf Clubs, Driving Range

Members and guests only. Golf lessons available. Walking permitted.

Fees:

Weekday: 18-hole: $45 Cart: $20
9-hole: (N/A) Cart: (N/A)
Weekend: 18-hole: $60 Cart: $20
9-hole: (N/A) Cart: (N/A)

Located north of Houston, west of Conroe on Hwy 105.

Greenbrier Golf & Country Club (6,457 yds) 254-853-2927

Route 2, Box 465
Moody, TX 76557
Contact: Jim Budziszewski
Description: A very rolling 18-hole public course that has a lot of trees on the back nine and lots of water. The course is 6,457 yards long. Food and drinks. **Par:** 70.
Rentals: Golf Carts, Pull Carts, Golf Clubs, Driving Range

Open to the public. Walking permitted. Golf lessons available.

Fees:

Weekday: 18-hole: $8.50 Cart: $9
9-hole: $5.50 Cart: $4
Weekend: 18-hole: $11 Cart: $9
9-hole: $7 Cart: $4

Located 15 miles west of Waco on Hwy 317.

Morton Country Club (5,853 yds) 806-266-5941

Route 2, Box 53
Morton, TX 79346
Contact: Fred New
Description: Out-of-town golfers are welcome to play this nine-hole private course. It has only two water hazards, no traps, and wide fairways with double tees. Food and drinks. **Par:** 35.
Rentals: Golf Carts, Pull Carts

Members and guests only. Golf lessons available. Walking permitted.

Fees:

Weekday: 18-hole: $10 Cart: $10
9-hole: (N/A) Cart: $3.75
Weekend: 18-hole: $15 Cart: $10
9-hole: (N/A) Cart: $3.75

Located east of town on FM 1780.

Mount Pleasant Country Club   (6,396 yds) 903-572-1804

1000 Country Club Drive
Mount Pleasant, TX 75455
Contact: Roy Stinson
Description: One of the best nine-hole
public courses in Texas. It is a hilly
course with trees, sand traps, water
hazards, and double tees. Food, drinks,
and pro shop. **Par:** 36.
Rentals: Golf Carts

Open to the public. Walking permitted.
Golf lessons available.

Fees:

Weekday: 18-hole: $8.75 Cart: $9.10
9-hole: (N/A) Cart: $5
Weekend: 18-hole: $17.50 Cart:
$9.10 9-hole: (N/A) Cart: $5

Located off I-30 on Greenhill Road.

Shadow Lake Golf Club   (1,186 yds) 903-527-1288

Route 3 Box 135
Mount Pleasant, TX 75455
Contact: Ken Smith/Coy Sevier
Description: Outstanding par 3 layout
built from scratch by owner Ken Smith,
who ran the bulldozer on the property
just off I-30. Very challenging short
game layout with the 118-yard fifth
hole a total island green. **Par:** 27.
Rentals: Golf Carts, Driving Range
Open to the public.

Fees:

Weekday: 18-hole: (N/A) Cart: (N/A)
9-hole: $10 Cart: $3
Weekend: 18-hole: (N/A) Cart: (N/A)
9-hole: $10 Cart: $3

Take first Mount Pleasant exit off I-30
East from Dallas. Take a right at the
first light; course is 2 miles on left.

Turtle Hill Golf Course   (6,510 yds) 940-759-4896

County Road 660
Highway 373 North
Muenster, TX 76252
Contact: Dick Murphy
Description: A neat nine-hole
semiprivate course that opened in July
1993 and added a second nine in
1995. A self-built course. It is hilly with
bentgrass greens, traps, and water.
Par: 36.
Rentals: Golf Carts, Pull Carts, Golf
Clubs, Driving Range

Open to the public. Walking permitted.
Golf lessons available.

Fees:

Weekday: 18-hole: $14.50 Cart: $8
9-hole: $8.10 Cart: $4
Weekend: 18-hole: $22 Cart: $8
9-hole: $11 Cart: $4

Located off Hwy 82 to Hwy 373 North.

Muleshoe Country Club
(6,054 yds) 806-272-4250

900 Country Club Drive
Muleshoe, TX 79347
Contact: Jeff Baker
Description: It is very possible to post a good score on this nine-hole public course thanks to flat fairways, bentgrass greens, and only two sand traps. There are some trees. Food and drinks. **Par:** 35.
Rentals: Golf Carts, Golf Clubs, Driving Range

Open to the public. Walking permitted.

Fees:

Weekday: 18-hole: $7 Cart: $9 9-hole: $4.50 Cart: $4.50
Weekend: 18-hole: $9 Cart: $9 9-hole: $9 Cart: $4.50

Located north of town.

Lake Creek Golf Course
(3,300 yds) 940-422-4458

340 W. Main Street
Munday, TX 76371
Contact: Bob Bowen
Description: A classic rural Texas nine-hole semiprivate course. The course is not very long but has the usual trees and water hazards along with some wind. **Par:** 35.
Rentals: Golf Carts
Open to the public. Walking permitted.

Fees:

Weekday: 18-hole: $10 Cart: $12 9-hole: (N/A) Cart: (N/A)
Weekend: 18-hole: $10 Cart: $12 9-hole: (N/A) Cart: (N/A)

Located four miles east of town on FM 222.

Echo Creek Country Club
(6,175 yds) 903-852-7094

6760 Ann Drive
Murchison, TX 75778
Contact: J.T. Andas
Description: A mid-length, semiprivate club. Tee times only needed on weekend. Clubhouse has restaurant, bar, lockers, meeting room, and pro shop. **Par:** 71.
Rentals: Golf Carts, Golf Clubs, Driving Range

Open to the public. Walking permitted.

Fees:

Weekday: 18-hole: $12 Cart: $18 9-hole: (N/A) Cart: (N/A)
Weekend: 18-hole: $18 Cart: $18 9-hole: (N/A) Cart: (N/A)

Located off FM 317 10 miles east of Athens or 22 miles west of Tyler.

Piney Woods Country Club   (6,187 yds) 409-569-6505

Highway 59
Nacogdoches, TX 75961
Contact: Dean Cole
Description: If you are playing well, you'll enjoy playing this 18-hole private course. It is pretty with trees, hilly fairways, small greens, and two water hazards. Food and drinks. **Par:** 72.
Rentals: Golf Carts, Driving Range

Members and guests only. Golf lessons available. Walking permitted.

Fees:

Weekday: 18-hole: $20 Cart: $18.23
9-hole: (N/A) Cart: $9.15
Weekend: 18-hole: $30 Cart: $18.23
9-hole: (N/A) Cart: $9.15

Located on Hwy 59 south of town.

Woodland Hills Golf Course   (6,610 yds) 409-564-2762

319 Woodland Hills Drive
Nacogdoches, TX 75961
Contact: J. David Sholar
Description: Tight 18 holes with trees and water in great East Texas setting. Clubhouse recently remodeled with large restaurant and pro shop. **Par:** 72.
Rentals: Golf Carts, Pull Carts, Golf Clubs, Driving Range
Open to the public. Walking permitted.

Fees:

Weekday: 18-hole: $12.50 Cart: $10
9-hole: (N/A) Cart: (N/A)
Weekend: 18-hole: $17.50 Cart: $10
9-hole: (N/A) Cart: (N/A)

Located three miles south of town on Hwy 59.

Bluebonnet Country Club   (6,707 yds) 409-894-2207

Route 2, Box 3471
Navasota, TX 77868
Contact: Blair Kline
Description: To post a good score on this 18-hole public course, golfers must hit good shots to avoid water on 15 holes, stay on the tight fairways, and avoid three-putting the large greens. Walking only on weekdays. **Par:** 72.
Rentals: Golf Carts, Pull Carts, Golf Clubs

Open to the public. Walking permitted.

Fees:

Weekday: 18-hole: $10.40 Cart: $9.61 9-hole: (N/A) Cart: (N/A)
Weekend: 18-hole: $26.69 Cart: (N/A)
9-hole: (N/A) Cart: (N/A)

Located off Hwy 6 in Navasota.

Navasota Municipal Golf Course   (6,000 yds) 409-825-7284

West Washington
Navasota, TX 77868
Contact: Charles Scott
Description: The converted par-4 sixth hole on this nine-hole public course into a par 5 is a highlight. Nonetheless, the entire course is open and short with water on five holes. **Par:** 35.
Rentals: Golf Carts, Pull Carts

Open to the public. Walking permitted.

Fees:

Weekday: 18-hole: $8 Cart: $14.50
9-hole: (N/A) Cart: $6.47
Weekend: 18-hole: $10 Cart: $14.50
9-hole: (N/A) Cart: $6.47

Located off I-45 west to Hwy 105.

Bandit   (6,950 yds) 888-923-7846

Long Creek Road
New Braunfels, TX 78130
Contact: Clint Alexander
Description: New public course opened in early 1998. Outstanding design follows Long Creek, with water on 11 holes. Very interesting holes. **Par:** 71.
Rentals: Golf Carts, Driving Range
Open to the public. Walking permitted.

Fees:

Weekday: 18-hole: $50 Cart: (N/A)
9-hole: (N/A) Cart: (N/A)
Weekend: 18-hole: $62 Cart: (N/A)
9-hole: (N/A) Cart: (N/A)

From I-35, take the Lake McQueeny/FM 725 exit, and go east on 725 for five miles. Club is on the left.

Landa Park Municipal Golf Course (6,103 yds) 830-608-2174

800 Golf Course Road
New Braunfels, TX 78132
Contact: Paul Pollard
Description: Even though the yards on this 18-hole popular public course are considered to be short, the course itself is a target course with water and traps. **Par:** 72.
Rentals: Golf Carts, Pull Carts, Golf Clubs

Open to the public. Walking permitted. Golf lessons available.

Fees:

Weekday: 18-hole: $23 Cart: (N/A)
9-hole: (N/A) Cart: $4.50
Weekend: 18-hole: $25 Cart: (N/A)
9-hole: (N/A) Cart: $4.50

Located off I-35, 25 miles northeast of San Antonio in New Braunfels city park off Hwy 46, next to Schlitterbahn

Lee's Par 3   **(1,100 yds) 830-620-4653**

P.O. Box 310059
New Braunfels, TX 78131-0059
Contact: Lee Maddox
Description: A strong, 1,100-yard
par-3 course that challenges the short
game and tee shots. Clubhouse has a
pro shop. **Par:** 27.
Rentals: Golf Clubs, Driving Range
Open to the public. Walking permitted.
Golf lessons available.

Fees:

Weekday: 18-hole: $8 Cart: (N/A)
9-hole: (N/A) Cart: (N/A)
Weekend: 18-hole: $8 Cart: (N/A)
9-hole: (N/A) Cart: (N/A)

From I-35, exit at FM 725. Go south
2.2 miles and turn right on Klein Road.

Sundance Golf Club   **(3,558 yds) 830-629-3817**

2294 Common St.
New Braunfels, TX 78130
Contact: Joseph Mendez
Description: Challenging executive
course to go along with outstanding
driving range and practice facility.
Golfers face par-3 and par-4 layouts
with water and rough. Course lights
visible from I-35 at Canyon Lake exit.
Par: 58.
Rentals: Golf Carts, Pull Carts, Driving
Range

Open to the public. Walking permitted.
Golf lessons available.

Fees:

Weekday: 18-hole: $12 Cart: $6
9-hole: (N/A) Cart: (N/A)
Weekend: 18-hole: $14 Cart: $6
9-hole: (N/A) Cart: (N/A)

Take Canyon Lake exit off I-35. Course
is one mile east of I-35.

Newgulf Golf Club   **(6,164 yds) 409-657-4639**

P.O. Box 441
Newgulf, TX 77462
Contact: Otis Myers
Description: This nine-hole semiprivate
course is owned by Texas Gulf Corp. It
does allow public golfers to play a flat
course with trees, no water, and double
tees. **Par:** 36.
Rentals: Golf Carts, Driving Range

Open to the public. Walking permitted.

Fees:

Weekday: 18-hole: $11.75 Cart: $12
9-hole: (N/A) Cart: $6
Weekend: 18-hole: $13.90 Cart: $12
9-hole: (N/A) Cart: $6

Located off Hwy 1301 to Newgulf.

Falls Golf & Country Club

(6,800 yds) 409-992-3123

1001 N. Falls Drive
New Ulm, TX 78950
Contact: Todd Coover
Description: Great scenery and great setting at this 18-hole semiprivate course with lots of water, tight fairways, and large undulating bentgrass greens. Food and drinks. **Par:** 71.
Rentals: Golf Carts, Golf Clubs, Driving Range

Open to the public. Walking permitted. Golf lessons available.

Fees:

Weekday: 18-hole: $47 Cart: (N/A)
9-hole: $15 Cart: $5
Weekend: 18-hole: $62 Cart: (N/A)
9-hole: $20 Cart: $5

Located north of Columbus off Hwy 109.

Indian Oaks Golf Club

(5,792 yds) 940-825-4213

West Highway 82
Nocona, TX 76255
Contact: Bob Crowley
Description: Although this is a short, 5,792-yard 18-hole course, it requires a perfect tee shot to post a good score on a hole. Trees guard the doglegs. Bentgrass greens. Snacks. **Par:** 70.
Rentals: Golf Carts, Pull Carts, Driving Range

Open to the public. Walking permitted. Golf lessons available.

Fees:

Weekday: 18-hole: $7.50 Cart: $7.50
9-hole: (N/A) Cart: $4.50
Weekend: 18-hole: $10 Cart: $7.50
9-hole: (N/A) Cart: $4.50

Located on Hwy 82 West.

Nocona Hills Country Club

(6,508 yds) 940-825-3444

179 Country Club Drive
Nocona, TX 76255
Contact: Doyle Wooten
Description: A very rolling 18-hole public course where the trees are the major hazard. No traps or water. Restaurant, 19th hole bar, and pro shop. **Par:** 71.
Rentals: Golf Carts, Pull Carts, Golf Clubs, Driving Range

Open to the public. Walking permitted. Golf lessons available.

Fees:

Weekday: 18-hole: $10 Cart: $7.50
9-hole: $5 Cart: $3.75
Weekend: 18-hole: $15 Cart: $7.50
9-hole: $6.25 Cart: $3.75

Located ten miles northeast of town on FM 3301.

Iron Horse Golf Course
(6,680 yds) 817-485-6666

6200 Skylark Circle
North Richland Hills, TX 76180
Contact: Jay Clements
Description: A very difficult 18-hole public course with lots of tough dogleg holes, few birdie par 5s, and one of the most difficult par 4s in North Texas. Railroad theme. **Par:** 70.
Rentals: Golf Carts, Pull Carts, Golf Clubs, Driving Range

Open to the public. Walking permitted. Golf lessons available.

Fees:

Weekday: 18-hole: $25 Cart: $10
9-hole: (N/A) Cart: (N/A)
Weekend: 18-hole: $36 Cart: $10
9-hole: (N/A) Cart: (N/A)

Located off Loop 820 to Glenview Drive.

Club at Mission Dorado
(7,135 yds) 915-561-8811

One Mission Blvd.
Odessa, TX 79760
Contact: Blake Bingham
Description: The 14th hole, a 445-yard par 4, is the most difficult hole on the Nike Tour, played here annually. The other holes are also tough. A great course. **Par:** 72.
Rentals: Golf Carts, Golf Clubs, Driving Range

Members and guests only. Golf lessons available. Walking permitted.

Fees:

Weekday: 18-hole: $50 Cart: $9.40
9-hole: (N/A) Cart: $4
Weekend: 18-hole: $50 without member Cart: $9.40 9-hole: (N/A) Cart: $4

Located on Mission Blvd. between Loop 588 and Hwy 80.

Odessa Country Club
(6,829 yds) 915-550-0899

7184 Club Drive
Odessa, TX 79760
Contact: Clay Kinnaird
Description: During the oil boom, golf pros would play in a pro-am here to make more money. It is a long course with greens protected by bunkers. Excellent clubhouse. **Par:** 72.
Rentals: Golf Carts, Pull Carts, Golf Clubs, Driving Range

Members and guests only. Golf lessons available. Walking permitted.

Fees:

Weekday: 18-hole: $20 Cart: $8
9-hole: (N/A) Cart: $4
Weekend: 18-hole: $30 Cart: $8
9-hole: (N/A) Cart: $4

Located east of Odessa on Business 20.

Ratliff Ranch Golf Links

(6,800 yds) 915-550-8181

7500 N. Grandview Avenue
Odessa, TX 79768
Contact: Chris deKenity
Description: Ranch land makes for tough golf holes. Several holes are hilly and have water hazards. Upscale, daily-fee course. Clubhouse has a pro shop and food. **Par:** 72.
Rentals: Golf Carts, Pull Carts, Golf Clubs, Driving Range

Open to the public. Walking permitted. Golf lessons available.

Fees:

Weekday: 18-hole: $12 Cart: $8
9-hole: $10 Cart: (N/A)
Weekend: 18-hole: $17 Cart: $8
9-hole: $15 Cart: (N/A)

> Located two miles north of Odessa on Grandview Road.

Sunset Country Club

(6,665 yds) 915-366-1061

9301 Andrews Hwy
Odessa, TX 79760
Contact: John Gordy
Description: Posting a good score on this 18-hole semiprivate course is doable because there are wide fairways and no water hazards or sand traps. Don't three-putt the large greens. **Par:** 72.
Rentals: Golf Carts, Pull Carts, Golf Clubs, Driving Range

Open to the public. Walking permitted. Golf lessons available.

Fees:

Weekday: 18-hole: $10 Cart: $7.50
9-hole: (N/A) Cart: $3.75
Weekend: 18-hole: $15 Cart: $7.50
9-hole: (N/A) Cart: $3.75

> Located north of town on Hwy 385.

Old Ocean Recreation Club

(3,105 yds) 409-647-9902

FM 1514
Old Ocean, TX 77463
Contact: Johnny Harget
Description: Even though the ocean is old, it does not come close to this nine-hole public course. Only one water hazard, lots of trees on flat fairways, and sand traps. Snacks. **Par:** 36.
Rentals: Golf Carts, Pull Carts, Golf Clubs, Driving Range

Open to the public. Walking permitted.

Fees:

Weekday: 18-hole: $10 Cart: $8
9-hole: (N/A) Cart: $4
Weekend: 18-hole: $12 Cart: $8
9-hole: (N/A) Cart: $4

> Located south of town on Hwy 35.

Olney Recreation & Country Club (7,200 yds) 940-564-2424

Country Club Road
Olney, TX 76374
Contact: Gilbert Brown
Description: There are five holes on this nine-hole public course that force carries over water hazards. The course is flat with trees. Double tees produce 18-hole layout. Clubhouse. **Par:** 36.
Rentals: Golf Carts, Driving Range

Open to the public. Walking permitted. Golf lessons available.

Fees:

Weekday: 18-hole: $7.50 Cart: $8
9-hole: (N/A) Cart: $3.15
Weekend: 18-hole: $15 Cart: $8
9-hole: (N/A) Cart: $3.15

Located south of Hwy 79.

Olton Country Club (3,400 yds) 806-285-2595

P.O. Box 424
Olton, TX 79064
Contact: Ned Kruger
Description: This nine-hole public course was constructed on the highest land in Lamb County. Because it is so high, the wind is a major problem, even though there are no traps. Water and bentgrass greens. **Par:** 36.
Rentals: Golf Carts, Golf Clubs

Open to the public. Walking permitted.

Fees:

Weekday: 18-hole: $6 Cart: $7.50
9-hole: (N/A) Cart: $3
Weekend: 18-hole: $10 Cart: $7.50
9-hole: (N/A) Cart: $3

Located on FM 168 South.

DuPont Employees Recreation Assn. (6,375 yds) 409-886-1779

2601 Irving
Orange, TX 77630
Contact: Salde Green
Description: An 18-hole private course that has a health club, basketball court, and racquetball court. The course is flat and open with water and traps around small greens. Snacks. **Par:** 71.
Rentals: Golf Carts, Golf Clubs, Driving Range

Members and guests only. Golf lessons available. Walking permitted.

Fees:

Weekday: 18-hole: $12 Cart: $10
9-hole: (N/A) Cart: $7.50
Weekend: 18-hole: $15 Cart: $10
9-hole: (N/A) Cart: $7.50

Located off I-10 on FM 1106.

Sunset Grove Country Club   (6,412 yds) 409-883-9454

2900 Sunset Drive
Orange, TX 77630
Contact: Jeff Cooper
Description: With a lot of trees and water on four holes of this 18-hole private course, golfers can get into trouble. Small greens and narrow fairways. Food and drinks. **Par:** 71.
Rentals: Golf Carts, Pull Carts

Members and guests only. Golf lessons available. Walking permitted.

Fees:

Weekday: 18-hole: $32 Cart: $9
9-hole: (N/A) Cart: (N/A)
Weekend: 18-hole: $38 Cart: $9
9-hole: (N/A) Cart: (N/A)

Located south of I-10, take Hwy 87 south to Sunset, then west to course.

Overton Municipal Golf Course   (5,632 yds) 903-834-6414

South Lakeside Drive
Overton, TX 75684
Contact: Joe Johnston
Description: Looking at the scorecard, golfers would think this nine-hole public course is easy. It's not because the greens are difficult to hit thanks to small size and elevation. No traps. **Par:** 35.
Rentals: Golf Carts, Pull Carts, Driving Range

Open to the public. Walking permitted.

Fees:

Weekday: 18-hole: $8 Cart: $10
9-hole: (N/A) Cart: $3.24
Weekend: 18-hole: $12 Cart: $10
9-hole: (N/A) Cart: $3.24

Located off FM 850.

Ozona Country Club   (6,052 yds) 915-392-2520

P.O. Box 1247
Ozona, TX 76943
Contact: Jim Green
Description: Out-of-town golfers are welcome at this nine-hole private course. It has double tees and small bentgrass greens. No water or traps. Food and drinks. **Par:** 35.
Rentals: Golf Carts, Driving Range

Members and guests only. Walking permitted.

Fees:

Weekday: 18-hole: $15 Cart: $5
9-hole: (N/A) Cart: $2.50
Weekend: 18-hole: $15 Cart: $5
9-hole: (N/A) Cart: $2.50

Located north of town on Hwy 163.

Paducah Golf Club

(6,024 yds) 806-492-2245

P.O. Box 914
Paducah, TX 79248
Contact: Rusty Jones
Description: Simple nine-hole par-36
course. Some trees, plenty of wind,
small greens. **Par:** 36.
Rentals: Golf Carts, Driving Range
Open to the public. Walking permitted.

Fees:

Weekday: 18-hole: $6 Cart: (N/A)
9-hole: $4 Cart: (N/A)
Weekend: 18-hole: $8 Cart: (N/A)
9-hole: $5 Cart: (N/A)

Located two miles south of town off FM
1038.

Palacios Golf Course

(3,088 yds) 512-972-2666

Drawer G
Palacios, TX 77465
Contact: Rene Lucio
Description: Wind is a major factor on
this nine-hole public course because it
is a seaside course. There are lots of
water hazards and mounds the wind
blows balls into. **Par:** 36.
Rentals: Golf Carts, Pull Carts, Golf
Clubs, Driving Range

Open to the public. Walking permitted.
Golf lessons available.

Fees:

Weekday: 18-hole: $7 Cart: $14
9-hole: $5 Cart: $7
Weekend: 18-hole: $7 Cart: $14
9-hole: $5 Cart: $7

Located on Hwy 35 South.

Eagle's Bluff Golf Course

(7,035 yds) 1-800-214-0462

100 Eagle Bluff Drive
Palestine, TX 75801
Contact: Golf Shop
Description: Outstanding resort course
opening in late 1998. One of the
newest, longest, and most scenic
courses in East TX. Several holes have
view of Lake Palestine from the bluffs
above. Hardwood trees everywhere
along with all manner of flowers and
greenery. A treat for the eyes if not the
scorecard. **Par:** 71.

Fees:

Weekday: 18-hole: $40 Cart: included
9-hole: $20 Cart: included
Weedend: 18-hole: $40 Cart: included
9-hole: $20 Cart: included

South on Hwy 69, right on Loop 323,
south on Hwy 155 to Palestine, left on
FM 344, then look for signs.

Meadowbrook Country Club   (6,000 yds) 903-723-7530

2130 Country Club Road
Palestine, TX 75801
Contact: Terry Brown
Description: A nine-hole course that is
short but testy. Clubhouse has a bar,
restaurant, lockers, showers, meeting
rooms, and tennis courts. **Par:** 36.
Rentals: Golf Carts, Golf Clubs, Driving
Range

Members and guests only. Golf lessons
available. Walking permitted.

Fees:

Weekday: 18-hole: $14 Cart: $9.75
9-hole: (N/A) Cart: $9.75
Weekend: 18-hole: $20 Cart: $9.75
9-hole: (N/A) Cart: $9.75

Located off Hwy 155, one block north
of FM 315.

Hidden Hills Public Golf Course   (6,403 yds) 806-669-5866

North Highway 70
Pampa, TX 79065
Contact: David Teichmann
Description: Even though a golfer hits
a tee shot down the middle of the
fairway on this 18-hole public course,
the second shot may not be level. The
greens are small. Snack bar and pro
shop. **Par:** 71.
Rentals: Golf Carts, Pull Carts, Golf
Clubs, Driving Range

Open to the public. Walking permitted.
Golf lessons available.

Fees:

Weekday: 18-hole: $10.50 Cart:
$7.50 9-hole: (N/A) Cart: $4.25
Weekend: 18-hole: $12 Cart: $7.50
9-hole: (N/A) Cart: $4.25

Located on Hwy 70 North.

Pamcel Golf Club   (6,506 yds) 806-663-4142

1700 E. Harvester Street
Pampa, TX 79066
Contact: Jim Bob Mitchell
Description: A nice nine-hole private
course with double tees that make it
almost like an 18-hole course. Wind is a
major factor with the short holes
playing long. **Par:** 35.
Rentals: Golf Carts

Members and guests only. Walking
permitted.

Fees:

Weekday: 18-hole: $10 Cart: $8
9-hole: (N/A) Cart: (N/A)
Weekend: 18-hole: $10 Cart: $8
9-hole: (N/A) Cart: (N/A)

Located southwest of town on Hwy 60.

Pampa Country Club

(7,067 yds) 806-665-8431

P.O. Box 2835
Pampa, TX 79066
Contact: Mickey Piersall
Description: Home of TOPO Texas
Invitational and Tri State Seniors
Championship. One of Texas' oldest
clubs, built in 1927. Clubhouse has
restaurant, bar, lockers, showers,
meeting rooms, tennis courts, and pro
shop. **Par:** 71.
Rentals: Golf Carts, Pull Carts, Driving
Range

Members and guests only. Golf lessons
available. Walking permitted.

Fees:

Weekday: 18-hole: $20 Cart: $8
9-hole: (N/A) Cart: (N/A)
Weekend: 18-hole: $20 Cart: $8
9-hole: (N/A) Cart: (N/A)

Located north on Hobart Street and
right on Harvester.

Panhandle Country Club

(3,029 yds) 806-537-3300

100 Pecan Street
Panhandle, TX 79068
Contact: Clint McMinn
Description: Shooting a good score
happens a lot on this nine-hole public
course because it is short with flat,
wide fairways, small trees, and only
three ponds. Double tees. **Par:** 36.
Rentals: Golf Carts

Open to the public. Walking permitted.
Golf lessons available.

Fees:

Weekday: 18-hole: $8.62 Cart: $7
9-hole: (N/A) Cart: (N/A)
Weekend: 18-hole: $12.93 Cart: $7
9-hole: (N/A) Cart: (N/A)

Located on the west side of town.

Elk Hollow Golf Course

(3,142 yds) 903-785-6585

2200 36th Street NE.
Paris, TX 75460
Contact: Mike Beezley
Description: At first glance, this
nine-hole public course looks easy, but
it is not, because the course is
reasonably long with a water hazard
and traps. Clubhouse. **Par:** 36.
Rentals: Golf Carts, Pull Carts, Golf
Clubs, Driving Range

Open to the public. Walking permitted.
Golf lessons available.

Fees:

Weekday: 18-hole: $8 Cart: $7.50
9-hole: (N/A) Cart: $4
Weekend: 18-hole: $10 Cart: $7.50
9-hole: (N/A) Cart: $4

Located on Hwy 195.

Paris Golf & Country Club   (6,143 yds) 903-785-6512

Route 6, Box 48B
Paris, TX 75462
Contact: Alan Norton
Description: A classic 18-hole course built in 1918. Traditional shot values have stood the test of golfing time. Clubhouse has restaurant and well-stocked pro shop. **Par:** 70. Members and guests only. Golf lessons available. Mandatory carts.

Fees:

Weekday: 18-hole: $20 Cart: $10
9-hole: (N/A) Cart: (N/A)
Weekend: 18-hole: $25 Cart: $10
9-hole: (N/A) Cart: (N/A)

Located three miles east of Paris on Hwy 195.

Pine Ridge Golf Course   (5,835 yds) 903-785-8076

P.O. Box 1309
Paris, TX 75461
Contact: Mike Larseinigue
Description: A short 18-hole public course that has water hazards and lots of trees. Few sand traps around mid-size greens. Opened in 1988. Clubhouse and pro shop. **Par:** 72.
Rentals: Golf Carts, Pull Carts, Golf Clubs, Driving Range

Open to the public. Walking permitted.

Fees:

Weekday: 18-hole: $9 Cart: $8 9-hole: $5 Cart: $4
Weekend: 18-hole: $11 Cart: $8
9-hole: $7 Cart: $4

Located two miles west of town on Hwy 195.

Baywood Country Club   (6,574 yds) 281-487-0050

5500 Genoa-Red Bluff Road
Pasadena, TX 77505
Contact: Donald St. Germaine
Description: The back nine of this 18-hole private course is constructed through woods and trees and the front nine is constructed around water. Sand traps protect small greens. Nice clubhouse. **Par:** 72.
Rentals: Golf Carts, Pull Carts, Golf Clubs, Driving Range

Members and guests only. Golf lessons available. Walking permitted.

Fees:

Weekday: 18-hole: $20 Cart: $9
9-hole: (N/A) Cart: $7
Weekend: 18-hole: $25 Cart: $9
9-hole: (N/A) Cart: $7

Located on Hwy 225.

Chemlake Golf Course   (3,085 yds) 281-474-4258

9502 Bayport Blvd.
Pasadena, TX 77507
Contact: Ron Wood
Description: A rather simple nine-hole private course with flat fairways that have trees but only four water hazards and no sand traps. No golf carts available. **Par:** 36.
Members and guests only. Walking permitted.

Fees:

Weekday: 18-hole: $5 Cart: (N/A)
9-hole: (N/A) Cart: (N/A)
Weekend: 18-hole: $5 Cart: (N/A)
9-hole: (N/A) Cart: (N/A)

Located on Bayport Road off Bary Blvd.

San Jacinto College Golf Course   (2,638 yds) 281-476-1880

8060 Spencer Hwy
Pasadena, TX 77505
Contact: Dean Evans
Description: This nine-hole public course is designed to get beginners into golf thanks to wide fairways, no water or traps, and short holes. Senior discounts. No riding carts. **Par:** 36.
Rentals: Pull Carts
Open to the public. Walking permitted. Golf lessons available.

Fees:

Weekday: 18-hole: $4 Cart: (N/A)
9-hole: (N/A) Cart: (N/A)
Weekend: 18-hole: $6 Cart: (N/A)
9-hole: (N/A) Cart: (N/A)

Located southwest of Houston off Fairmont Parkway on college campus.

Country Place Golf Club   (6,756 yds) 713-436-1533

3123 Flower Field Lane
Pearland, TX 77584
Contact: Mike Hoelzer Sr.
Description: A short 18-hole course that has fast rounds with carts. Clubhouse has a restaurant, lockers, and pro shop. **Par:** 72.
Rentals: Golf Carts, Golf Clubs, Driving Range
Members and guests only. Golf lessons available. Mandatory carts.

Fees:

Weekday: 18-hole: $21.35 Cart: $10
9-hole: $10 Cart: $7.50
Weekend: 18-hole: $27 Cart: $10
9-hole: $12.50 Cart: $7.50

Located off Hwy 288 south 6½ miles past Hwy 610; turn left on McHard.

Golfcrest Country Club   (7,051 yds) 713-485-4550

2509 Country Club Drive
Pearland, TX 77581
Contact: David Pilsner
Description: A very long 18-hole
private course with lots of
out-of-bounds, pine trees, and water on
11 holes. The greens are protected by
53 sand traps. The course is windy.
Par: 72.
Rentals: Golf Carts, Golf Clubs, Driving
Range

Members and guests only. Golf lessons
available. Walking permitted.

Fees:

Weekday: 18-hole: $30 Cart: $9
9-hole: (N/A) Cart: (N/A)
Weekend: 18-hole: $35 Cart: $9
9-hole: (N/A) Cart: (N/A)

Located on Hwy 35 off FM 518.

Southwyck Golf Club   (7,015 yds) 713-436-9999

2901 Clubhouse Drive
Pearland, TX 77584
Contact: Louis Gantz
Description: Playing this 7,015-yard
18-hole public course can be tough. A
Scottish links-style with water on 13
holes and lots of traps. Walking only on
weekdays. **Par:** 72.
Rentals: Golf Carts, Golf Clubs, Driving
Range

Open to the public. Walking permitted.

Fees:

Weekday: 18-hole: $35 Cart: (N/A)
9-hole: (N/A) Cart: (N/A)
Weekend: 18-hole: $44 Cart: (N/A)
9-hole: (N/A) Cart: (N/A)

Located off Hwy 288 east to FM 518.

Reeves County Golf Course   (6,132 yds) 915-447-2858

88 Starley Drive
Pecos, TX 79772
Contact: Royce Cassell
Description: The only 11-hole course
in Texas. The front nine is the original
nine and the back nine is 1-2 to 12-13
and 4, skip 5, and play on in. The
greens are small. Pro shop. **Par:** 70.
Rentals: Golf Carts, Pull Carts, Golf
Clubs, Driving Range

Open to the public. Walking permitted.
Golf lessons available.

Fees:

Weekday: 18-hole: $5 Cart: $8 9-hole:
(N/A) Cart: $3.15
Weekend: 18-hole: $7 Cart: $8 9-hole:
(N/A) Cart: $3.15

Located south of I-20.

Indian Oaks Golf Course   (5,208 yds) 903-498-3564

7574 Lee Lane
Peeltown, TX 75143
Contact: Ken Andrews
Description: A short 18-hole public course with lots of trees, water, no traps, and hills. Clubhouse has a snack bar and pro shop. Very unique setting. **Par:** 71.
Rentals: Golf Carts, Driving Range
Open to the public. Walking permitted.

Fees:

Weekday: 18-hole: $18.25 Cart: $5
9-hole: $6 Cart: (N/A)
Weekend: 18-hole: $25 Cart: (N/A)
9-hole: (N/A) Cart: (N/A)

Located off Hwy 148 eight miles from Kemp.

Perryton Municipal Golf Course   (6,431 yds) 806-435-5381

P.O. Box 707
Perryton, TX 79070
Contact: Tim Schiffelbein
Description: Being a long 18-hole semiprivate course makes this course tough, but it is more difficult thanks to thick rough, bentgrass greens, and out-of-bounds. Pro shop. **Par:** 72.
Rentals: Golf Carts, Pull Carts, Golf Clubs, Driving Range

Open to the public. Walking permitted.
Golf lessons available.

Fees:

Weekday: 18-hole: $8 Cart: $10
9-hole: (N/A) Cart: $3.50
Weekend: 18-hole: $11 Cart: $10
9-hole: (N/A) Cart: $3.50

Located off Hwy 83 on Hwy 143 South.

Blackhawk Golf Club   (7,100 yds) 512-251-9000

2714 Kelly Lane
Pflugerville, TX 78660
Contact: Chris Fox
Description: Even though this 18-hole public course is 7,100 yards long, it gets more difficult thanks to large three-putt bentgrass greens and water on 14 holes. Links-style next to an old dairy farm. Pro shop. **Par:** 72.
Rentals: Golf Carts, Golf Clubs, Driving Range

Open to the public. Walking permitted.
Golf lessons available.

Fees:

Weekday: 18-hole: $16 Cart: $9
9-hole: (N/A) Cart: $4.50
Weekend: 18-hole: $31 Cart: (N/A)
9-hole: (N/A) Cart: $4.50

Located in northeast Plugerville off FM 685 and Kelly Lane.

Plantation Country Club   (6,767 yds) 956-781-6613

2503 Palmer Drive
Pharr, TX 78577
Contact: Adolfo Moya
Description: It is real easy to lose golf balls on this 18-hole semiprivate course thanks to water on all 18 holes. No sand traps, undulating greens, and flat fairways. **Par:** 72.
Rentals: Golf Carts, Pull Carts, Golf Clubs, Driving Range

Open to the public. Walking permitted.

Fees:

Weekday: 18-hole: $13 Cart: $7
9-hole: $8 Cart: $4
Weekend: 18-hole: $15.16 Cart: $7
9-hole: $8 Cart: $4

Located south of town on Hwy 281 East.

Tropic Star Park   (3,038 yds) 956-787-5957

1401 S. Cage Blvd.
Pharr, TX 78577
Contact: Park Manager
Description: This nine-hole private par-3 course is part of a mobile home and RV vehicle park. Anybody renting a spot on RV vacation can play the course free. Holes are 70 to 150 yards. **Par:** 27.

Members and guests only. Walking permitted.

Fees:

Weekday: 18-hole: $2 Cart: (N/A)
9-hole: (N/A) Cart: (N/A)
Weekend: 18-hole: $2 Cart: (N/A)
9-hole: (N/A) Cart: (N/A)

Located south of town on Hwy 281.

Princedale Golf Club   (2,858 yds) 903-856-3737

Dangerfield Highway
Pittsburg, TX 75686
Contact: Barbara Milam
Description: A short nine-hole semiprivate course that does allow out-of-county golfers to play. It is a hilly course with trees and some water. **Par:** 36.
Rentals: Golf Carts
Open to the public. Walking permitted.

Fees:

Weekday: 18-hole: $14 Cart: $12
9-hole: (N/A) Cart: $6
Weekend: 18-hole: $20 Cart: $12
9-hole: (N/A) Cart: $6

Located on Hwy 11 seven miles east of Hwy 271.

Plainview Country Club

(6,287 yds) 806-293-2445

2902 W. Fourth Street
Plainview, TX 79072
Contact: Pete Peterson
Description: There are short par 4s and short par 5s on this 18-hole public course. A river and lake make up the difference as do small bentgrass greens. New clubhouse. **Par:** 71.
Rentals: Golf Carts, Pull Carts, Golf Clubs, Driving Range

Open to the public. Walking permitted. Golf lessons available.

Fees:

Weekday: 18-hole: $15.15 Cart: $10
9-hole: (N/A) Cart: $4.06
Weekend: 18-hole: $22.73 Cart: $10
9-hole: (N/A) Cart: $4.06

Located on West 4th St.

Chase Oaks Golf Club

(27 hs) 972-517-7777

7201 Chase Oaks Blvd.
Plano, TX 75025
Contact: Ann Sowieja
Blackjack Course Description: A 27-hole public course that is a very difficult public course in Dallas/Fort Worth. The Blackjack 18 course is a championship target golf course. **Par:** 72 (6,016 yards).

Sawtooth Course Description:
Playing the Sawtooth nine-hole course twice is like playing a full 18-hole course. The holes change on each nine with different tees. The clubhouse is

like a country club with a restaurant and pro shop. **Par:** 36 (6,782 yards).
Rentals: Golf Carts, Golf Clubs, Driving Range
Open to the public. Walking permitted. Golf lessons available.

Fees:

Weekday: 18-hole: $49 Cart: (N/A)
9-hole: (N/A) Cart: (N/A)
Weekend: 18-hole: $65 Cart: (N/A)
9-hole: (N/A) Cart: (N/A)

Located just west of U.S. 75 off exit 31 in north Plano.

Gleneagles Country Club

(36 hs) 972-867-8888

5401 W. Park Ave.
Plano, TX 75093
Contact: Grey Smith
Kings Course Description: A very difficult 36-hole private club. The Kings Course is a tough course with target greens and elevated, recently replanted greens. The clubhouse is one of the largest in Dallas/Fort Worth with a huge pro shop and a great locker room.
Par: 72 (6,707 yards).

Queens Course Description: The Queens Course is more difficult than the Kings. Both are target golf courses demanding perfect golf shots, but there is more water on the Queens Course.
Par: 71 (6,901 yards).

Rentals: Golf Carts, Golf Clubs, Driving Range
Members and guests only. Golf lessons available. Mandatory carts.

Fees:

Weekday: 18-hole: $81.18 Cart: (N/A)
9-hole: (N/A) Cart: (N/A)
Weekend: 18-hole: $97.43 Cart: (N/A)
9-hole: (N/A) Cart: (N/A)

Take Park exit off Dallas North Tollway. Turn right (east). Course is one mile down on left.

Los Rios Country Club

(6,507 yds) 972-424-8913

1700 Country Club Drive
Plano, TX 75074
Contact: Joe Hager
Description: An 18-hole semiprivate club in east Plano. Lots of water hazards make golf balls sleep with the fishes on this course. The par-35 front nine is tougher. Club has tennis courts, pool, restaurant, pro shop, and lockers.
Par: 71.
Rentals: Golf Carts, Golf Clubs, Driving Range

Members and guests only. Golf lessons available. Walking permitted.

Fees:

Weekday: 18-hole: $25 Cart: (N/A)
9-hole: (N/A) Cart: (N/A)
Weekend: 18-hole: $41 Cart: (N/A)
9-hole: (N/A) Cart: (N/A)

Located off 14th St. east of U.S. 75 (Central Expressway). Turn north on Los Rios Blvd.

Pecan Hollow Golf Course

(6,782 yds) 972-423-5444

4501 E. 14th St.
Plano, TX 75074
Contact: Steve Heidelberg
Description: The last three holes are 400-yard+ par 4s. It is possible to blow a good round after playing 15 somewhat easier holes. Good city golf. Clubhouse has snack bar and pro shop. **Par:** 72.
Rentals: Golf Carts, Pull Carts, Golf Clubs, Driving Range

Open to the public. Walking permitted. Golf lessons available.

Fees:

Weekday: 18-hole: $15 Cart: $9
9-hole: (N/A) Cart: (N/A)
Weekend: 18-hole: $19 Cart: $9
9-hole: (N/A) Cart: (N/A)

Located east of U.S. 75 on E. 14th St. (FM 544).

Ridgeview Ranch Golf Course

(7,025 yds) 972-390-1039

2701 Ridgeview Drive
Plano, TX 75025
Contact: Brett Fletcher
Description: New course co-owned by the City of Plano. Features hills, trees, and plenty of mounding; reminds golfer of a Hill Country layout. Local graveyard fronts one green. Carts required weekends/holidays. **Par:** 72.
Rentals: Golf Carts, Driving Range

Open to the public. Walking permitted. Golf lessons available.

Fees:

Weekday: 18-hole: $42 Cart: (N/A)
9-hole: (N/A) Cart: (N/A)
Weekend: 18-hole: $53 Cart: (N/A)
9-hole: (N/A) Cart: (N/A)

Take Custer north to Ridgeview Drive.

Pleasanton Country Club

(6,529 yds) 830-569-3486

1801 McGuffin Drive
Pleasanton, TX 78064
Contact: Mike Yanity
Description: The oak trees on this 18-hole semiprivate course are 300 years old and tighten up the fairways. A new nine was opened in March 1994 to make it an 18-hole course. Lots of water. **Par:** 72.
Rentals: Golf Carts, Pull Carts

Open to the public. Walking permitted.

Fees:

Weekday: 18-hole: $14.95 Cart: $7.50 9-hole: $8 Cart: $6
Weekend: 18-hole: $17.10 Cart: $7.50 9-hole: $10 Cart: $6

Located on Hwy 97.

Babe Zaharias Golf Course   (6,827 yds) 409-722-8286

3500 Jimmy Johnson Blvd
Port Arthur, TX 77642
Contact: Ed Campbell
Description: Wind causes problems on
this links-style 18-hole public course,
but the fairways are wide with large
greens. No sand traps and water only
on nine holes. Good clubhouse. **Par:**
72.
Rentals: Golf Carts, Pull Carts, Golf
Clubs, Driving Range

Open to the public. Walking permitted.
Golf lessons available.

Fees:

Weekday: 18-hole: $7.50 Cart: $8
9-hole: (N/A) Cart: $5
Weekend: 18-hole: $9.40 Cart: $8
9-hole: (N/A) Cart: $5

Located on 75th St. off Hwy 69.

Port Arthur Country Club   (6,755 yds) 409-796-1311

P.O. Box 486
Port Arthur, TX 77640
Contact: Tommy Eller
Description: The public is allowed to
play this 18-hole semiprivate course on
Mondays only. Taylor's Bayou runs
through eight holes. There are pine
trees, small greens, and sand traps.
Food. **Par:** 72.
Rentals: Golf Carts, Pull Carts, Golf
Clubs, Driving Range

Open to the public. Walking permitted.
Golf lessons available.

Fees:

Weekday: 18-hole: $15 Cart: $8
9-hole: $7.50 Cart: $4
Weekend: 18-hole: $20 Cart: $8
9-hole: $10 Cart: $4

Located west on Hwy 73.

Bentwood Golf Club   (6,903 yds) 281-354-GOLF

19980 Bentwood Oaks Drive
Porter, TX 77365
Contact: Phil Davis
Description: Challenging and scenic
semipublic course located just north of
Houston. Former site of Doug Sanders
celebrity event. Features 58 traps,
water on five holes. Look for giant
clock tower at entrance. **Par:** 72.
Open to the public. Walking permitted.

Fees:

Weekday: 18-hole: $30 Cart: $10
9-hole: (N/A) Cart: (N/A)
Weekend: 18-hole: $40 Cart: $10
9-hole: (N/A) Cart: (N/A)

Located on Hwy 59 between Kingwood
and FM 1314 exits.

Jim Paul Golf Course ### (1,100 yds) 210-943-3131

Garcia Street
Port Isabel, TX 78578
Contact: Golf Shop
Description: The former outdoor
Executive par-3 course is now a nice
18-hole par-3 course with four lakes,
palm trees, and holes ranging from 44
to 146 yards. Most are 90 to 110
yards. **Par:** 54.
Rentals: Golf Clubs

Open to the public. Walking permitted.

Fees:

Weekday: 18-hole: $6.50 Cart: (N/A)
9-hole: (N/A) Cart: (N/A)
Weekend: 18-hole: $6.50 Cart: (N/A)
9-hole: (N/A) Cart: (N/A)

Located on Garcia St.

South Padre Island Country Club ### (6,931 yds) 956-943-5678

1 Golf House Road
Port Isabel, TX 78578
Contact: Brent Goodger
Description: First 18-hole course
located on South Padre Island. Several
holes border causeway with view of Gulf
of Mexico in background. Plenty of
sand, water, and palm trees with great
scenery everywhere. **Par:** 72.
Rentals: Golf Carts, Driving Range

Open to the public. Walking permitted.
Golf lessons available.

Fees:

Weekday: 18-hole: $40 Cart: $9
9-hole: $24 Cart: $9
Weekend: 18-hole: $45 Cart: $9
9-hole: $27 Cart: $9

Located off South Padre Causeway.

North Shore Country Club ### (6,800 yds) 512-643-1546

801 E. Broadway
Portland, TX 78374
Contact: Damon Solle
Description: A dramatic 18-hole
private course with four holes on the
back nine running along Corpus Christi
Bay. Former site of the Nike Tour South
Texas Open. Out-of-town golfers
welcome. **Par:** 72.

Rentals: Golf Carts, Golf Clubs, Driving
Range
Members and guests only. Golf lessons
available. Walking permitted.

Fees:

Weekday: 18-hole: $38 Cart: $15
9-hole: (N/A) Cart: $8
Weekend: 18-hole: $50 Cart: $15
9-hole: (N/A) Cart: $8

Located on Hwy 181 North.

Hatch Bend Country Club

(3,300 yds) 512-552-3037

Meadow Lane
Port Lavaca, TX 77979
Contact: John Jones
Description: A simple nine-hole
semiprivate course. It has normal
double tees to play 18 holes. The
fairways are narrow with lots of trees,
but the course is not long. **Par:** 36.
Rentals: Golf Carts, Pull Carts

Open to the public. Walking permitted.

Fees:

Weekday: 18-hole: $10.68 Cart:
$8.01 9-hole: (N/A) Cart: $3.75
Weekend: 18-hole: $10.68 Cart:
$8.01 9-hole: (N/A) Cart: $3.75

Located south of town on Hwy 35.

Caprock Golf Course

(5,700 yds) 806-495-3029

Cleche Road
Post, TX 79356
Contact: Pro Shop
Description: Golfers face a lot of blind
tee shots on this nine-hole public course
because of strong hills. No traps, small
greens, and water. Pro shop. **Par:** 35.
Rentals: Golf Carts, Pull Carts, Golf
Clubs, Driving Range

Open to the public. Walking permitted.
Golf lessons available.

Fees:

Weekday: 18-hole: $7 Cart: $9 9-hole:
(N/A) Cart: $3.50
Weekend: 18-hole: $10 Cart: $9
9-hole: (N/A) Cart: $3.50

Located northwest of Post on Hwy 84.

Tanglewood Resort

(7,001 yds) 903-786-2968

Tanglewood Drive
Pottsboro, TX 75076
Contact: Mike Fish
Description: A go-for-broke course
with water and traps. Resort has rooms,
villa, and restaurants. Great views of
Lake Texoma from elevated greens.
Par: 72.
Rentals: Golf Carts, Golf Clubs, Driving
Range
Open to the public. Walking permitted.
Golf lessons available.

Fees:

Weekday: 18-hole: $44 Cart: (N/A)
9-hole: (N/A) Cart: (N/A)
Weekend: 18-hole: $55 Cart: (N/A)
9-hole: (N/A) Cart: (N/A)

Located north of Dallas; take U.S. 75
north to Denison and go west on Hwy
120 then follow signs.

Quanah Country Club
(3,200 yds) 940-663-2069

P.O. Box 86
Quanah, TX 79252
Contact: Mike Lamberton
Description: In order to shoot a good score on this short nine-hole private course, golfers must two-putt the large bentgrass greens. Double tees make for 18 holes. **Par:** 36.
Rentals: Driving Range

Members and guests only. Walking permitted.

Fees:

Weekday: 18-hole: $12 Cart: $9
9-hole: (N/A) Cart: (N/A)
Weekend: 18-hole: $25 Cart: $9
9-hole: (N/A) Cart: (N/A)

Located off Hwy 287 northeast of town.

Tawakoni Golf Club
(6,691 yds) 903-447-2981

Highway 276
Quinlan, TX 75474
Contact: John Lively
Description: This 18-hole semiprivate course is along Lake Tawakoni, but the lake doesn't come into play. There are water hazards on six holes, and the fairways are wide and flat. Watery clubhouse views. **Par:** 72.
Rentals: Golf Carts, Pull Carts, Golf Clubs, Driving Range

Open to the public. Walking permitted. Golf lessons available.

Fees:

Weekday: 18-hole: $10 Cart: $8
9-hole: (N/A) Cart: $4
Weekend: 18-hole: $20 Cart: $8
9-hole: (N/A) Cart: $4

From Terrell, take Hwy 34 north to Hwy 276. Turn right on Hwy 276 for 8½ miles.

Rancho Viejo Resort & Country Club (6,847 yds) 956-350-4359

1 Rancho Viejo Drive
Rancho Viejo, TX 78575
Contact: Robert Lindsay
El Diablo Course Description: The El Diablo Course is more difficult than the El Angel. The front nine plays into the strong wind, there is more water, and the course is longer. Great resort setting. **Par:** 70.

Rentals: Golf Carts, Driving Range
Open to the public. Golf lessons available. Mandatory carts.

Fees:

Weekday: 18-hole: $40 Cart: $12
9-hole: $20 Cart: $6
Weekend: 18-hole: $40 Cart: $12
9-hole: $20 Cart: $6

Rancho Viejo Resort & Country Club (6,518 yds) 956-350-4359

1 Ranch Viejo Drive
Rancho Viejo, TX 78575
Contact: Robert Lindsay
El Angel Course Description: A
36-hole resort/private club. Resort
guests and members of USGA country
clubs are welcome. The El Angel Course
is links-style with wide open fairways.
There is strong wind and out-of-bounds.
Par: 70.
Rentals: Golf Carts, Golf Clubs, Driving
Range

Members and guests only. Golf lessons
available. Mandatory carts.

Fees:

Weekday: 18-hole: $40 Cart: $12
9-hole: $20 Cart: $6
Weekend: 18-hole: $40 Cart: $12
9-hole: $20 Cart: $6

Located 15 miles north of town on Hwy
77, follow signs to course.

Randolph Oaks AFB Golf Course (7,172 yds) 210-652-4653

P.O. Box 188
Bldg 1300
Randolph AFB, TX 78148
Contact: Ed Schieber
Description: A 7,172-yard 18-hole
military course that has lots of water,
trees, and elevated greens. The fairways
are flat and there is not much rough.
Food and pro shop. **Par:** 72.
Rentals: Golf Carts, Pull Carts, Golf
Clubs, Driving Range

Members and guests only. Walking
permitted.

Fees:

Weekday: 18-hole: $9 Cart: $7.50
9-hole: (N/A) Cart: $4
Weekend: 18-hole: $10 Cart: $7.50
9-hole: (N/A) Cart: $4

Located east of San Antonio off I-10
east on Anderson Loop (1604) north.

Rankin Country Club (6,235 yds) 915-693-2834

Highway 67
Rankin, TX 79778
Contact: Golf Shop
Description: Like all rural West Texas
nine-hole semiprivate courses, the wind
can make this course play rather tough.
It has double tees to set up a decent
18-hole round. **Par:** 36.
Open to the public. Walking permitted.

Fees:

Weekday: 18-hole: $4 Cart: (N/A)
9-hole: (N/A) Cart: (N/A)
Weekend: 18-hole: $6 Cart: (N/A)
9-hole: (N/A) Cart: (N/A)

Located off Hwy 67 on Midland Truck
Road.

Raymondville Municipal Golf Course (5,980 yds) 956-689-9904

142 S. 7th St.
Raymondville, TX 78580
Contact: Benny Serna
Description: To shoot a good score on this short nine-hole public course, golfers must avoid tricky putts on the large greens not protected by sandtraps. Flat, open fairways. **Par:** 36.
Rentals: Golf Carts, Pull Carts, Driving Range

Open to the public. Walking permitted.

Fees:

Weekday: 18-hole: $4.78 Cart: $8.50
9-hole: (N/A) Cart: $4.19
Weekend: 18-hole: $5.84 Cart: $8.50
9-hole: (N/A) Cart: $4.19

Located on Business Hwy 77 South.

Red Oak Valley Golf Course (5,911 yds) 972-617-3249

Route 1
P.O. Box 801
Red Oak, TX 75154
Contact: Monty Kelton
Description: A short 18-hole public course that has lots of wide fairways, no sand traps, and bermuda grass greens. Hilly holes play longer. **Par:** 70.
Rentals: Golf Carts, Pull Carts, Golf Clubs, Driving Range

Open to the public. Walking permitted.

Fees:

Weekday: 18-hole: $8 Cart: $8 9-hole: (N/A) Cart: $8.50
Weekend: 18-hole: $12 Cart: $8
9-hole: (N/A) Cart: $8.50

Located east of I-35E south of Dallas off exit 408. Visible from I-35.

Refugio County Country Club (2,904 yds) 512-526-5554

Woodsboro Highway
Refugio, TX 78377
Contact: Peggy Chambers
Description: Posting a good score is possible on this nine-hole semiprivate course because it is short with no sand traps, wide fairways, and smaller greens. Water on six holes. **Par:** 35.
Rentals: Golf Carts, Pull Carts

Open to the public. Walking permitted.

Fees:

Weekday: 18-hole: $7 Cart: $7 9-hole: (N/A) Cart: $3.50
Weekend: 18-hole: $10 Cart: $7
9-hole: (N/A) Cart: $3.50

Located on Hwy 77 South.

Canyon Creek Country Club
(6,648 yds) 972-231-3083

625 Lookout Drive
Richardson, TX 75080
Contact: Matt Sanders
Description: A good score will be on the front nine. The back nine is hilly and tight. Club has food, drinks, tennis, and pro shop. **Par:** 70.
Rentals: Golf Carts, Golf Clubs, Driving Range

Members and guests only. Golf lessons available. Mandatory carts.

Fees:

Weekday: 18-hole: $25 Cart: $21
9-hole: (N/A) Cart: $7
Weekend: 18-hole: $50 Cart: $21
9-hole: (N/A) Cart: $7

Located 2 miles west of U.S. 75 between Campbell Rd. and Renner Rd.

Practice Tee
(1,050 yds) 972-235-6540

2950 Waterview
Richardson, TX 75080
Contact: Kevin Bleiler
Description: A perfect facility to improve your golf game. Good lessons on the driving range and a nice par 3 to help your short game. **Par:** 27.
Rentals: Golf Clubs, Driving Range
Open to the public. Walking permitted. Golf lessons available.

Fees:

Weekday: 18-hole: $11 Cart: (N/A)
9-hole: $6 Cart: (N/A)
Weekend: 18-hole: $14 Cart: (N/A)
9-hole: $8 Cart: (N/A)

Located on Waterview Drive north of Campbell Road and next to UT-Dallas.

Sherrill Park Golf Course — (36 hs) 972-234-1416

2001 E. Lookout Drive
Richardson, TX 75082
Contact: Ronny Glanton
Course No. 1 Description: Excellent 36-hole public course with tough trees and mounds. No. 1 course was totally redone for fall 1997. **Par:** 72 (6,800 yards).

Course No. 2 Description: The second 18 is shorter than the first 18 but has more water hazards and tighter fairways. Clubhouse has a snack bar and pro shop. Redesigned course opens with par 3. Very interesting public golf. **Par:** 70 (6,083 yards).

Rentals: Golf Carts, Pull Carts, Golf Clubs, Driving Range
Open to the public. Walking permitted. Golf lessons available.

Fees:

Weekday: 18-hole: $22 Cart: $10
9-hole: $14 Cart: $8
Weekend: 18-hole: $30 Cart: $10
9-hole: $17 Cart: $8

Located east of U.S. 75, take Campbell Rd. east to Jupiter Rd. then north.

Fort Bend Country Club — (6,346 yds) 281-342-8368

P.O. Box 126
Richmond, TX 77469
Contact: Eddie Carter
Description: An old-style 18-hole private course designed in 1952 with narrow fairways lined with pecan trees. The greens are small. Food and a pro shop. **Par:** 71.
Rentals: Golf Carts, Driving Range

Members and guests only. Golf lessons available. Walking permitted.

Fees:

Weekday: 18-hole: $16.50 Cart: $7.50 9-hole: (N/A) Cart: $3.25
Weekend: 18-hole: $22.50 Cart: $7.50 9-hole: (N/A) Cart: $3.25

Located on Hwy 59 eight miles south of Sugar Land.

Old Orchard Golf Club

(27 hs) 281-277-3300

13134 FM 1464 Road
Richmond, TX 77469
Contact: Jackie Montgomery
Description: There is quite a difference among the three nines on this 27-hole public course. The Stables and Barns nines are long with pecan trees and water. The Range nine is open links-style. Great variety. **Par:** 72.
Rentals: Golf Carts, Golf Clubs, Driving Range

Open to the public. Walking permitted. Golf lessons available.

Fees:

Weekday: 18-hole: $40 Cart: (N/A)
9-hole: (N/A) Cart: (N/A)
Weekend: 18-hole: $50 Cart: (N/A)
9-hole: (N/A) Cart: (N/A)

Take U.S. 59 to Hwy 6, west to Hwy 90, then left on FM 1464 and right to club entrance.

Pecan Grove Plantation Country Club

(27 hs) 281-342-9940

3000 Plantation Drive
Richmond, TX 77469
Contact: John Saffle
Description: All three nines on this 27-hole private course are tough. Playing the Plantation and Grove nines is more than 7,000 yards long. The Pecan nine is short with wide traps. Out-of-bounds on all 27 holes. **Par:** 72.
Rentals: Golf Carts, Golf Clubs, Driving Range

Members and guests only. Golf lessons available. Walking permitted.

Fees:

Weekday: 18-hole: $25 Cart: $10
9-hole: (N/A) Cart: $5
Weekend: 18-hole: $35 Cart: $10
9-hole: (N/A) Cart: $5

Located southwest of Houston, Hwy 59 to Hwy 90, eight miles to FM 359.

Lakewood Recreation Center

(5,748 yds) 254-643-7792

Route 1
Rising Star, TX 76471
Contact: Bruce Rivers
Description: Even though this nine-hole public course is short, with oak trees and water hazards on five holes, it plays tougher. Also, bentgrass greens are fast. **Par:** 36.
Rentals: Golf Carts, Pull Carts, Golf Clubs

Open to the public. Walking permitted. Golf lessons available.

Fees:

Weekday: 18-hole: $8 Cart: $12
9-hole: (N/A) Cart: $8
Weekend: 18-hole: $10 Cart: $12
9-hole: (N/A) Cart: $8

Located six miles east of Cross Plains on Hwy 36.

Rising Star Golf Club

(6,342 yds) 254-643-4653

Country Road 266 South
Rising Star, TX 76471
Contact: Pat McManus
Description: New public 18-hole layout
with gently rolling terrain, water, trees
and bentgrass greens. Very scenic
location in Central Texas area. **Par:** 72.
Rentals: Golf Carts, Driving Range
Open to the public.

Fees:

Weekday: 18-hole: $10 Cart: $7
9-hole: (N/A) Cart: (N/A)
Weekend: 18-hole: $14 Cart: $7
9-hole: (N/A) Cart: (N/A)

Two miles south of Rising Star off
Country Road 266; visible from
highway.

Roaring Springs Ranch Golf Club   (5,856 yds) 806-348-7267

P.O. Box 71
Roaring Springs, TX 79256
Contact: Gary Smith
Description: A very popular nine-hole
private course because it is short with
no water or traps, and extra large
bentgrass greens. Three-putts are
common and can blow up the score.
Pro shop. **Par:** 36.
Rentals: Golf Carts, Pull Carts

Members and guests only. Walking
permitted.

Fees:

Weekday: 18-hole: $11 Cart: $20
9-hole: (N/A) Cart: $10
Weekend: 18-hole: $12 Cart: $20
9-hole: (N/A) Cart: $10

South on Hwy 70 two to three miles.

Mountain Creek Golf Club

(2,856 yds) 915-453-2317

P.O. Box 700
Robert Lee, TX 76945
Contact: Jessie Flores
Description: A short nine-hole public
course that has trees on flat fairways.
Golfers must hit over a creek on three
holes, and double tees make an 18-hole
round better. Snacks. **Par:** 36.
Rentals: Golf Carts, Golf Clubs, Driving
Range

Open to the public. Walking permitted.
Golf lessons available.

Fees:

Weekday: 18-hole: $7 Cart: $8 9-hole:
(N/A) Cart: $4
Weekend: 18-hole: $12 Cart: $8
9-hole: (N/A) Cart: $4

Located west of Hwy 280 and Hwy
158.

Rockdale Country Club   (6,459 yds) 512-446-4013

P.O. Box 166
Rockdale, TX 76567
Contact: Jim Barton
Description: A typical nine-hole rural Texas course with no sand traps, three water hazards, and large greens. Fairways are wide. Food, drinks, and pro shop. **Par:** 36.
Rentals: Golf Carts, Driving Range

Members and guests only. Golf lessons available. Walking permitted.

Fees:

Weekday: 18-hole: $9 Cart: $8.50
9-hole: (N/A) Cart: $6
Weekend: 18-hole: $12.50 Cart: $8.50 9-hole: (N/A) Cart: $6

Located west of Bryan on Hwy 79.

Live Oak Country Club   (5,908 yds) 512-729-8551

318 Country Club Drive
Rockport, TX 78336
Contact: Tim Tillman
Description: A simple nine-hole rural Texas private course with flat fairways slightly protected by oak trees. Only two water hazards and two sand traps. Small greens. **Par:** 36.
Rentals: Golf Carts, Pull Carts, Golf Clubs, Driving Range

Members and guests only. Walking permitted.

Fees:

Weekday: 18-hole: $15 Cart: $7
9-hole: (N/A) Cart: (N/A)
Weekend: 18-hole: $20 Cart: $7
9-hole: (N/A) Cart: (N/A)

Located off FM 881 West.

Rockport Country Club   (6,439 yds) 512-729-4182

101 Champion Drive
Rockport, TX 78382
Contact: Thane Emerson
Description: The best course in the area. This 18-hole private course has water on 14 holes, lots of trees, and sand traps protecting large and small greens. Food, drinks, pro shop, and swimming. **Par:** 71.
Rentals: Golf Carts, Golf Clubs, Driving Range

Members and guests only. Golf lessons available. Walking permitted.

Fees:

Weekday: 18-hole: $50 Cart: (N/A)
9-hole: (N/A) Cart: (N/A)
Weekend: 18-hole: $50 Cart: (N/A)
9-hole: (N/A) Cart: (N/A)

Located on Hwy 35.

Rocksprings Country Club

(5,863 yds) 830-683-4224

P.O. Box 175
Rocksprings, TX 78880
Contact: Charles Carson
Description: The only sand green golf course in Texas. The greens are round and have a carpet strip to putt on. It is a unique nine-hole course open to out-of-town golfers. **Par:** 36.
Rentals: Golf Carts, Driving Range

Members and guests only. Walking permitted.

Fees:

Weekday: 18-hole: (N/A) Cart: (N/A)
9-hole: (N/A) Cart: (N/A)
Weekend: 18-hole: (N/A) Cart: (N/A)
9-hole: (N/A) Cart: (N/A)

Located six miles south of Rocksprings on Hwy 55, turn right past the airport.

Buffalo Creek Golf Club

(7,018 yds) 972-771-4003

300 Country Club Drive
P.O. Box 910
Rockwall, TX 75087
Contact: Mick Griffin
Description: One of the best public courses in the Dallas area. Water hazards and long holes make for challenges. A Weiskopf/Morrish design opened in 1992. **Par:** 71.
Rentals: Golf Carts, Golf Clubs, Driving Range

Open to the public. Walking permitted. Golf lessons available.

Fees:

Weekday: 18-hole: $59.50 Cart: (N/A)
9-hole: (N/A) Cart: (N/A)
Weekend: 18-hole: $79.50 Cart: (N/A)
9-hole: (N/A) Cart: (N/A)

Located east of I-30 in Rockwall off Ridge Road.

Shores Country Club

(7,138 yds) 972-771-0301

2600 Champion Drive
Rockwall, TX 75087
Contact: Rusty Locke
Description: A neat 18-hole course constructed on the side of Lake Ray Hubbard. Water hazards are on 14 holes. Clubhouse has restaurant, bar, lockers, and pro shop. **Par:** 72.
Rentals: Golf Carts, Golf Clubs, Driving Range

Open to the public. Walking permitted. Golf lessons available.

Fees:

Weekday: 18-hole: $35 Cart: (N/A)
9-hole: (N/A) Cart: (N/A)
Weekend: 18-hole: $45 Cart: (N/A)
9-hole: (N/A) Cart: (N/A)

Located north of Rockwall on Hwy 205.

Brazoria Bend Golf Club

(6,480 yds) 281-431-2954

2315 County Road 57
Rosharon, TX 77583
Contact: Ron Hollowell
Description: This nine-hole public course is not very long but has pine trees guarding narrow fairways, large three-putt greens, triple tees, no sand traps, and one water hazard. Senior discounts. **Par:** 36.
Rentals: Golf Carts, Pull Carts, Golf Clubs, Driving Range

Open to the public. Walking permitted. Golf lessons available.

Fees:

Weekday: 18-hole: $9 Cart: $7.50
9-hole: (N/A) Cart: $4.75
Weekend: 18-hole: $12 Cart: $7.50
9-hole: (N/A) Cart: $4.75

Located on Hwy 288.

Forest Creek Golf Club

(7,084 yds) 512-388-2874

99 Twin Ridge Road
Round Rock, TX 78664
Contact: Lindsay Bowman
Description: A real long, 7,084-yard 18-hole course north of Austin. Good test with plenty of traps, trees, water, and mounds. Simple clubhouse with food and pro shop. **Par:** 72.
Rentals: Golf Carts, Golf Clubs, Driving Range

Open to the public. Walking permitted. Golf lessons available.

Fees:

Weekday: 18-hole: $39 Cart: (N/A)
9-hole: (N/A) Cart: (N/A)
Weekend: 18-hole: $50 Cart: (N/A)
9-hole: (N/A) Cart: (N/A)

Located 4½ miles east of I-35 off Hwy 79.

Aaki Ranch International

(6,327 yds) 972-636-2254

846 FM 2453
Royse City, TX 75189
Contact: Kirk Froelich
Description: New 18-hole champion-ship course open to public along with private memberships available. Several challenging holes include water, trees, and undulating greens. Don't overlook this small city gem. **Par:** 71.
Rentals: Golf Carts, Golf Clubs, Driving Range

Open to the public.

Fees:

Weekday: 18-hole: $15 Cart: $10
9-hole: (N/A) Cart: (N/A)
Weekend: 18-hole: $25 Cart: $10
9-hole: (N/A) Cart: (N/A)

Located seven miles east of Rockwall in Royse City; take FM 2453 east from Rockwall to course.

Birmingham Golf Club   (5,745 yds) 903-683-9518

P.O. Box 728
Rusk, TX 75785
Contact: Mark Raiborn
Description: There is a lake in the
middle of this nine-hole public course,
but it is not in play unless there are
some bad shots. The course is hilly and
the fairways narrow. Snacks. **Par:** 36.
Rentals: Golf Carts, Pull Carts, Golf
Clubs, Driving Range

Open to the public. Walking permitted.

Fees:

Weekday: 18-hole: $10 Cart: $7
9-hole: (N/A) Cart: $5
Weekend: 18-hole: $14 Cart: $7
9-hole: (N/A) Cart: $5

Located on Hwy 84 South.

Mill Creek Golf & Country Club   (6,486 yds) 800-736-3441

1401 S. Ridge Road
Salado, TX 76571
Contact: Mike Cameron
Description: One of the most beautiful
golf courses in Texas. Allows golfers
staying in the Mill Creek Inn to play.
Course designed by Robert Trent Jones
Jr. **Par:** 71.
Rentals: Golf Carts, Golf Clubs, Driving
Range

Members and guests only. Golf lessons
available. Mandatory carts.

Fees:

Weekday: 18-hole: $35 Cart: $12
9-hole: (N/A) Cart: $8
Weekend: 18-hole: $45 Cart: $12
9-hole: (N/A) Cart: $8

Take Salado exit 285 off I-35 and
follow signs.

Rayburn County Country Club   (27 hs) 800-882-1442

P.O. Drawer 100
Sam Rayburn, TX 75951
Contact: Lisa Barrow
Description: A very interesting 27-hole
resort course. The Green nine is the
shortest but most difficult, designed by
Bob von Hagge. Robert Trent Jones did
the Blue nine. The Gold nine has little
water, but sand on every hole. **Par:** 72.
Rentals: Golf Carts, Golf Clubs, Driving
Range

Open to the public. Walking permitted.

Fees:

Weekday: 18-hole: $31.88 Cart: (N/A)
9-hole: (N/A) Cart: $5
Weekend: 18-hole: $47.82 Cart: (N/A)
9-hole: (N/A) Cart: $5

Located off Hwy 96 on West Hwy 255.

Bentwood Country Club   (6,900 yds) 915-944-8575

2111 Clubhouse Lane
San Angelo, TX 76904
Contact: Kyle Kolls
Description: A good-looking 18-hole private course. Constructed next to houses that create lots of out-of-bounds. Course plays into the wind and the par 5s are downwind. Clubhouse. **Par:** 72.
Rentals: Golf Carts, Golf Clubs, Driving Range

Members and guests only. Golf lessons available. Walking permitted.

Fees:

Weekday: 18-hole: $20 Cart: $8.50
9-hole: (N/A) Cart: $4
Weekend: 18-hole: $30 Cart: $8.50
9-hole: (N/A) Cart: $4

Located southwest off Loop 306.

Quick Sand Golf Club   (7,171 yds) 915-482-8337

2305 Pulliam St.
San Angelo, TX 76905
Contact: Don Bryant
Description: Good public West Texas layout which opened in 1996. Architect was Michael Hartage, who placed water on three holes on both the front and back nines. Course name comes from 105 bunkers on 18 holes. **Par:** 72.
Rentals: Golf Carts, Pull Carts, Golf Clubs, Driving Range

Open to the public. Walking permitted. Golf lessons available.

Fees:

Weekday: 18-hole: $25 Cart: $9
9-hole: (N/A) Cart: (N/A)
Weekend: 18-hole: $28 Cart: $9
9-hole: (N/A) Cart: (N/A)

Located on Pulliam St., north of downtown.

Riverside Golf Club   (6,356 yds) 915-653-6130

2600 N. Randolph
San Angelo, TX 76903
Contact: Joey Allen
Description: Posting a good score is very possible on this neat 18-hole public course because the fairways are flat and there are no sand traps. However, a golfer must keep the ball dry. **Par:** 72.
Rentals: Golf Carts, Pull Carts, Golf Clubs, Driving Range

Open to the public. Walking permitted. Golf lessons available.

Fees:

Weekday: 18-hole: $9 Cart: $6.50
9-hole: (N/A) Cart: $4
Weekend: 18-hole: $12 Cart: $6.50
9-hole: (N/A) Cart: $4

Located off Hwy 87 North on W. 29th St.

San Angelo Country Club — (6,600 yds) 915-655-3144

1609 Country Club Road
San Angelo, TX 76904
Contact: Steve Wheelis
Description: Golfers are forced to hit a lot of layup tee shots on this 18-hole private course because of two creeks running through the course and hilly fairways. Boat harbor for fun. **Par:** 71
Rentals: Golf Clubs, Driving Range

Members and guests only. Golf lessons available. Walking permitted.

Fees:

Weekday: 18-hole: $35 Cart: $8.62
9-hole: (N/A) Cart: $4.31
Weekend: 18-hole: $50 Cart: $8.62
9-hole: (N/A) Cart: $4.31

Located on U.S. Hwy 87.

Santa Fe Park Golf Course — (5,200 yds) 915-651-7227

111 River Road
San Angelo, TX 76902
Contact: Mike Terrazas
Description: A short nine-hole executive course next to Concho River. No traps protecting small greens but there are big trees and out-of-bounds. No tee time required. **Par:** 34.
Rentals: Pull Carts

Open to the public. Walking permitted. Golf lessons available.

Fees:

Weekday: 18-hole: $5 Cart: (N/A)
9-hole: (N/A) Cart: (N/A)
Weekend: 18-hole: $7 Cart: (N/A)
9-hole: (N/A) Cart: (N/A)

Located on Business Hwy 67 in center of town.

Alamo Country Club — (4,515 yds) 210-696-4000

9700 Rochelle Road
San Antonio, TX 78240
Contact: Mac Wylie
Description: Popular par-3 layout to go with outstanding practice facility. Only double-decker driving range in South Texas. Course offers chance for golfers to work on short game with range and good par 3s plus par 4s.
Par: 65.
Rentals: Pull Carts, Driving Range

Open to the public. Walking permitted. Golf lessons available.

Fees:

Weekday: 18-hole: $18 Cart: $8
9-hole: (N/A) Cart: (N/A)
Weekend: 18-hole: $18 Cart: $8
9-hole: (N/A) Cart: (N/A)

Located off Babcock Road 1 1/2 miles northwest of Huebner Road.

Brackenridge Golf Course
(6,182 yds) 210-226-5612

2315 Avenue B
San Antonio, TX 78215
Contact: Richard Holcott
Description: The most historic course in Texas. First public 18 holes, first grass greens. Site of first PGA Texas Open, Mike Souchak's all-time 72 PGA scoring record. Clubhouse is a living golf museum. Worth a trip! **Par:** 72.
Rentals: Golf Carts, Pull Carts

Open to the public. Walking permitted.

Fees:

Weekday: 18-hole: $14 Cart: $18
9-hole: (N/A) Cart: $4.75
Weekend: 18-hole: $17 Cart: $18
9-hole: (N/A) Cart: $9

Located one block off Broadway near downtown.

Brooks AFB Golf Club
(3,387 yds) 210-536-2140

Bldg 821
Brooks AFB
San Antonio, TX 78235
Contact: Al Beck
Description: A nice nine-hole military course that has double tees and short par 4s and par 5s. The fairways are wide open, and the greens are bentgrass. Senior discount. Food and pro shop. **Par:** 36.

Rentals: Golf Carts, Pull Carts, Golf Clubs, Driving Range
Members and guests only. Golf lessons available. Walking permitted.

Fees:

Weekday: 18-hole: $12 Cart: $7
9-hole: $7 Cart: $3.50
Weekend: 18-hole: $14 Cart: $7
9-hole: $10 Cart: $3.50

Take I-37 to Military Drive.

Canyon Springs
(7,077 yds) 210-497-1770

24400 Canyon Golf Road
San Antonio, TX 78258
Contact: Terry Olivarri
Description: Beautiful new course carved out of the San Antonio Hill Country. Located on highest point of land in San Antonio with every hole presenting a new view of surroundings. Large, undulated greens allow good putters to excel. Great daily-fee

adventure, best new addition of '98. **Par:** 72.

Fees:

Weekday: 18-hole: $80 Cart: included
9-hole: (N/A) Cart: (N/A)
Weekend: 18-hole: $90 Cart: included
9-hole: (N/A) Cart: (N/A)

North of Hwy 1604, take Stone Oak exit, go north three miles, and take left on Evans to Canyon Springs development.

Cedar Creek Municipal Golf Course (7,158 yds) 210-695-5050

8250 Vista Colina
San Antonio, TX 78255
Contact: Steve Lennon
Description: A very long 18-hole public course that has up and down fairways with mounds. Great views and great golf bargin for a city-owned course. Easy to lose balls. **Par:** 72.
Rentals: Golf Carts, Pull Carts, Golf Clubs, Driving Range

Open to the public. Walking permitted. Golf lessons available.

Fees:

Weekday: 18-hole: $18 Cart: $9
9-hole: (N/A) Cart: $5
Weekend: 18-hole: $21 Cart: $9
9-hole: (N/A) Cart: $5

> Located off Loop 1604 on Kyle Seale Parkway.

Club at Sonterra (36 hs) 210-491-9900

901 Sonterra
San Antonio, TX 78258
Contact: Gary Bailey
Sunburst Course Description: A 36-hole club with target golf courses. Sunburst Course is the toughest of the two. Target golf design by Devlin/von Haage. Very pretty and very challenging with elevated par 3 over pond. **Par:** 72 (7,070 yards).

Deer Canyon Course Description:
Deer Canyon is shorter but very tight with trees and plenty of sand. No water. Great private course combination. **Par:** 72 (6,535 yards).

Rentals: Golf Carts, Golf Clubs, Driving Range
Members and guests only. Golf lessons available. Mandatory carts.

Fees:

Weekday: 18-hole: $50 Cart: $12
9-hole: (N/A) Cart: (N/A)
Weekend: 18-hole: $55 Cart: $12
9-hole: (N/A) Cart: (N/A)

> Located ½ mile north of Loop 1604. Take Stone Oak Parkway exit; course is one mile west of Hwy 281.

Dominion Country Club   (6,785 yds) 210-698-1146

One Dominion Drive
San Antonio, TX 78257
Contact: Marc DeWall
Description: Ranked as the best
clubhouse in Texas, The Dominion hosts
a Senior PGA Tour event. Clubhouse
has to be seen to believed, but it's
luxury at its very best. **Par:** 72.
Rentals: Golf Carts, Golf Clubs, Driving
Range

Members and guests only. Golf lessons
available. Mandatory carts.

Fees:

Weekday: 18-hole: $75 Cart: $10
9-hole: $100 Cart: $15
Weekend: 18-hole: $75 Cart: $10
9-hole: $100 Cart: $15

Take I-10 west to Leon Springs exit.

Gateway Hills Golf Course   (6,917 yds) 210-671-3466

Bldg 2901
Lackland AFB
San Antonio, TX 78236
Contact: Judy Stillman
Description: A reasonably long
18-hole military course that is hilly with
lots of sand traps, large greens, and
plenty of trees. Water is only on two
holes. Food. **Par:** 72.
Rentals: Golf Carts, Pull Carts, Golf
Clubs, Driving Range

Members and guests only. Golf lessons
available. Walking permitted.

Fees:

Weekday: 18-hole: $15 Cart: $7
9-hole: $8 Cart: $4
Weekend: 18-hole: $18 Cart: $7
9-hole: $10 Cart: $5

Located on Lackland AFB off Military
Drive.

Hill Country Golf Club   (6,913 yds) 210-647-1234

9800 Hyatt Resort Drive
San Antonio, TX 78251
Contact: Bud Zius
Description: Very nice Texas golf
resort with a long, challenging course.
Very pretty layout, especially in the
spring. Plenty of mounding, high rough,
water, and cactus. **Par:** 72.
Rentals: Golf Carts, Golf Clubs, Driving
Range

Open to the public. Walking permitted.
Golf lessons available.

Fees:

Weekday: 18-hole: $100 Cart: (N/A)
9-hole: $50 Cart: (N/A)
Weekend: 18-hole: $100 Cart: (N/A)
9-hole: $55 Cart: (N/A)

Go west on Hwy 151. Club is on access
road past Westover Hills Blvd.

Kelly AFB Golf Course (6,869 yds) 210-977-5100

Bldg 871
Kelly AFB
San Antonio, TX 78241
Contact: Frank Hurt
Description: A somewhat long 18-hole military course with lots of water, trees on the front nine, sand traps, and mounds on the back nine. Some holes play off of tall hills to wide fairways. **Par:** 72.
Rentals: Golf Carts, Pull Carts, Golf Clubs, Driving Range

Members and guests only. Walking permitted.

Fees:

Weekday: 18-hole: $14 Cart: $7
9-hole: $7 Cart: $5
Weekend: 18-hole: $14 Cart: $7
9-hole: $7 Cart: $5

Take I-37 south, exit McClelland to Kelly AFB main gate.

La Cantera Golf Club (7,135 yds) 800-446-5387

16641 La Cantera Parkway
San Antonio, TX 78256
Contact: Mike Soltau
Description: Site of PGA's La Cantera Texas Open. Named best new course in America by *Golf Digest* for 1995. Sweeping views of Hill Country and downtown San Antonio. Great public course pampering. **Par:** 72.
Rentals: Golf Carts, Golf Clubs, Driving Range

Open to the public. Golf lessons available. Mandatory carts.

Fees:

Weekday: 18-hole: $95 Cart: (N/A)
9-hole: (N/A) Cart: (N/A)
Weekend: 18-hole: $105 Cart: (N/A)
9-hole: (N/A) Cart: (N/A)

From downtown, take I-10 west to La Cantera Pkwy, then left 1.2 miles.

Mission Del Lago Municipal G.C. (7,007 yds) 210-627-2522

P.O. Box 14526
San Antonio, TX 78214-0526
Contact: Rubin Cedillo
Description: A links-style 18-hole public course that has wide open fairways. It is a very long course with 125 sand traps, 11 water hazards, and greens that are elevated. **Par:** 72.
Rentals: Golf Carts, Pull Carts, Golf Clubs, Driving Range

Open to the public. Walking permitted. Golf lessons available.

Fees:

Weekday: 18-hole: $14 Cart: $9
9-hole: (N/A) Cart: $4.72
Weekend: 18-hole: $17 Cart: $9
9-hole: (N/A) Cart: $4.72

South of Loop 410 off Roosevelt Ave.

Northern Hills Country Club   (6,536 yds) 210-655-8026

13202 Scarsdale
San Antonio, TX 78217
Contact: Brian Byers
Description: Even though this 18-hole private course is somewhat short, golfers must play well on the long par 3s to shoot a good score. There is water, traps, and undulating greens. **Par:** 72.
Rentals: Golf Carts, Golf Clubs, Driving Range

Members and guests only. Golf lessons available. Walking permitted.

Fees:

Weekday: 18-hole: $35 Cart: (N/A)
9-hole: $16 Cart: $7
Weekend: 18-hole: $45 Cart: (N/A)
9-hole: $20 Cart: $7

> Take Wetmore north off Loop 410 to Thousand Oaks. Turn right to Park Crossing, left to club.

Oak Hills Country Club   (6,653 yds) 210-349-5151

5403 Fredericksburg Road
San Antonio, TX 78229
Contact: Warren Chancellor
Description: Former site of PGA Tour's Texas Open. Considered to be one of the best golf courses in San Antonio. Classic design by golf architect A.W. Tillinghast has stood the test of time. **Par:** 71.
Rentals: Golf Carts, Driving Range
Members and guests only. Golf lessons

available. Walking permitted.

Fees:

Weekday: 18-hole: $100 Cart: (N/A)
9-hole: (N/A) Cart: (N/A)
Weekend: 18-hole: $100 Cart: (N/A)
9-hole: (N/A) Cart: (N/A)

> Located off Loop 410 West, on Fredericksburg Road (B.R. 87) near Callaghan Road.

Olmos Basin Golf Course   (6,894 yds) 210-826-4041

7022 N. McCullough
San Antonio, TX 78216
Contact: Jerry Hill
Description: Golfers enjoy playing this 18-hole public course because it is a solid city course with out-of-bounds, large greens, sand traps, only three creeks, and open fairways. Very popular with local golfers. **Par:** 72.
Rentals: Golf Carts, Pull Carts, Golf Clubs

Open to the public. Walking permitted.

Fees:

Weekday: 18-hole: $14 Cart: $9
9-hole: $6 Cart: $3
Weekend: 18-hole: $17 Cart: $9
9-hole: $8 Cart: $4

> Take Hwy 281 north, exit West Basse Road, and turn right on McCullough. Course is on the right.

Pecan Valley Golf Club
(7,116 yds) 210-333-9018

4700 Pecan Valley Drive
San Antonio, TX 78223
Contact: Greg Carroll
Description: *Golf Digest* ranks this course as one of the top 50 public courses in America. It hosted the 1968 PGA championship won by Julius Boros. A shot-maker's delight. Lots of trees, water, and traps. **Par:** 72.
Rentals: Golf Carts, Golf Clubs, Driving Range

Open to the public. Walking permitted. Golf lessons available.

Fees:

Weekday: 18-hole: $35 Cart: (N/A)
9-hole: (N/A) Cart: (N/A)
Weekend: 18-hole: $42 Cart: (N/A)
9-hole: (N/A) Cart: (N/A)

Take Pecan Valley exit off I-35. Cross freeway; three miles to club at Pecan Valley and Southcross.

Quarry Golf Club
(6,740 yds) 210-824-4500

444 E. Basse Road
San Antonio, TX 78209
Contact: Todd McCabe
Description: A great 18-hole public course opened in December 1993. One of the most unique courses in the state with the entire back nine inside a rock quarry. Great experience for any golfer. **Par:** 71.
Rentals: Golf Carts, Golf Clubs, Driving Range

Open to the public. Walking permitted. Golf lessons available.

Fees:

Weekday: 18-hole: $75 Cart: (N/A)
9-hole: $37 Cart: (N/A)
Weekend: 18-hole: $85 Cart: (N/A)
9-hole: $42 Cart: (N/A)

Located off Hwy 281 North and Basse Road.

Riverside Municipal Golf Course
(6,602 yds) 210-533-8371

203 McDonald
San Antonio, TX 78210
Contact: Roy Truesdale
Description: The San Antonio River runs though this 18-hole public course. Great downtown views from course. The front nine is tight, the back nine is open. There also is a neat par-3 course from 76 to 130 yards. **Par:** 72.
Rentals: Golf Carts, Pull Carts, Golf Clubs

Open to the public. Walking permitted.

Fees:

Weekday: 18-hole: $14 Cart: $9
9-hole: $7 Cart: $5.75
Weekend: 18-hole: $17 Cart: $9
9-hole: $8.50 Cart: $5.75

Take I-10 to Roosevelt Drive, turn south to McDonald Road.

San Antonio Country Club
(6,774 yds) 210-824-8863

4100 N. New Braunfels
San Antonio, TX 78209
Contact: Chuck Westergard
Description: Former British Open
champion Bill Rogers is director of golf
at this traditional 18-hole private course
constructed in 1907. Small greens are
undulating, and the rough is tough.
Fancy clubhouse. **Par:** 72.
Rentals: Golf Carts, Pull Carts, Golf
Clubs, Driving Range

Members and guests only. Golf lessons
available. Walking permitted.

Fees:

Weekday: 18-hole: $53.88 Cart: (N/A)
9-hole: (N/A) Cart: $3.29
Weekend: 18-hole: $64.75 Cart: (N/A)
9-hole: (N/A) Cart: $3.29

East of Hwy 281 & McCullough in
Terrell Hills.

San Pedro Driving Range & Par 3
(944 yds) 210-349-5113

6102 San Pedro
San Antonio, TX 78216
Contact: Ron Gardner
Description: Improving your short
game is quite possible playing this
nine-hole public par-3 course. The holes
range from 80 to 134 yards with large
greens, no traps, and lots of trees.
Par: 27.
Rentals: Club Rentals, Driving Range

Open to the public. Walking permitted.
Golf lessons available.

Fees:

Weekday: 18-hole: $3 Cart: (N/A)
9-hole: $3 Cart: (N/A)
Weekend: 18-hole: $4 Cart: (N/A)
9-hole: $3.50 Cart: (N/A)

Located south of Loop 410.

Seven Oaks Hotel & Sports Club
(1,300 yds) 800-346-5866

1400 Austin Hwy
San Antonio, TX 78209
Contact: Jim Kennedy
Description: Staying at this hotel
located between downtown San Antonio
and the airport allows you to play this
short par-3 course for free. One pond,
two traps, and short holes. Non-guests
welcome. **Par:** 27.
Open to the public. Walking permitted.

Fees:

Weekday: 18-hole: $4 Cart: (N/A)
9-hole: (N/A) Cart: (N/A)
Weekend: 18-hole: $5 Cart: (N/A)
9-hole: (N/A) Cart: (N/A)

Located 12 miles north of downtown on
Austin Hwy (B.R. 81).

Silverhorn Golf Club

(6,922 yds) 210-545-5300

1100 Bitters Road
San Antonio, TX 78216
Contact: Rick Deloach
Description: Course opening delayed by money woes, but golfers will find it's well worth the wait. Great change of pace from front nine which plays around a Corps of Engineers lake to backside with traps and trees. **Par:** 72.
Rentals: Golf Carts, Golf Clubs, Driving Range

Open to the public. Golf lessons available. Mandatory carts.

Fees:

Weekday: 18-hole: $75 Cart: (N/A)
9-hole: (N/A) Cart: (N/A)
Weekend: 18-hole: $75 Cart: (N/A)
9-hole: (N/A) Cart: (N/A)

Go west on Bitters Road from northbound Hwy 281; turn left on Partridge Trail.

Willow Springs Golf Course

(7,218 yds) 210-226-6721

202 Coliseum Road
San Antonio, TX 78219
Contact: John Erwin
Description: Perhaps the longest par 5 in Texas is on this 18-hole public course. It is the 663-yard second hole with water on the left side. Very old and historic course. Check out the snack bar's great Mexican food. **Par:** 72.
Rentals: Golf Carts, Pull Carts, Golf Clubs

Open to the public. Walking permitted.

Fees:

Weekday: 18-hole: $14 Cart: $9
9-hole: $8 Cart: $4.75
Weekend: 18-hole: $17 Cart: $9
9-hole: $9 Cart: $4.75

Located east of downtown near Joe Freeman Coliseum.

Windcrest Golf Club

(4,780 yds) 210-655-1421

8600 Midcrown
San Antonio, TX 78239
Contact: Dick Hickenbottom
Description: Even though this nine-hole private course is short, it has strong double tees, tight fairways lined with trees, small greens guarded by sand traps, and water. **Par:** 34.
Rentals: Golf Carts, Pull Carts, Golf Clubs

Members and guests only. Walking permitted.

Fees:

Weekday: 18-hole: $12 Cart: $6
9-hole: $7 Cart: $3
Weekend: 18-hole: $12 Cart: $6
9-hole: $9 Cart: $3

Located east of I-35 off Walzem Road.

Woodlake Golf & Country Club (6,691 yds) 210-661-6124

6500 Woodlake Parkway
San Antonio, TX 78244
Contact: Ray Metz
Description: Site of Ben Crenshaw's first PGA victory at Texas Open. Course tough thanks to water on 13 holes and 45 sand traps protecting elevated greens. Restaurant and bar. **Par:** 72.
Rentals: Golf Carts, Golf Clubs, Driving Range

Members and guests only. Golf lessons available. Walking permitted.

Fees:

Weekday: 18-hole: $32 Cart: (N/A)
9-hole: (N/A) Cart: (N/A)
Weekend: 18-hole: $43.70 Cart: (N/A)
9-hole: (N/A) Cart: (N/A)

From downtown, take I-35 north to Rittimon Road. Stay right to Hwy 78, then right at light to clubhouse.

Fairway Farm (7,500 yds) 409-275-5458

P.O. Box 575
San Augustine, TX 75972
Contact: Andy Stephens
Description: Golfers consider this extremely long 18-hole semiprivate course to be a monster. Lots of water on a 7,500-yard course with rolling fairways. It was ranked in the 1950s as a top course in the country. **Par:** 71.
Rentals: Golf Carts, Golf Clubs, Driving Range

Open to the public. Walking permitted. Golf lessons available.

Fees:

Weekday: 18-hole: $15 Cart: $7
9-hole: $7.50 Cart: $3.50
Weekend: 18-hole: $20 Cart: $7
9-hole: $10 Cart: $3.50

Located east of town.

Stephen F. Austin Country Club (6,567 yds) 409-885-2811

38 Park Road
San Felipe, TX 77473
Contact: Bob Browne
Description: This 18-hole public course runs along the Brazos River. It provides five water hazards. The back nine greens are protected by mounds, and there are out-of-bounds and trees. **Par:** 70.
Rentals: Golf Carts, Pull Carts, Golf Clubs

Open to the public. Walking permitted.

Fees:

Weekday: 18-hole: $15 Cart: $10
9-hole: $4.90 Cart: $4.33
Weekend: 18-hole: $23 Cart: $10
9-hole: $8.13 Cart: $4.33

Located on Park Road off FM 1458.

Aquarena Springs Golf Club   (2,602 yds) 512-245-7593

1351 Post Road
San Marcos, TX 78666
Contact: Cory Kelly
Description: The longest hole on this nine-hole public executive course is only 355 yards. Four holes do go over water, and the greens are very simple to hit. **Par:** 34.
Rentals: Golf Carts, Pull Carts, Golf Clubs

Open to the public. Walking permitted.

Fees:

Weekday: 18-hole: $9 Cart: $8 9-hole: (N/A) Cart: $4
Weekend: 18-hole: $11 Cart: $8 9-hole: (N/A) Cart: $4

> Located near course owner Southwest Texas State.

Quail Creek Country Club   (6,424 yds) 512-353-1665

P.O. Drawer 2329
San Marcos, TX 78666
Contact: John Ferguson Jr.
Description: All golfers are welcome to play this 18-hole semiprivate course. Golfers not playing with members must ride in carts. The course is rolling with trees and large three-putt greens. **Par:** 72.
Rentals: Golf Carts, Pull Carts, Golf Clubs, Driving Range

Open to the public. Walking permitted. Golf lessons available.

Fees:

Weekday: 18-hole: $30.70 Cart: $10 9-hole: (N/A) Cart: $5
Weekend: 18-hole: $38.17 Cart: $10 9-hole: (N/A) Cart: $5

> Located 30 miles south of Austin, 1½ miles off Bastrop Hwy from I-35.

San Saba Municipal Golf Course   (6,397 yds) 915-372-3212

Golf Course Road
San Saba, TX 76877
Contact: Larry McNeely
Description: A former nine-hole course that added a new nine in 1990. The new nine is not as tough as the original nine which has more trees than any nine holes in Texas. **Par:** 72.
Rentals: Golf Carts, Pull Carts, Golf Clubs, Driving Range

Open to the public. Walking permitted. Golf lessons available.

Fees:

Weekday: 18-hole: $10 Cart: $19 9-hole: $5 Cart: $4
Weekend: 18-hole: $15 Cart: $19 9-hole: $8 Cart: $4

> Located off Hwy 190 East.

Cypress Creek Country Club

(3,330 yds) 903-860-2155

Route 1
P.O. Box 95
Scroggins, TX 75480
Contact: A.J. Clinton
Description: A very hilly nine-hole public course that has water hazards on four of the nine holes. No sand traps, wide fairways, and trees. Double tees. Food and drinks. **Par:** 36.
Rentals: Golf Carts, Driving Range

Open to the public. Walking permitted.

Fees:

Weekday: 18-hole: $14 Cart: $7
9-hole: (N/A) Cart: $5
Weekend: 18-hole: $20 Cart: $7
9-hole: (N/A) Cart: $5

Located south of Mount Vernon on Hwy 115.

River Ridge Golf Club

(27 hs) 409-885-3333

3133 Brazos Oak Lane
Sealy, TX 77474
Contact: Brent Blackburn
Description: Stunning new 27-hole Jay Rivere design by the banks of the Brazos River just outside of Houston. River Ridge includes the River Course, the Parkland Course, and the Ridge Course. Several holes are located on the banks of the Brazos with more

manmade water and bunkers. Great scenic test! **Par:** 71/72.
Open to the public. Club and cart rentals available.

Fees:

Weekday: $55 (Cart included)
Weekend: $65 (Cart included)

From downtown Houtson take 1-10 West to exit 725, Micak Rd. Left on Chew Rd and south to Brazos Oak Ln.

Chaparral Country Club

(7,008 yds) 830-379-6313

300 Chaparral Drive
Seguin, TX 78155
Contact: Hank Hendrickson
Description: Out-of-town golfers are welcome to play this very long 18-hole semiprivate course, but they must make tee times to play. The course has very long par 3s and out-of-bounds. Food. **Par:** 72.
Rentals: Golf Carts, Golf Clubs, Driving Range

Open to the public. Walking permitted. Golf lessons available.

Fees:

Weekday: 18-hole: $21.60 Cart: $9.16 9-hole: (N/A) Cart: (N/A)
Weekend: 18-hole: $29.17 Cart: $9.16 9-hole: (N/A) Cart: (N/A)

Located off I-10 East. Take Alternate 90 exit to Hwy 725, then past four-way stop; look for sign on right.

Max Starcke Park Golf Course   (6,721 yds) 830-401-2490

1400 S. Guadalupe
Seguin, TX 78155
Contact: Biff Alexander
Description: Because this 18-hole
public course is somewhat long with 10
water holes, out-of-bounds, and 24 sand
traps, golfers have to play very well to
card a good score. **Par:** 71.
Rentals: Golf Carts, Pull Carts, Golf
Clubs, Driving Range
Open to the public. Walking permitted.
Golf lessons available.

Fees:

Weekday: 18-hole: $10 Cart: $9
9-hole: (N/A) Cart: $3.75
Weekend: 18-hole: $13 Cart: $9
9-hole: (N/A) Cart: $3.75

Located off I-10 east of San Antonio.
Take exit 603, go south on Hwy 90,
then right on Guadalupe.

Gaines County Golf Course   (6,685 yds) 915-758-3808

P.O. Box 308
Seminole, TX 79360
Contact: Shaun McDonald
Description: The front nine on this
18-hole public course is very hard
because of strong south wind. The front
nine is in a valley mound. The back nine
has trees and no traps. **Par:** 72.
Rentals: Golf Carts, Pull Carts, Golf
Clubs, Driving Range

Open to the public. Walking permitted.
Golf lessons available.

Fees:

Weekday: 18-hole: $12.50 Cart: $8
9-hole: (N/A) Cart: $4.25
Weekend: 18-hole: $17.50 Cart: $8
9-hole: (N/A) Cart: $4.25

Located 10 miles north on Hwy 385.

Seymour Golf & Country Club   (3,300 yds) 940-888-2833

P.O. Box 386
Seymour, TX 76380
Contact: Jeff Borie
Description: The operators of this
nine-hole private course recently
renovated the greens, adding bentgrass
greens. The course has a lot of blind
shots which make it tough. **Par:** 35.
Members and guests only. Walking
permitted.

Fees:

Weekday: 18-hole: $10 Cart: (N/A)
9-hole: (N/A) Cart: (N/A)
Weekend: 18-hole: $10 Cart: (N/A)
9-hole: (N/A) Cart: (N/A)

Located on Throckmorton Hwy.

Shamrock Country Club   (6,439 yds) 806-256-5151

900 S. Wall
Shamrock, TX 79079
Contact: Ric Butler
Description: Tee shots on this
nine-hole public course tend to run a
long way thanks to hard fairways and
rolling hills. No sand traps, three water
holes, and bentgrass greens. **Par:** 36.
Open to the public. Walking permitted.

Fees:

Weekday: 18-hole: $7.50 Cart: $18
9-hole: (N/A) Cart: $9
Weekend: 18-hole: $10 Cart: $18
9-hole: (N/A) Cart: $9

Located south of town on Hwy 83.

Sheppard AFB Golf Course   (7,100 yds) 940-676-6369

900 First Ave.
Bldg 4490
Sheppard AFB, TX 76311
Contact: Mike O'Donnell
Description: This is one of the longest
18-hole private military golf courses in
Texas. Level fairways lost trees due to a
tornado but 56 sand traps and winding
creek make course tough on the back
nine. **Par:** 72.
Rentals: Golf Carts, Pull Carts, Golf
Clubs, Driving Range

Members and guests only. Golf lessons
available. Walking permitted.

Fees:

Weekday: 18-hole: $15 Cart: $7.50
9-hole: $6 Cart: $4.50
Weekend: 18-hole: $16 Cart: $7.50
9-hole: $7 Cart: $4.50

Located in Wichita Falls off 1st Avenue
on base.

Woodlawn Country Club   (6,700 yds) 903-893-3240

P.O. Box 1303
Sherman, TX 75091
Contact: Sale Omohundro
Description: Water is a major factor
on seven holes of this private club. The
greens are elevated. Woodlawn home to
Senior PGA star Miller Barber. **Par:** 71.
Rentals: Golf Carts
Members and guests only. Golf lessons
available. Walking permitted.

Fees:

Weekday: 18-hole: $30 Cart: $8.50
9-hole: (N/A) Cart: $4.25
Weekend: 18-hole: $40 Cart: $8.50
9-hole: (N/A) Cart: $4.25

Located off U.S. 75 to Woodlake exit to
club.

Silsbee Country Club
(3,203 yds) 409-385-4372

P.O. Box 982
Silsbee, TX 77656
Contact: Robert Alvarro
Description: A classic nine-hole golf course. Clubhouse has a restaurant, bar, lockers, showers, tennis courts, meeting room, and pro shop. **Par:** 36.
Rentals: Golf Carts, Pull Carts, Golf Clubs, Driving Range

Members and guests only. Golf lessons available. Walking permitted.

Fees:

Weekday: 18-hole: $10 Cart: $6.91
9-hole: $10 Cart: $3.92
Weekend: 18-hole: $15 Cart: $6.91
9-hole: $15 Cart: $3.92

Located on Hwy 418 15 minutes from Beaumont.

Valley Lodge Golf Club
(6,572 yds) 281-346-1426

614 Horseshoe
Simonton, TX 77476
Contact: Mike White
Description: Golfers consider this nine-hole semiprivate course to be great. It is a hilly course with elevated greens and five water hazards plus thousands of pecan trees. **Par:** 36.
Rentals: Golf Carts, Pull Carts, Golf Clubs, Driving Range

Open to the public. Walking permitted. Golf lessons available.

Fees:

Weekday: 18-hole: $14 Cart: $8
9-hole: $9 Cart: $5
Weekend: 18-hole: $14 Cart: $8
9-hole: $9 Cart: $5

Located west of Houston on Wrangler Road off FM 1093.

Sinton Municipal Golf Course
(6,678 yds) 512-364-9013

Waelder Park
Sinton, TX 78387
Contact: Bill Evans
Description: A very good 18-hole rural course where all levels of golfers post a good score thanks to wide fairways, no sand traps, slight water, and one-putt greens. **Par:** 72.
Rentals: Golf Carts, Pull Carts, Golf Clubs, Driving Range

Open to the public. Walking permitted. Golf lessons available.

Fees:

Weekday: 18-hole: $7 Cart: $7 9-hole: (N/A) Cart: (N/A)
Weekend: 18-hole: $8 Cart: $7 9-hole: (N/A) Cart: (N/A)

Located north of town on Hwy 181.

Slaton Golf Club

(6,305 yds) 806-828-3269

Route 2
P.O. Box 158B
Slaton, TX 79364
Contact: Ned Kygar
Description: Shooting a good score is possible on this nine-hole public course. The fairways are wide open with light trees and bentgrass greens. Some water. **Par:** 35.
Open to the public. Walking permitted.

Fees:

Weekday: 18-hole: $7 Cart: $8 9-hole: (N/A) Cart: $4
Weekend: 18-hole: $10 Cart: $8 9-hole: (N/A) Cart: $4

Located three miles north of town on Golf Course Road.

Snyder Country Club

(6,175 yds) 915-573-7101

P.O. Box 925
Snyder, TX 79550
Contact: Rick Mammolite
Description: A reasonable nine-hole private course with great bentgrass greens, light rough, and some trees. Two lakes are on the course. Restaurant, bar, and pro shop. **Par:** 36.
Rentals: Golf Carts, Driving Range

Members and guests only. Golf lessons available. Walking permitted.

Fees:

Weekday: 18-hole: $15 Cart: $7.50 9-hole: $9 Cart: $3.75
Weekend: 18-hole: $20 Cart: $7.50 9-hole: $12 Cart: $3.75

Located on Lubbock Hwy north of town.

Western Texas College Golf Course (6,064 yds) 915-573-9291

6200 South College Avenue
Snyder, TX 79549
Contact: Rick Kahlich
Description: A big pond sits in the middle of five holes on this nine-hole public course. There are big greens and the course is rolling. Student discounts. Pro shop. **Par:** 35.
Rentals: Golf Carts, Golf Clubs, Driving Range

Open to the public. Walking permitted. Golf lessons available.

Fees:

Weekday: 18-hole: $8.50 Cart: $7.75 9-hole: (N/A) Cart: $3
Weekend: 18-hole: $13.50 Cart: $7.75 9-hole: (N/A) Cart: $3

Located on the college campus.

Sonora Golf Course   (6,500 yds) 915-387-3680

1612 Golf Course
Sonora, TX 76950
Contact: Steve Alexander
Description: Even though this
nine-hole public course is not very long,
it is easy to post a crummy score
because the bentgrass greens are so
large. Three-putts are common. **Par:**
36.
Rentals: Golf Carts, Golf Clubs, Driving
Range

Open to the public. Walking permitted.
Golf lessons available.

Fees:

Weekday: 18-hole: $12 Cart: $7.50
9-hole: $8 Cart: $3.25
Weekend: 18-hole: $18 Cart: $7.50
9-hole: $10 Cart: $3.25

Located on I-10; take the Sonora exit.

Idylwild Golf Club   (6,727 yds) 409-753-2521

1100 E. Pine Shadows Drive
Sour Lake, TX 77659
Contact: Mike Smith
Description: This 18-hole semiprivate
course was cut into a pine and
hardwood forest. It is extremely tight
and has water hazards on 13 holes.
Food. **Par:** 72.
Rentals: Golf Carts, Pull Carts, Golf
Clubs, Driving Range

Open to the public. Walking permitted.
Golf lessons available.

Fees:

Weekday: 18-hole: $10 Cart: $8.50
9-hole: (N/A) Cart: $3.25
Weekend: 18-hole: $20 Cart: $8.50
9-hole: (N/A) Cart: $3.25

Located west of Beaumont on Hwy
105.

Timarron Golf Club   (7,000 yds) 817-481-7529

1400 Byron Nelson Parkway
Southlake, TX 76092
Contact: Charlie Mabie
Description: Scenic public course built
in new housing development. Golf
legend Byron Nelson contributed to
design. Extensive mounding with trees
and water. 18th hole is par 5 with
island green. Great pro shop. **Par:** 72.
Rentals: Golf Carts, Golf Clubs, Driving
Range

Open to the public. Golf lessons
available. Mandatory carts.

Fees:

Weekday: 18-hole: $50 Cart: (N/A)
9-hole: (N/A) Cart: (N/A)
Weekend: 18-hole: $65 Cart: (N/A)
9-hole: (N/A) Cart: (N/A)

Take Hwy 114 to E. Southlake, left two
miles to Whitechapel, left to E.
Continental, left to Byron Nelson.

Hansford Golf Club

(2,900 yds) 806-659-2233

P.O. Box 335
Spearman, TX 79081
Contact: Jody Spearman
Description: The double tees on this nine-hole public course are very neat. The 250-yard par-4 third hole is a 161-yard par 3 on the back nine. Flat bentgrass greens. Student discount. **Par:** 36.
Rentals: Golf Carts, Pull Carts, Golf Clubs, Driving Range

Open to the public. Walking permitted. Golf lessons available.

Fees:

Weekday: 18-hole: $8 Cart: $8 9-hole: (N/A) Cart: $3.50
Weekend: 18-hole: $12 Cart: $8 9-hole: (N/A) Cart: $3.50

Located on Hardesty Hwy (FM 2387).

Barton Creek Resort & C.C.

(6,622 yds) 830-693-7581

1800 Clubhouse Hill Drive
Spicewood, TX 78669
Contact: Brian Dees
Description: In 1991, Barton Creek purchased a private club designed by Arnold Palmer. Barton Creek Resort guests and members can play a true go-for-broke course with lots of water. **Par:** 71.
Rentals: Golf Carts, Golf Clubs, Driving Range

Members and guests only. Golf lessons available. Walking permitted.

Fees:

Weekday: 18-hole: $95 Cart: (N/A) 9-hole: (N/A) Cart: (N/A)
Weekend: 18-hole: $95 Cart: (N/A) 9-hole: (N/A) Cart: (N/A)

Take Haynie Flat Road off Hwy 71. Go right four miles to stop sign. Club is on right.

Pedernales Golf Club

(3,330 yds) 512-264-1489

Route 1, Briarcliff II
Spicewood, TX 78669
Contact: Larry Trader
Description: Legendary Hill Country layout owned by country music legend Willie Nelson. Great views from elevated location with lake in the background. Look out for Willie, who plays here often. **Par:** 36.
Rentals: Golf Carts

Open to the public. Walking permitted. Golf lessons available.

Fees:

Weekday: 18-hole: $17.50 Cart: (N/A) 9-hole: (N/A) Cart: (N/A)
Weekend: 18-hole: $22.50 Cart: (N/A) 9-hole: (N/A) Cart: (N/A)

Located three miles north of Hwy 71 off Bee Creek Road and FM 2322.

Cypresswood Golf Club   (54 hs) 281-821-6300

21602 Cypresswood Drive
Spring, TX 77373
Contact: Christino Martinez
Creek Course Description: The Creek Course is much longer and more demanding of long drives. Designed by Rick Forester in 1986. Named by *Golf Digest* as one of the top new courses in America when it opened. Booming business. **Par:** 72 (6,937 yards).

Cypress Course Description: Good 54-hole complex. Course has plenty of water along with tree and trap trouble. **Par:** 72 (6,906 yards).
Rentals: Golf Carts, Pull Carts, Golf Clubs, Driving Range
Open to the public. Walking permitted. Golf lessons available.

Fees:

Weekday: 18-hole: $47 Cart: $11.50
9-hole: (N/A) Cart: (N/A)
Weekend: 18-hole: $55.50 Cart: $11.50 9-hole: (N/A) Cart: (N/A)

Legends Course Description: The newest offering from this highly popular public golf complex. Keith Forester, who has done outstanding work in San Antonio and Dallas, brought together water and trees in this classic design. **Par:** 72 (7,150 yards).
Rentals: Golf Carts, Golf Clubs, Driving Range
Open to the public. Walking permitted. Golf lessons available.

Fees:

Weekday: 18-hole: $65 Cart: (N/A)
9-hole: (N/A) Cart: (N/A)
Weekend: 18-hole: $75 Cart: (N/A)
9-hole: (N/A) Cart: (N/A)

Located between I-45 and Hwy 59 on FM 1960, north on Cypresswood Drive.

Raveneaux Country Club   (36 hs) 281-370-6370

9415 Cypresswood Drive
Spring, TX 77379
Contact: Matt Swanson
Old Course Description: A 36-hole private course. The Old Course is longer than the New Course but has wide open fairways and not as much water. Small greens. Food, drinks, and pool. **Par:** 71 (6,695 yards).

New Course Description: Even though the New Course is shorter than the Old Course, it is more difficult with lots of water, trees, small greens, sand traps, and tight fairways. Raveneaux is a target golf course. Nice club. **Par:** 71 (6,515 yards).

Rentals: Golf Carts, Golf Clubs, Driving Range
Members and guests only. Golf lessons available. Walking permitted.

Fees:

Weekday: 18-hole: $40 Cart: $11
9-hole: (N/A) Cart: $7
Weekend: 18-hole: $60 Cart: $11
9-hole: (N/A) Cart: $7

Located north of FM 1960 near Champions.

Willow Creek Golf Club   (6,921 yds) 281-376-4061

24525 Northcrest
Spring, TX 77379
Contact: Brett Baske
Description: The front nine on this 18-hole semiprivate course is par 36. The back nine is par 37. Lots of trees, tough greens, water, and out-of-bounds on narrow fairways. **Par:** 73.
Rentals: Golf Carts, Golf Clubs, Driving Range
Private club. Walking permitted. Golf lessons available.

Fees:

Weekday: 18-hole: $40 Cart: $11
9-hole: (N/A) Cart: $5.50
Weekend: 18-hole: $45 Cart: $11
9-hole: (N/A) Cart: $5.50

Located off I-45 and FM 2920. Go west to Kuykendahl, right on Spring-Steuber, right on Northcrest, and left to club.

WindRose Golf Club   (7,203 yds) 281-370-8900

6235 Pine Street
Spring, TX 77379
Contact: Martin Stroman
Description: Great new daily-fee addition to Houston golf scene. Course designed by Rick Forester, who did first two layouts at Cypresswood. Course features mounding and more slopes than you'd expect at Southeast TX location. Some risk-reward opportunities. **Par:** 72.

Fees:

Weekday: 18-hole: $50 Cart: included
9-hole: (N/A) Cart: (N/A)
Weekend: 18-hole: $60 Cart: included
9-hole: (N/A) Cart: (N/A)

Take 2920 Tomball exit off I-45 in Spring. Take a left on 2920 and a left on Kuykendahl, follow signs to course.

Rebecca Creek Golf Course   (6,470 yds) 830-885-7495

10101 Rebecca Creek Road
Spring Branch, TX 78070
Contact: Mike Cassidy
Description: Public layout in highly scenic Hill Country location. Watch out for tricky holes with plenty of trees and native brush. Homey clubhouse to view scenery. **Par:** 72.
Rentals: Golf Carts
Open to the public. Walking permitted.

Fees:

Weekday: 18-hole: $20 Cart: $8
9-hole: (N/A) Cart: (N/A)
Weekend: 18-hole: $25 Cart: $8
9-hole: (N/A) Cart: (N/A)

North of San Antonio off Hwy 281. Look for the giant golf ball.

Spur Golf Course   (3,663 yds) 806-271-4355

P.O. Box 1083
Spur, TX 79370
Contact: Golf Shop
Description: Good 9-hole test with some trees, traps, and hidden trouble. Greens can pose a problem to the unwary with plenty of wind to deal with. Locals have an advantage over visitors because of hometown knowledge. **Par:** 35.
Rentals: Golf Carts

Open to the public.

Fees:

Weekday: 18-hole: (N/A) Cart: (N/A)
9-hole: $7 Cart: $7
Weekend: 18-hole: (N/A) Cart: (N/A)
9-hole: $9 Cart: $7

One mile east of town on Main Street. Turn right to course.

Stamford Golf & Country Club   (3,331 yds) 915-773-5001

P.O. Box 289
Stamford, TX 79553
Contact: Golf Shop
Description: Small West Texas private club with trees, plenty of sand and one water hazard. Locals have the advantage on the putting greens knowledge, but course can yield low scores. **Par:** 35.
Rentals: Golf Carts

Fees:

Weekday: 18-hole: (N/A) Cart: (N/A)
9-hole: $10.50 Cart: $10
Weekend: 18-hole: (N/A) Cart: (N/A)
9-hole: $12 Cart: $10

Course is one mile west of town off Hwy 277; turn right on Route 6 and look for small sign.

Martin County Country Club   (6,200 yds) 915-756-2556

P.O. Box 651
Stanton, TX 79782
Contact: Eldon Hopkins
Description: The bentgrass greens on this nine-hole private course are easy to three-putt. The course itself is wide open and flat with no traps and young trees. Out-of-county golfers welcome.
Par: 36.
Rentals: Golf Carts

Members and guests only. Walking permitted.

Fees:

Weekday: 18-hole: $7 Cart: $6 9-hole: $7 Cart: $3
Weekend: 18-hole: $12 Cart: $8
9-hole: $8 Cart: $3

Located south of Hwy 80.

Legends Golf Club   (6,400 yds) 254-968-2200

137 Ben Hogan Drive
Stephenville, TX 76401
Contact: Liz Albracht
Description: A short but challenging 18-hole course inspired by Ben Hogan. Clubhouse has a restaurant, bar, and pro shop. Course open to legends and regular hackers. **Par:** 72.
Rentals: Golf Carts, Driving Range

Open to the public. Walking permitted. Golf lessons available.

Fees:

Weekday: 18-hole: $12 Cart: $18
9-hole: (N/A) Cart: $9
Weekend: 18-hole: $18 Cart: $18
9-hole: (N/A) Cart: $9

Located off Hwy 8 in Stephenville.

Tejas Golf Course

(6,134 yds) 940-965-3904

P.O. Box 326
Stephenville, TX 76401
Contact: Steve Thieman
Description: Even though this nine-hole public course has flat fairways, there is very thick rough and tight trees. The greens are small with no traps. Water on four holes. Double tees. **Par:** 36.
Rentals: Golf Carts, Pull Carts, Golf Clubs

Open to the public. Walking permitted. Golf lessons available.

Fees:

Weekday: 18-hole: $8 Cart: $15
9-hole: (N/A) Cart: $3.25
Weekend: 18-hole: $11 Cart: $15
9-hole: (N/A) Cart: $3.25

Located on Hwy 281 West.

Stratford Country Club

(3,172 yds) 806-396-2259

P.O. Box 662
Stratford, TX 79084
Contact: Golf Shop
Description: A private nine-hole course that is open only to members and golfers from out of town. Large bentgrass greens, few sand traps, and rolling buffalo grass fairways. **Par:** 36.
Rentals: Golf Carts, Driving Range

Members and guests only. Walking permitted.

Fees:

Weekday: 18-hole: $8 Cart: $8 9-hole: (N/A) Cart: $4
Weekend: 18-hole: $15 Cart: $8
9-hole: (N/A) Cart: $4

Located west of town on Hwy 54.

Greatwood Golf Club

(7,034 yds) 281-343-9999

6767 Greatwood Parkway
Sugar Land, TX 77479
Contact: Tommy Blancas
Description: This 18-hole public course is extremely long. That makes it tough, and three-putting on the large greens adds more strokes. There are 14 water holes. **Par:** 72.
Rentals: Golf Carts, Golf Clubs, Driving Range

Open to the public. Golf lessons available. Mandatory carts.

Fees:

Weekday: 18-hole: $44 Cart: (N/A)
9-hole: (N/A) Cart: (N/A)
Weekend: 18-hole: $58.44 Cart: (N/A)
9-hole: (N/A) Cart: (N/A)

Located on the southwest corner of Hwy 59 and Greatwood Parkway.

Riverbend Country Club   (6,712 yds) 281-269-2527

1214 Dulles
Sugar Land, TX 77478
Contact: Kevin Hood
Description: This 18-hole private
course is reasonably long but is difficult
thanks to large three-putt greens, 11
water holes, and lots of trees. Food and
drinks. **Par:** 72.
Rentals: Golf Carts, Golf Clubs, Driving
Range

Members and guests only. Golf lessons
available. Walking permitted.

Fees:

Weekday: 18-hole: $35 Cart: $8
9-hole: (N/A) Cart: $5
Weekend: 18-hole: $55 Cart: $8
9-hole: (N/A) Cart: $5

Located off U.S. 59, take
Airport-Kirkwood exit and turn on
Dulles.

Sugar Creek Country Club   (27 hs) 281-494-9135

420 Sugar Creek Blvd.
Sugar Land, TX 77478
Contact: J.D. Murchinson
Description: This is a 27-hole Robert
Trent Jones-designed private course.
The nines are named Robert, Trent, and
Jones. Trent and Jones are tough with
tough par 3s over water with traps in
front. **Par:** 72.
Rentals: Golf Carts, Golf Clubs, Driving
Range

Members and guests only. Golf lessons
available. Walking permitted.

Fees:

Weekday: 18-hole: $35 Cart: $13
9-hole: $17.50 Cart: $5
Weekend: 18-hole: $55 Cart: $13
9-hole: $35 Cart: $5

Take U.S. 59 to Sugar Creek Blvd.
Course is on right.

Sweetwater Country Club   (36 hs) 281-980-4653

4400 Palm Royale
Sugar Land, TX 77479
Contact: John Kennedy
Pecan Course Description: A 36-hole private course. The Pecan Course has lots of water on 14 holes and big greens that are easy to three-putt. The course is 7,100 yards long. **Par:** 72 (7,152 yards).

Cypress Course Description: The Cypress Course is a lot shorter than the Pecan Course, but it is extremely tight with water on 13 holes and mounds on the fairway to make it a target course. Clubhouse has food, bar, and tennis. **Par:** 71 (6,687 yards).

Fees:

Weekday: 18-hole: $35 Cart: $11
9-hole: (N/A) Cart: $5.50
Weekend: 18-hole: $60 Cart: $11
9-hole: (N/A) Cart: $5.50
Rentals: Golf Carts, Golf Clubs, Driving Range
Members and guests only. Golf lessons available. Walking permitted.

Located off Hwy 59 on Sweetwater Blvd. exit.

Sulphur Springs Country Club   (6,800 yds) 903-885-4861

Route 1
P.O. Box 340
Sulphur Springs, TX 75482
Contact: Tony Martin
Description: It is quite common for all levels of golfers to shoot a good score on this 18-hole semiprivate course. The course is short but hilly with no sand traps, wide fairways, and not much water. Pool. **Par:** 72.
Rentals: Golf Carts, Pull Carts, Golf Clubs, Driving Range

Open to the public. Walking permitted. Golf lessons available.

Fees:

Weekday: 18-hole: $18.50 Cart: $7.50 9-hole: (N/A) Cart: $3.25
Weekend: 18-hole: $23.50 Cart: $7.50 9-hole: (N/A) Cart: $3.25

Take exit 127 from eastbound I-30; take access road two miles, and turn right.

Sundown Municipal Golf Course   (6,626 yds)   806-229-6186

600 W. Richardson
Sundown, TX 79372
Contact: Scott Nichols
Description: A long nine-hole public course ranked as one of the top nine-hole courses in Texas. Bentgrass greens with two flags from front and back nine and double tees. **Par:** 35.
Rentals: Golf Carts, Pull Carts, Driving Range

Open to the public. Walking permitted. Golf lessons available.

Fees:

Weekday: 18-hole: $8 Cart: $7 9-hole: (N/A) Cart: $3.50
Weekend: 18-hole: $12 Cart: $7 9-hole: (N/A) Cart: $3.50

> Located west of the only stoplight in town.

Lake Sweetwater Golf Course   (6,557 yds)   915-235-8816

Route 3, FM 1856
Sweetwater, TX 79556
Contact: Jack Newton
Description: Good, solid 18-hole public course near town lake. Scenic surroundings with some trees, bermuda greens, and traps. Wind can be a factor. **Par:** 71.
Rentals: Golf Carts, Driving Range

Open to the public. Walking permitted. Golf lessons available.

Fees:

Weekday: 18-hole: $8 Cart: $9 9-hole: (N/A) Cart: (N/A)
Weekend: 18-hole: $11 Cart: $11 9-hole: (N/A) Cart: (N/A)

> Exit 249 off of FM 1856 on Lake Sweetwater. Look for small sign..

Sweetwater Country Club   (6,362 yds)   915-235-8093

1901 Country Club Drive
Sweetwater, TX 79556
Contact: Don Timm
Description: Posting a good score on this 18-hole semiprivate course requires good putting on the small and fast rolling bentgrass greens. Also, the rough is very thick. Food, drinks, and pro shop. **Par:** 71.
Rentals: Golf Carts, Driving Range

Open to the public. Walking permitted.

Fees:

Weekday: 18-hole: $15 Cart: $12.75 9-hole: (N/A) Cart: $7.25
Weekend: 18-hole: $20 Cart: $12.75 9-hole: (N/A) Cart: $7.25

> Located off I-20.

T-Bar Country Club (6,180 yds) 806-998-5305

P.O. Box 415
Tahoka, TX 79373
Contact: Cherry Gandy
Description: The development of a new set of double tees makes playing 18 holes on this nine-hole private course great. There are bentgrass greens, few trees, no traps, and water. Out-of-town golfers welcome. **Par:** 36.

Members and guests only. Walking permitted.

Fees:

Weekday: 18-hole: $7.44 Cart: (N/A) 9-hole: (N/A) Cart: (N/A)
Weekend: 18-hole: $7.44 Cart: (N/A) 9-hole: (N/A) Cart: (N/A)

Located on Hwy 380, west of town.

Mustang Creek Golf Course (2,600 yds) 512-365-1332

Washington Hts
Taylor, TX 76574
Contact: Mike McCowan
Description: This short executive nine-hole semiprivate course has no bunkers, small greens, and hilly fairways. Only two water hazards. Senior discounts. Friendly pro shop. **Par:** 34.
Rentals: Golf Carts, Pull Carts, Golf Clubs

Open to the public. Walking permitted.

Fees:

Weekday: 18-hole: $6 Cart: $7 9-hole: (N/A) Cart: $3.75
Weekend: 18-hole: $9 Cart: $7 9-hole: (N/A) Cart: $3.75

Located off U.S. 79 on Hwy 95.

Big Cedar Golf Club (3,600 yds) 254-739-5600

Route 2 Box 234
Teague, TX 75860
Contact: Ken Moss
Description: New owners are making positive changes on this nice nine-hole public course. There are hills, lots of trees, and four ponds. Snacks, drinks, and pro shop. **Par:** 36.
Rentals: Golf Carts, Driving Range

Open to the public. Walking permitted.

Fees:

Weekday: 18-hole: $10 Cart: $10.75 9-hole: (N/A) Cart: $5
Weekend: 18-hole: $15 Cart: $21.50 9-hole: (N/A) Cart: $5

Located off I-45 exit Fairfield west.

Sammons Park Golf Course   (6,100 yds) 254-778-8282

2220 W. Ave. D
Temple, TX 76504
Contact: Bob Burns
Description: Water is a major hazard on this 18-hole public course. The water comes into play on 15 holes. Golfers must hit good shots to keep their score dry. **Par:** 70.
Rentals: Golf Carts, Pull Carts, Golf Clubs, Driving Range

Open to the public. Walking permitted. Golf lessons available.

Fees:

Weekday: 18-hole: $10.50 Cart: $8.75 9-hole: $6.50 Cart: $5
Weekend: 18-hole: $13.75 Cart: $8.75 9-hole: $6.50 Cart: $5

> Located off I-35 on H Ave. to D Ave. West.

Temple Junior College Golf Course (2,760 yds) 254-773-0888

2501 S. 1st Street
Temple, TX 76501
Contact: Paul Gullion
Description: The first two holes on this nine-hole public course are par 3s. It can be tough to be even par after two holes. The rest of the holes are lined with pine trees. No water. **Par:** 34.
Rentals: Golf Carts, Pull Carts, Golf Clubs

Open to the public. Walking permitted. Golf lessons available.

Fees:

Weekday: 18-hole: $5 Cart: $5 9-hole: (N/A) Cart: $2.50
Weekend: 18-hole: $6 Cart: $5 9-hole: (N/A) Cart: $2.50

> Located next to VA Hospital on South 1st St.

Wildflower Country Club   (7,000 yds) 254-771-1177

4902 Wildflower Lane
Temple, TX 76502
Contact: Bill Euler
Description: A very long 18-hole private course with five back nine holes along water. Great views. Contoured greens set up three-putts, and the first hole is a 608-yard par 5. **Par:** 72.
Rentals: Golf Carts, Golf Clubs, Driving Range

Members and guests only. Golf lessons available. Walking permitted.

Fees:

Weekday: 18-hole: $28 Cart: $9 9-hole: (N/A) Cart: $5.50
Weekend: 18-hole: $33 Cart: $9 9-hole: (N/A) Cart: $5.50

> Take Midway exit off I-35. Go west one mile then turn right on Wildflower Ln.

Lajitas Resort Golf Course   (6,200 yds) 915-424-3211

Star Route 70
Box 400
Terlingua, TX 79852
Contact: Fred Shely
Description: There is a hotel and three motels near this nine-hole resort course that has water on five holes, thick fairways, and double tees. No sand traps. **Par:** 35.
Rentals: Golf Carts, Pull Carts, Golf Clubs, Driving Range

Open to the public. Walking permitted. Golf lessons available.

Fees:

Weekday: 18-hole: $10 Cart: $6.50
9-hole: (N/A) Cart: $4
Weekend: 18-hole: $14 Cart: $6.50
9-hole: (N/A) Cart: $4

Located west of town on Hwy 170 from Hwy 118 South.

Oak Grove Golf Course   (6,374 yds) 972-563-8553

2000 Colquitt Road
Terrell, TX 75160
Contact: John Lawson
Description: Trees more than 60 years old protect this short nine-hole public course. Four holes have water and all holes have double tees. Food and drinks. **Par:** 35.
Rentals: Golf Carts, Pull Carts, Golf Clubs

Open to the public. Walking permitted. Golf lessons available.

Fees:

Weekday: 18-hole: $11 Cart: $3
9-hole: $10 Cart: $3
Weekend: 18-hole: $12.50 Cart: $3
9-hole: $10 Cart: $3

Located east of Dallas off Hwy 80 to Hwy 205.

Northridge Country Club   (6,471 yds) 903-792-9331

120 Bill Rogers Drive
Texarkana, TX 75503
Contact: Rick Rogers
Description: Playing a round on Northridge is like riding a roller coaster. It is so hilly, 6,471 yards from the back tees is like 7,000 yards. **Par:** 71.
Rentals: Golf Carts, Golf Clubs, Driving Range

Members and guests only. Golf lessons available. Walking permitted.

Fees:

Weekday: 18-hole: $50 Cart: $10
9-hole: (N/A) Cart: (N/A)
Weekend: 18-hole: $50 Cart: $10
9-hole: (N/A) Cart: (N/A)

Located north of I-30 off Summer Hill North to Bill Rogers Drive.

Oak Grove Golf Club
(6,274 yds) 903-831-6249

Red River Army Depot
Texarkana, TX 75507-5000
Contact: Tonya Dillard
Description: With water hazards on four holes of this nine-hole military course, it is easy to get penalty strokes. Also, the fairways are very tight with trees. **Par:** 36.
Rentals: Golf Carts, Pull Carts, Driving Range

Members and guests only. Walking permitted.

Fees:

Weekday: 18-hole: $8 Cart: $14
9-hole: (N/A) Cart: $7
Weekend: 18-hole: $12 Cart: $14
9-hole: (N/A) Cart: $7

Located west of Hooks on Hwy 82.

Bayou Golf Club
(6,835 yds) 409-643-5850

2800 Ted Dudley Drive
Texas City, TX 77590
Contact: Tom Ashworth
Description: Joe Finger designed this public course that is very challenging at 6,835 yards. The range has a practice putting and chipping green. Food and drinks. **Par:** 72.
Rentals: Golf Carts, Pull Carts, Golf Clubs, Driving Range

Open to the public. Walking permitted. Golf lessons available.

Fees:

Weekday: 18-hole: $11 Cart: $8.66
9-hole: $11 Cart: $5.41
Weekend: 18-hole: $13 Cart: $8.66
9-hole: $13 Cart: $5.41

Located off I-45 south of Houston to Texas City.

Stewart Peninsula Golf Course
(5,300 yds) 972-625-8700

100 Cottonwood Springs Circle
The Colony, TX 75056
Contact: Lance Allen
Description: Unique course located on Lake Lewisville in fast-growing area. Course uses two-flag system on nine greens, much like Starr Hollow in Tolar. Holes either par 3 or 4, but very challenging layout with great views of nearby lake. Nice addition. **Par:** 66.

Fees:

Weekday: 18-hole: $22 Cart: $28
9-hole: (N/A) Cart: (N/A)
Weedend: 18-hole: $28 Cart: $28
9-hole: (N/A) Cart: (N/A)

Take Main Street into The Colony off Highway 121. Go past three lights to North Colony Blvd., and go left for about a mile.

Montgomery County Golf Center   (3,200 yds) 409-273-4002

P.O. Box 8264
The Woodlands, TX 77387
Contact: Jim Price
Description: One of the best par-3
courses in Texas with lots of trees, long
and short holes, and water hazards.
Club repair shop, snacks, and golf pro.
Par: 27.
Open to the public. Walking permitted.
Golf lessons available.

Fees:

Weekday: 18-hole: $9.50 Cart: (N/A)
9-hole: $6.75 Cart: (N/A)
Weekend: 18-hole: $12 Cart: (N/A)
9-hole: $6.75 Cart: (N/A)

Located off I-45 exit 83 west, north of
The Woodlands.

TPC-Woodlands   (7,018 yds) 281-367-7285

1730 S. Millbend Drive
The Woodlands, TX 77380
Contact: Gary Rippy
Description: The site of the Shell
Houston Open. It is one of the toughest
TPC courses in the U.S. It has lots of
water hazards demanding great shots to
hit the green. Closing combo of par-4
17th, par-5 18th great. **Par:** 72.
Rentals: Golf Carts, Golf Clubs, Driving
Range

Open to the public. Walking permitted.
Golf lessons available.

Fees:

Weekday: 18-hole: $85 Cart: (N/A)
9-hole: (N/A) Cart: (N/A)
Weekend: 18-hole: $105 Cart: (N/A)
9-hole: (N/A) Cart: (N/A)

Take I-45 to Woodlands Parkway exit,
west on Grogan's Mill, left to S.
Millbend.

The Woodlands Arnold Palmer Course   (27 hs) 281-367-5554

100 Grand Fairway
The Woodlands, TX 77380
Contact: John Phillips
Description: A classic 27-hole private
Arnold Palmer go-for-broke course with
water hazards on 13 holes demanding
layups or go-for-broke. A new nine holes
opened in fall of 1995. Great private
club golf. **Par:** 72 (7,184 yards).
Rentals: Golf Carts, Golf Clubs, Driving
Range

Members and guests only. Golf lessons
available. Walking permitted.

Fees:

Weekday: 18-hole: $32 Cart: $10
9-hole: (N/A) Cart: $6.50
Weekend: 18-hole: $37 Cart: $10
9-hole: (N/A) Cart: $6.50

Take I-45 to Woodlands Parkway to
Cochrans Crossing, then right.

The Woodlands Resort & Country Club (36 hs) 281-367-1100

2301 N. Millbend Drive
The Woodlands, TX 77380
Contact: Brad Myer
West Course Description: The West Course hosted the Houston Open before the TPC was built. It is a strong course with well-placed water hazards, sand traps protecting the greens, and narrow fairways. **Par:** 72 (6,881 yards).
Rentals: Golf Carts, Golf Clubs, Driving Range
Members and guests only. Golf lessons available. Walking permitted.

Fees:

Weekday: 18-hole: $32 Cart: $10
9-hole: $15 Cart: $6.50
Weekend: 18-hole: $37 Cart: $10
9-hole: $20 Cart: $6.50

North Course Description: The North Course of this 36-hole private course is open to guests of the resort. It is a tough course with hilly fairways and water hazards. The fairways are tight and narrow. Lots of sand traps. **Par:** 72 (6,881 yards).

Fees:

Weekday: 18-hole: $40 Cart: $11.50
9-hole: $20 Cart: $8
Weekend: 18-hole: $45 Cart: $11.50
9-hole: $35 Cart: $8

Located off I-45 north of Houston.

Throckmorton Country Club   (3,144 yds) 954-849-3131

P.O. Box 335
Throckmorton, TX 76083
Contact: Glen Boyd
Description: A lot of golf tournaments are played on this rural nine-hole public course because it is so tough thanks to water on all nine holes, tight fairways, and small greens. **Par:** 35.
Open to the public. Walking permitted.

Fees:

Weekday: 18-hole: $3.50 Cart: (N/A)
9-hole: (N/A) Cart: (N/A)
Weekend: 18-hole: $3.50 Cart: (N/A)
9-hole: (N/A) Cart: (N/A)

Located off Hwy 380 South.

Starr Hollow Golf Course

(5,955 yds) 254-835-4398

Route 1
P.O. Box 176
Tolar, TX 76476
Contact: Jim Wood
Description: A lake runs along the edge of the first five holes of this lovely nine-hole private course. The ninth green is a replica of the state of Texas. Double flags and tees. **Par:** 36.
Rentals: Golf Carts

Members and guests only. Golf lessons available. Walking permitted.

Fees:

Weekday: 18-hole: $25 Cart: $18
9-hole: (N/A) Cart: $9
Weekend: 18-hole: $35 Cart: $18
9-hole: (N/A) Cart: $9

Located on Hwy 56 north of town.

Tomball Country Club

(6,201 yds) 281-351-5102

22303 Walden Way
Tomball, TX 77375
Contact: Kenny Rucker
Description: A good-looking Houston-area nine-hole private course with five water hazards, small greens protected by sand traps, and tight fairways. Pro shop. **Par:** 35.
Rentals: Golf Carts, Pull Carts, Driving Range

Members and guests only. Walking permitted.

Fees:

Weekday: 18-hole: $15 Cart: $7
9-hole: (N/A) Cart: (N/A)
Weekend: 18-hole: $25 Cart: $7
9-hole: (N/A) Cart: (N/A)

Located northwest of Houston on FM 149.

Treeline Golf Club

(5,370 yds) 281-376-1542

17505 N. Eldridge Pkwy
Tomball, TX 77375
Contact: Joe Demaret
Description: An 18-hole par-68 course that is challenging with trees. Playing the course makes you precise with your approach shots. Clubhouse and pro shop. **Par:** 68.
Rentals: Golf Carts, Pull Carts, Golf Clubs, Driving Range

Open to the public. Walking permitted. Golf lessons available.

Fees:

Weekday: 18-hole: $16 Cart: $9.50
9-hole: $9 Cart: $5
Weekend: 18-hole: $22.50 Cart: $9.50 9-hole: $11 Cart: $5

Located off Hwy 249 four miles north of Willowbrook Mall.

Trinity Plantation Country Club   (3,205 yds) 409-594-2583

Highway 19 South
Trinity, TX 75862
Contact: Michael Craig
Description: A challenging nine-hole course at 3,205 yards long. Senior and student discounts. Club repair in clubhouse, plus lockers and pro shop. **Par:** 36.
Rentals: Golf Carts, Pull Carts, Golf Clubs, Driving Range

Open to the public. Walking permitted. Golf lessons available.

Fees:

Weekday: 18-hole: $11 Cart: $7.50
9-hole: (N/A) Cart: $4
Weekend: 18-hole: $14 Cart: $7.50
9-hole: (N/A) Cart: $4

Take I-45 to Huntsville, exit 113 Hwy 19 to FM 3453.

Westwood Shores Country Club   (6,791 yds) 409-594-9172

Route 4, Box 3650
Trinity, TX 75862
Contact: Scott A. Carmody
Description: Even though this 18-hole private club is reasonably long, it is not too difficult thanks to wide fairways and good greens. There are some out-of-bounds. **Par:** 72.
Rentals: Golf Carts, Pull Carts, Golf Clubs, Driving Range

Members and guests only. Golf lessons available. Walking permitted.

Fees:

Weekday: 18-hole: $18 Cart: $18
9-hole: (N/A) Cart: $9
Weekend: 18-hole: $25 Cart: $18
9-hole: (N/A) Cart: $9

Located north of Houston off I-45 to Hwy 356.

Trophy Club Country Club

500 Trophy Club Drive
Trophy Club, TX 75262
Contact: Dion Carver
Hills Course Description: Arthur Hills designed second 18-hole layout which opened in 1996. Course places strong value on long, straight iron shots with some sand, water, and smaller trees. Good variety from Hogan course. **Par:** 72 (6,942 yards).
Hogan Course Description: The original 18-hole course is the only layout designed by Ben Hogan. A second 18-hole tract was opened in 1996, designed by architect Arthur Hills. **Par:** 72 (6,953 yards).
Rentals: Golf Carts, Driving Range
Members and guests only. Golf lessons available. Walking permitted.

Fees:

Weekday: 18-hole: $25 Cart: $15
9-hole: (N/A) Cart: (N/A)
Weekend: 18-hole: $35 Cart: $15
9-hole: (N/A) Cart: (N/A)

> Located on Hwy 114, 15 miles west of DFW Airport.

Hilltop Country Club

P.O. Box 455
Troup, TX 75789
Contact: Liz Langston
Description: It is possible to shoot a good score on this nine-hole semi-private course thanks to shorter holes. The fairways are tight but there's only one water hazard. **Par:** 35.
Rentals: Golf Carts, Pull Carts
Open to the public. Walking permitted.

Fees:

Weekday: 18-hole: $10 Cart: $15
9-hole: (N/A) Cart: $4
Weekend: 18-hole: $15 Cart: $15
9-hole: (N/A) Cart: $4

> Located northwest of town on Hwy 135.

Tule Lake Golf Course

P.O. Box 843
Tulia, TX 79088
Contact: Lou Hardy
Description: Double tees make an 18-hole round on this nine-hole semiprivate course more challenging. Lots of trees on the hilly fairways and bentgrass greens. Food. **Par:** 36.
Rentals: Golf Carts, Driving Range

Open to the public. Walking permitted.

Fees:

Weekday: 18-hole: $9 Cart: $7.50
9-hole: (N/A) Cart: $3.48
Weekend: 18-hole: $15 Cart: $7.50
9-hole: (N/A) Cart: $3.48

> Located three miles northeast of Tulia.

Bellwood Country Club   (6,863 yds) 903-597-4871

800 Bellwood Golf Road
Tyler, TX 75709
Contact: Golf Shop
Description: High scenic public East
Texas layout, wanders through trees,
water hazards, and scenic terrain.
Watch out for water on several holes
with tricky Bermuda greens. **Par:** 72.
Rentals: Golf Carts, Golf Clubs, Driving
Range
Open to the public.

Fees:

Weekday: 18-hole: $35 Cart: $10
9-hole: (N/A) Cart: (N/A)
Weekend: 18-hole: $45 Cart: $10
9-hole: (N/A) Cart: (N/A)

Take Loop 323 South to Hwy 31 West
(to Athens). Stay on Hwy 31 three
miles and take Bellwood/Bellwood
Lake exit to course on right.

Briarwood Golf Club   (6,210 yds) 903-593-7741

4511 Briarwood
Tyler, TX 75709
Contact: Justin Orbin
Description: A short 18-hole
semiprivate course with very fast greens
and tight rolling fairways lined with
trees. Only three water hazards. Food,
drinks, and pro shop. **Par:** 71.
Rentals: Golf Carts, Pull Carts, Driving
Range

Open to the public. Walking permitted.
Golf lessons available.

Fees:

Weekday: 18-hole: $19 Cart: $10
9-hole: $14.50 Cart: $5
Weekend: 18-hole: $27 Cart: $10
9-hole: $16.50 Cart: $5

Located south on Loop 323 to
Briarwood.

Cross Creek Golf Club   (6,100 yds) 903-597-4871

P.O. Box 50
Route 11
Tyler, TX 75709
Contact: Club Manager
Description: One of the oldest 18-hole
public courses in Texas. The creek
crosses six holes, and the other holes
are hilly and tight. Senior discounts.
Par: 70.
Open to the public. Walking permitted.

Fees:

Weekday: 18-hole: $8 Cart: $4 9-hole:
(N/A) Cart: $5
Weekend: 18-hole: $12 Cart: $5
9-hole: (N/A) Cart: $5

Located off Loop 323 West to Hwy 31
West.

Hollytree Country Club
(6,670 yds) 903-581-7723

6700 Hollytree Drive
Tyler, TX 75703
Contact: Chris Hudson
Description: A mid-length but tough 18-hole private club with several water hazards and big trees on dogleg corners. A very nice private clubhouse. **Par:** 72.
Rentals: Golf Carts, Golf Clubs, Driving Range

Members and guests only. Golf lessons available. Walking permitted.

Fees:

Weekday: 18-hole: $25 Cart: $11
9-hole: (N/A) Cart: $5
Weekend: 18-hole: $50 Cart: $11
9-hole: (N/A) Cart: $5

Located south of Loop 323 off Hwy 69 to Grande Road.

Willow Brook Country Club
(6,503 yds) 903-592-8229

3205 W. Erwin
Tyler, TX 75702
Contact: Jim Wise
Description: This 18-hole private course was constructed in 1924 which makes it a very traditional golf course with hills, traps, and narrow fairways. The course has been redesigned. Food and drinks. **Par:** 71.
Rentals: Golf Carts, Pull Carts, Driving Range

Members and guests only. Golf lessons available. Walking permitted.

Fees:

Weekday: 18-hole: $30 Cart: $9
9-hole: (N/A) Cart: $5
Weekend: 18-hole: $40 Cart: $9
9-hole: (N/A) Cart: $5

Located off Loop 323 on W. Erwin (Hwy 64).

Memorial Park Golf Course
(3,000 yds) 830-278-6155

329 E. Garden St.
Uvalde, TX 78801
Contact: David Bessire
Description: A traditional rural Texas nine-hole course built in 1943. No tee times required. Clubhouse has a locker room, showers, meeting rooms, and pro shop. **Par:** 35.
Rentals: Golf Carts, Pull Carts, Golf Clubs

Open to the public. Walking permitted. Golf lessons available.

Fees:

Weekday: 18-hole: $10 Cart: $15
9-hole: $8 Cart: $13.16
Weekend: 18-hole: $12 Cart: $15
9-hole: $10 Cart: $13.16

Located on Hwy 90 East across from Civic Center.

Mountain View Golf Course

(6,283 yds) 915-283-2628

Golf Course Drive
Van Horn, TX 79855
Contact: J.B. Hart
Description: Tough nine-hole course with water on seven holes and bentgrass greens. Clubhouse has snacks, food, small concession, and pro shop. **Par:** 36.
Rentals: Golf Carts, Pull Carts
Open to the public. Walking permitted.

Fees:

Weekday: 18-hole: $6 Cart: $8 9-hole: (N/A) Cart: (N/A)
Weekend: 18-hole: $8 Cart: $8 9-hole: (N/A) Cart: (N/A)

Located on Golf Course Drive I-10 exit, south one mile.

Oldham County Country Club

(6,500 yds) 806-267-2595

P.O. Box 465
Vega, TX 79092
Contact: Jim Basford
Description: A public nine-hole course that is easy to get on. No tee times required. First come/first serve. Strong Panhandle wind can make bogies easy and pars hard. **Par:** 36.
Rentals: Golf Carts, Pull Carts, Golf Clubs, Driving Range

Open to the public. Walking permitted. Golf lessons available.

Fees:

Weekday: 18-hole: $8 Cart: $8 9-hole: $6 Cart: $8
Weekend: 18-hole: $9 Cart: $8 9-hole: $6 Cart: $8

Located 5 miles south of city off Hwy 385.

Hillcrest Country Club

(6,169 yds) 940-552-5406

44 Country Club Road
Vernon, TX 76384
Contact: Jeffrey Case
Description: Water is not a major factor on this nine-hole private course. The challenge is elevated bentgrass greens protected by traps. The fairways are tight. Out-of-town golfers welcome. **Par:** 35.
Rentals: Golf Carts, Driving Range

Members and guests only. Golf lessons available. Walking permitted.

Fees:

Weekday: 18-hole: $15 Cart: $7.50 9-hole: (N/A) Cart: $6
Weekend: 18-hole: $20 Cart: $7.50 9-hole: (N/A) Cart: $6

Located off Hwy 287.

Colony Creek Country Club — (6,261 yds) 512-576-0020

301 Colony Creek Drive
Victoria, TX 77904
Contact: David Turrentine
Description: Narrow fairways and lots of water make this short 18-hole public course tougher. Also out-of-bounds, sand traps, and strong wind. Walking restricted before noon on weekends. **Par:** 71.
Rentals: Golf Carts, Driving Range

Open to the public. Walking permitted at certain times. Golf lessons available.

Fees:

Weekday: 18-hole: $30 Cart: $7
9-hole: (N/A) Cart: $3.50
Weekend: 18-hole: $35 Cart: $7
9-hole: (N/A) Cart: $3.50

Located off Hwy 59, take John Stockbauer exit to Colony Creek.

Riverside Golf Course — (27 hs) 512-573-4521

302 McCright Drive
P.O. Box 2234
Victoria, TX 77901
Contact: Steve Dermit
Description: All three nines on this 27-hole public course are narrow with lots of trees, water, and sand traps protecting large, three-putt greens. The Red and White nines are longer, but the Blue is tough. **Par:** 72.

Rentals: Golf Carts
Open to the public. Walking permitted.

Fees:

Weekday: 18-hole: $10 Cart: $6
9-hole: (N/A) Cart: $3
Weekend: 18-hole: $12 Cart: $6
9-hole: (N/A) Cart: $3

Located off Hwy 59.

Victoria Country Club — (6,870 yds) 512-575-6161

14 Spring Creek Road
Victoria, TX 77904
Contact: Alan Wooley
Description: The major factor on this 18-hole private course is very thick rough. Only eight holes have water. Another factor is large bentgrass greens. Food, drinks, and pro shop. **Par:** 72.
Rentals: Golf Carts, Golf Clubs, Driving Range

Members and guests only. Golf lessons available. Walking permitted.

Fees:

Weekday: 18-hole: $30 Cart: $9
9-hole: (N/A) Cart: (N/A)
Weekend: 18-hole: $40 Cart: $9
9-hole: (N/A) Cart: (N/A)

Located off Hwy 59.

Riverwood Golf Course

(6,771 yds) 409-768-1710

Front Street
Vidor, TX 77662
Contact: Howard Barlow
Description: One creek hits seven holes on this 18-hole public course. With a lot of trees making fairways tight and large three-putt greens, the course is tough. Snacks. **Par:** 71.
Rentals: Golf Carts, Pull Carts

Open to the public. Walking permitted.

Fees:

Weekday: 18-hole: $6.45 Cart: $15
9-hole: (N/A) Cart: $7.50
Weekend: 18-hole: $7.50 Cart: $15
9-hole: (N/A) Cart: $7.50

Located on Hwy 105 east of Beaumont.

Wildwood Golf Club

(6,696 yds) 409-834-2940

P.O. Box 903
Village Mills, TX 77663
Contact: Mike Kent
Description: This 18-hole semiprivate course has well-placed sand traps and water hazards on five holes that make the course tougher. Also, the fairways are open but wooded. Large greens. **Par:** 72.
Rentals: Golf Carts, Pull Carts, Golf Clubs, Driving Range

Open to the public. Walking permitted. Golf lessons available.

Fees:

Weekday: 18-hole: $15 Cart: $8
9-hole: (N/A) Cart: $4
Weekend: 18-hole: $20 Cart: $8
9-hole: (N/A) Cart: $4

Located off Hwy 65.

Better Golf, Inc.

(2,700 yds) 254-848-4831

Route 1
P.O. Box 715
Waco, TX 76712
Contact: Ray Lamb
Description: This is one of the best places in Central Texas to improve your game. The facility was expanded to indoor and outdoor teaching rooms. The lighted par-3 course is long with tight holes. **Par:** 27.

Open to the public. Walking permitted. Golf lessons available.

Fees:

Weekday: 18-hole: $5 Cart: (N/A)
9-hole: (N/A) Cart: $3
Weekend: 18-hole: $5 Cart: (N/A)
9-hole: (N/A) Cart: $3

Located on Hwy 6 West.

Bogey's Par 3 Golf

(2,748 yds) 254-754-4401

5500 Old Steinbeck Bend Road
Waco, TX 76708
Contact: Jesse Hancock
Description: A perfect place to improve your short game. Bogies are possible if you don't have a good short game, but after a lot of practice on all 18 holes, you will be better. New clubhouse. **Par:** 54.
Rentals: Golf Carts, Pull Carts, Golf Clubs, Driving Range

Open to the public. Walking permitted. Golf lessons available.

Fees:

Weekday: 18-hole: $6 Cart: $6 9-hole: $4 Cart: $3
Weekend: 18-hole: $7 Cart: $6 9-hole: $4 Cart: $3

Take MLK exit from northbound I-35; turn left. Course is on left past Lake Shore Drive.

Cottonwood Creek Golf Course

(7,200 yds) 254-752-2474

5200 Bagby
Waco, TX 76711
Contact: Cary Maddox
Description: This fairly new 18-hole course is one of the best in Waco. It is long with hilly fairways and greens. Six water hazards on the front nine and four on the back. Rebuilt greens. **Par:** 72.
Rentals: Golf Carts, Pull Carts, Golf Clubs, Driving Range

Open to the public. Walking permitted. Golf lessons available.

Fees:

Weekday: 18-hole: $10.83 Cart: $8 9-hole: $8.65 Cart: $5.51
Weekend: 18-hole: $14 Cart: $8 9-hole: $9 Cart: $5.51

Located west of I-35 on New Road.

Heather Run Golf & Fishing Club

(6,382 yds) 254-772-8100

1600 Western Oaks Drive
Waco, TX 76712
Contact: Jerry Swain
Description: A short, semiprivate 18-hole course with tight fairways. Newly renamed course. Clubhouse has nice facilities. **Par:** 70.
Rentals: Golf Carts, Pull Carts, Golf Clubs, Driving Range
Open to the public. Walking permitted. Golf lessons available.

Fees:

Weekday: 18-hole: $21 Cart: $10.25 9-hole: (N/A) Cart: (N/A)
Weekend: 18-hole: $26 Cart: $11.85 9-hole: (N/A) Cart: (N/A)

Located north on Hwy 6 off I-35 to Bosque Blvd. and left to Western Oaks Drive.

James Connally Golf Course   (6,975 yds) 254-799-6561

7900 Concord Road
Waco, TX 76715
Contact: Kenneth Duron
Description: Designed by Ralph
Plummer, a great Texas golf architect.
Connally is a long, good course.
Clubhouse has snack bar and pro shop.
Par: 72.
Rentals: Golf Carts, Pull Carts, Golf
Clubs, Driving Range

Open to the public. Walking permitted.
Golf lessons available.

Fees:

Weekday: 18-hole: $9.75 Cart: $10
9-hole: $5 Cart: $8.50
Weekend: 18-hole: $13 Cart: $10
9-hole: $5 Cart: $8.75

> Located two miles north of Hwy 84 on
> Aviation Parkway at old Connally Air
> Force Base near TSTI.

Lake Waco Country Club   (6,640 yds) 254-756-2161

5608 Flat Rock Road
Waco, TX 76708
Contact: Larry Salter
Description: A great private club with
challenging 18-hole course and 18-hole
par-3 course. Lake Waco is visible.
Clubhouse has restaurant, lockers, and
pro shop. **Par:** 72.
Rentals: Golf Carts, Driving Range

Members and guests only. Golf lessons
available. Walking permitted.

Fees:

Weekday: 18-hole: $22.50 Cart: $9
9-hole: (N/A) Cart: (N/A)
Weekend: 18-hole: $30 Cart: $9
9-hole: (N/A) Cart: (N/A)

> Located north of Lake Waco near the
> airport.

Ridgewood Country Club   (6,469 yds) 254-772-2050

7300 Fish Pond Road
Waco, TX 76710
Contact: Jimmy Cunningham
Description: With small bentgrass
greens, this 18-hole private course
plays tougher than its length. The
course is also hilly with sand traps.
Restaurant, bar, and pro shop. **Par:** 71.
Rentals: Golf Carts, Driving Range

Members and guests only. Golf lessons
available. Walking permitted.

Fees:

Weekday: 18-hole: $35 Cart: $10
9-hole: $17.50 Cart: $5
Weekend: 18-hole: $40 Cart: $10
9-hole: $20 Cart: $5

> Located southwest of town on Hwy 6.

Waller Country Club   (3,000 yds)   409-931-3335

15357 Penick Road
Waller, TX 77484
Contact: Barbara Beaumont
Description: With six lakes on this nine-hole semiprivate course, it is easy to lose golf balls. The fairways are mid-length with pine trees. Snack bar and pro shop. **Par:** 35.
Rentals: Golf Carts, Pull Carts, Golf Clubs, Driving Range

Open to the public. Walking permitted.

Fees:

Weekday: 18-hole: $10 Cart: $10
9-hole: (N/A) Cart: $10
Weekend: 18-hole: $15 Cart: $15
9-hole: (N/A) Cart: $15

Located northwest of Houston on Hwy 290.

Waxahachie Country Club   (3,500 yds)   972-937-3521

1920 W. 287 Business
Waxahachie, TX 75165
Contact: Chance Blythe
Description: Course runs around two lakes that can grab mis-hit golf shots. Tee shots on the par-4 14th hole can't be too long or the ball will go into the lake. **Par:** 70.
Rentals: Golf Carts, Golf Clubs, Driving Range

Members and guests only. Walking permitted.

Fees:

Weekday: 18-hole: $9.50 Cart: $7.50
9-hole: (N/A) Cart: $4
Weekend: 18-hole: $22.50 Cart: $7.50 9-hole: (N/A) Cart: $4

Located east of I-35E off exit 401B.

Canyon West Golf Club   (6,613 yds)   817-599-4653

4701 Quanah Hill Road
Weatherford, TX 76087
Contact: Charley Mack
Description: Golfer-friendly new course location that offers players of all skill levels a chance to succeed. Several elevation changes provide scenic vistas with traps and some water.

Fees:

Weekday: 18-hole: $50 Cart: included
9-hole: (N/A) Cart: (N/A)
Weekend: 18-hole: $65 Cart: included
9-hole: (N/A) Cart: (N/A)

Located off I-20 outside of Weatherford; take Exit 403 to Quanah Hill Road.

Horseshoe Bend Country Club   (5,630 yds)   817-594-6454

305 Lipton Trail
Weatherford, TX 76086-9670
Contact: Vicki Hale
Description: If a golfer is playing well on this nine-hole semiprivate course, he or she will shoot a good score because it is short with large greens and only one water hazard. Food and drink. **Par:** 36.
Rentals: Golf Carts, Golf Clubs, Driving Range

Open to the public. Walking permitted.

Fees:

Weekday: 18-hole: $10 Cart: $15
9-hole: $6 Cart: $8
Weekend: 18-hole: $14 Cart: $15
9-hole: $8 Cart: $8

Located on FM 1884.

Live Oak Country Club   (6,102 yds)   817-594-7596

1734 Bethel Road
Weatherford, TX 76086
Contact: Golf Shop
Description: Putting on the bentgrass greens on this nine-hole semiprivate course is great. The course is wide open and tight with doglegs, water, and traps. Senior discounts. **Par:** 36.
Rentals: Golf Carts, Pull Carts, Driving Range

Open to the public. Walking permitted. Golf lessons available.

Fees:

Weekday: 18-hole: $11 Cart: $7
9-hole: $7 Cart: $7
Weekend: 18-hole: $16 Cart: $7
9-hole: $11 Cart: $7

Located on Bethel Road south.

Weimar Golf Club   (6,190 yds)   409-725-8624

Route 3, P.O. Box 295
Weimar, TX 78962
Contact: Christian Milroy
Description: A very pretty nine-hole public course with lots of trees along very wide open fairways. Water only comes into play on three holes. Medium greens. Pro shop. **Par:** 36.
Rentals: Golf Carts, Pull Carts, Golf Clubs

Open to the public. Walking permitted.

Fees:

Weekday: 18-hole: $7.54 Cart: $12
9-hole: (N/A) Cart: $6
Weekend: 18-hole: $12 Cart: $12
9-hole: (N/A) Cart: $6

Located ½ mile east of town on Hwy 90.

Wellington Country Club   (3,435 yds) 806-447-5050

P.O. Box 904
Wellington, TX 79095
Contact: Golf Shop
Description: A simple nine-hole public course that has no sand traps and just a little bit of water. Drinks available from pro shop. **Par:** 36.
Rentals: Golf Carts
Open to the public. Walking permitted.

Fees:

Weekday: 18-hole: $8 Cart: $7.50
9-hole: (N/A) Cart: $4
Weekend: 18-hole: $12 Cart: $7.50
9-hole: (N/A) Cart: $4

Located two miles northeast of Wellington.

Tierra Santa Golf Club   (7,100 yds) 800-838-5769

1901 Club De Amistad
Weslaco, TX 78596
Contact: J.P. Van Tilburg
Description: First upscale daily-fee golf course to come to Rio Grande Valley. Course features water, palm trees, sand, and highly scenic views. Head pro Carl Baker is former South Texas PGA president. **Par:** 72.
Rentals: Golf Carts, Pull Carts, Golf Clubs, Driving Range

Open to the public. Walking permitted. Golf lessons available.

Fees:

Weekday: 18-hole: $20 Cart: $9.50
9-hole: (N/A) Cart: (N/A)
Weekend: 18-hole: $23 Cart: $9.50
9-hole: (N/A) Cart: (N/A)

Take FM 1015 two miles south of Business 83 in Weslaco.

Village Executive Golf Course   (1,563 yds) 956-968-6516

P.O. Box 1309
Weslaco, TX 78570
Contact: Ray McGregor
Description: Playing this nine-hole executive course can result in good scores. A lake is in the middle of the course but easy to avoid. Not many trees and no traps. **Par:** 31.
Rentals: Golf Clubs, Driving Range
Open to the public. Walking permitted.

Fees:

Weekday: 18-hole: $7 Cart: (N/A)
9-hole: $5 Cart: (N/A)
Weekend: 18-hole: $7.50 Cart: (N/A)
9-hole: $5 Cart: (N/A)

Located on FM 1015 south of Business 83.

Columbia Lakes Resort & Conference (6,697 yds) 409-345-5455

188 Freeman Blvd.
West Columbia, TX 77486
Contact: Gene Amman
Description: Redesigned by Tom Fazio, the course is a smart layout. Club has a resort where guests can play. Great Southeast Texas setting with great practice facilities. **Par:** 72.
Rentals: Golf Carts, Pull Carts, Golf Clubs, Driving Range

Members and guests only. Golf lessons available. Walking permitted.

Fees:

Weekday: 18-hole: $60 Cart: (N/A)
9-hole: (N/A) Cart: (N/A)
Weekend: 18-hole: $75 Cart: (N/A)
9-hole: (N/A) Cart: (N/A)

Located southwest of Houston; take Hwy 288 to Hwy 35 and go west.

Wharton Country Club   (5,963 yds) 409-532-5940

1149 Country Club Drive
Wharton, TX 77488
Contact: John Reyna
Description: This short and hilly nine-hole private course has narrow fairways. The creek is only wet after strong rains. Great Southeast Texas setting with great practice facilities. Food, drinks, and pro shop. **Par:** 35.
Rentals: Golf Carts, Golf Clubs

Members and guests only. Mandatory carts.

Fees:

Weekday: 18-hole: $12 Cart: $18
9-hole: (N/A) Cart: (N/A)
Weekend: 18-hole: $15 Cart: $18
9-hole: (N/A) Cart: (N/A)

Located on Hwy 59 off Old Lane City Road.

Lake Whitney Golf Club   (6,697 yds) 254-694-2313

Route 1, Box 2075
Whitney, TX 76692
Contact: David Ohrn
Description: Not a real long 18-hole public course, but the course will play a bit longer because of rolling hills. The greens are difficult to hit because they are elevated. **Par:** 70.
Rentals: Golf Carts, Pull Carts, Golf Clubs, Driving Range

Open to the public. Walking permitted. Golf lessons available.

Fees:

Weekday: 18-hole: $8.50 Cart: $8
9-hole: (N/A) Cart: $4
Weekend: 18-hole: $9 Cart: $8 9-hole: (N/A) Cart: $4

Located off FM 993, three miles north.

White Bluff on Lake Whitney   (36 hs) 254-694-3656

No. 4 White Bluff Road
Whitney, TX 76692
Contact: Brad Wells
Description: This 36-hole semiprivate
resort course added a new 18 holes in
1995 to let others in. Condos are for
rent. Challenging course is wide open
with bentgrass greens and
out-of-bounds. **Par:** 72 (6,866 yards).
Rentals: Golf Carts, Golf Clubs, Driving
Range

Open to the public. Walking permitted.
Golf lessons available.

Fees:

Weekday: 18-hole: $34 Cart: (N/A)
9-hole: (N/A) Cart: (N/A)
Weekend: 18-hole: $49 Cart: (N/A)
9-hole: (N/A) Cart: (N/A)

Located on FM 933 North.

LaVista Golf & Country Club   (6,163 yds) 940-855-0771

2000 Northeast Loop 11
Wichita Falls, TX 76305
Contact: Kip Cotton
Description: This 18-hole public
course is rather simple with only three
water hazards, wide fairways, and sand
traps. Small bentgrass greens are tough
to hit. Snacks and pro shop. **Par:** 72.
Rentals: Golf Carts, Pull Carts, Golf
Clubs, Driving Range

Open to the public. Walking permitted.
Golf lessons available.

Fees:

Weekday: 18-hole: $8.50 Cart: $8.50
9-hole: (N/A) Cart: $4.50
Weekend: 18-hole: $10.50 Cart:
$8.50 9-hole: (N/A) Cart: $4.50

Located off Hwy 287 to Northeast Loop
11.

Weeks Park Municipal Golf Course (6,470 yds) 940-767-6107

4400 Lake Park Drive
Wichita Falls, TX 76302
Contact: Dick Weston
Description: This short 18-hole public
course can set up good scores. There is
water on eight holes, only one sand
trap, and few trees, so there is not a lot
of trouble. **Par:** 72.
Rentals: Golf Carts, Pull Carts, Golf
Clubs

Open to the public. Walking permitted.
Golf lessons available.

Fees:

Weekday: 18-hole: $10 Cart: $8.50
9-hole: (N/A) Cart: $4.29
Weekend: 18-hole: $12.50 Cart:
$8.50 9-hole: (N/A) Cart: $4.29

Located off Business 281 to Jacksboro.

Wichita Falls Country Club
(6,700 yds) 940-767-1486

1701 Hamilton Blvd.
Wichita Falls, TX 76308
Contact: Bruce Cotton
Description: The course was recently remodeled with two more lakes from eight acres recently purchased. It is tight with lots of water. Very nice clubhouse. **Par:** 72.
Rentals: Golf Carts, Pull Carts, Golf Clubs, Driving Range

Members and guests only. Golf lessons available. Walking permitted.

Fees:

Weekday: 18-hole: $40 Cart: $10
9-hole: (N/A) Cart: $4.50
Weekend: 18-hole: $60 Cart: $10
9-hole: (N/A) Cart: $4.50

Located south of town on Midwestern Parkway.

Texas National Country Club
(6,700 yds) 409-856-4233

P.O. Box 585
Willis, TX 77378
Contact: Greg Harvell
Description: The birthplace of the Texas Golf Hall of Fame, now at The Woodlands. This 18-hole course is neat with narrow fairways, a creek running through the course, and sand traps. **Par:** 72.
Rentals: Golf Carts, Golf Clubs, Driving Range

Open to the public. Walking permitted. Golf lessons available.

Fees:

Weekday: 18-hole: $16 Cart: $20
9-hole: (N/A) Cart: $4.50
Weekend: 18-hole: $21 Cart: $20
9-hole: (N/A) Cart: $4.50

Located off I-45 north of Houston; exit east on FM 2432.

Squaw Creek Golf Course
(6,749 yds) 940-441-8185

1605 Ranch House Road
Willow Park, TX 76086
Contact: Lynn Vaughn
Description: A semiprivate long 18-hole course with lots of hills and 12 holes on the creek. Clubhouse has grill and pro shop with some lockers. **Par:** 71.
Rentals: Golf Carts, Pull Carts, Golf Clubs, Driving Range

Open to the public. Walking permitted. Golf lessons available.

Fees:

Weekday: 18-hole: $21 Cart: $8
9-hole: (N/A) Cart: $4
Weekend: 18-hole: $26 Cart: $8
9-hole: (N/A) Cart: $4

Located west of Fort Worth off I-20 West exit 418.

Woodcreek Resort Golf Course   (6,470 yds) 512-847-9700

1 Woodcreek Drive
Wimberley, TX 78676
Contact: Michael Bertagna
Description: A nice 18-hole semiprivate course with narrow, rolling fairways, out-of-bounds, and water hazards that create layup holes. Small greens. Lodge and condos for vacation rent. **Par:** 72.
Rentals: Golf Carts, Pull Carts, Golf Clubs
Open to the public. Walking permitted. Golf lessons available.

Fees:

Weekday: 18-hole: $20 Cart: $10
9-hole: $12 Cart: $6
Weekend: 18-hole: $24 Cart: $10
9-hole: $14 Cart: $6

Located approximately 18 miles northwest of San Marcos on Ranch Road 12.

Winters Country Club   (2,698 yds) 915-754-4679

Route 3, Box 14
Winters, TX 79567
Contact: Rich King
Description: Looking at the scorecard on this nine-hole semiprivate course will make golfers think it's easy. However, five holes are on top of a hill and four holes are in the valley. **Par:** 34.
Rentals: Golf Carts

Open to the public. Walking permitted.

Fees:

Weekday: 18-hole: $7 Cart: $14
9-hole: (N/A) Cart: $7
Weekend: 18-hole: $10 Cart: $14
9-hole: (N/A) Cart: $7

Located on Ballenger Hwy in Winters.

Webb Hill Country Club   (6,749 yds) 903-496-2221

Route 1
P.O. Box 190 A
Wolfe City, TX 75496
Contact: Charles Ranly
Description: Golfers playing this 18-hole private course face a whole lot of blind shots over hills. Out-of-town golfers welcome to deal with large greens and water hazards. Food and drinks. **Par:** 72.

Rentals: Golf Carts, Driving Range
Members and guests only. Golf lessons available. Walking permitted.

Fees:

Weekday: 18-hole: $17 Cart: $10
9-hole: (N/A) Cart: $4.25
Weekend: 18-hole: $37 Cart: $10
9-hole: (N/A) Cart: $4.25

Located off Hwy 34, south of town.

Dogwood Hills Country Club   (3,600 yds) 409-283-8725

150 Highway 190 West
Woodville, TX 75979
Contact: Dave Youngblood
Description: A nice nine-hole rural
Texas public course that has hilly and
tight fairways, small greens, sand traps,
and water on two holes. Snack bar and
pro shop. **Par:** 36.
Rentals: Golf Carts, Pull Carts, Golf
Clubs

Open to the public. Walking permitted.

Fees:

Weekday: 18-hole: $7.50 Cart: $8
9-hole: (N/A) Cart: $4
Weekend: 18-hole: $12 Cart: $8
9-hole: (N/A) Cart: $4

Located three miles west of town on
Hwy 190.

Woodbridge Golf Club   (7,000 yds) 972-429-5100

7400 Country Club Drive
Wylie, TX 75098
Contact: TBD
Description: Great new North Texas
addition scheduled to be future home of
the Northern Texas PGA when it opens
in August 1999. Texas architect Lee
Singletary designed a very challenging
course out of this heavily wooded tract
of land. There is a natural creek which
runs through the property along with
several man-made lakes. Rolling terrain
with several mounds. **Par:** 72.

Fees:

Weekday: 18-hole: $40 Cart: included
9-hole: (N/A) Cart: (N/A)
Weekend: 18-hole: $60 Cart: included
9-hole: (N/A) Cart: (N/A)

From Dallas, go north on U.S. Hwy 75
to U.S. 190 (George Bush Tollway),
east on U.S. 190 to Hwy 78, north on
Hwy 78, four miles on the right.

McAlister's Two-Hole Ranch & C.C.   (3,201 yds) 903-383-7707

Route 1 Box 228
Yantis, TX 79272
Contact: Mike McAlister
Description: The most unique golf
course in the region. Mike McAlister
owned a ranch south of Sulphur Springs
and personally built a nine-hole par-36
course playing on only two greens.
Invited golfers play free. **Par:** 36.
Rentals: Golf Carts

Members and guests only. Mandatory
carts.

Fees:

Weekday: 18-hole: (N/A) Cart: (N/A)
9-hole: (N/A) Cart: (N/A)
Weekend: 18-hole: (N/A) Cart: (N/A)
9-hole: (N/A) Cart: (N/A)

Located in Hopkins County south of
Sulphur Springs.

Yoakum Municipal Golf Course   (5,920 yds) 512-293-5682

703 Southwell
Yoakum, TX 77995
Contact: Tom Chilek
Description: Nine-hole public course
that's a favorite hangout for local
golfers. Clubhouse has a meeting room,
pro shop, and tennis courts. **Par:** 36.
Rentals: Golf Carts, Pull Carts, Golf
Clubs

Open to the public. Walking permitted.
Golf lessons available.

Fees:

Weekday: 18-hole: $5.50 Cart: $13
9-hole: (N/A) Cart: $7
Weekend: 18-hole: $7.25 Cart: $13
9-hole: (N/A) Cart: $7

Located 30 miles south of I-10 off Hwy
77A, just outside of Victoria.

Yorktown Country Club   (6,300 yds) 512-564-9191

Country Club Road
Yorktown, TX 78164
Contact: Warner Borth
Description: Out-of-town golfers are
welcome at this nine-hole private
course. A creek runs through the
course. The fairways are tight with
trees, no traps, and out-of-bounds.
Par: 35.
Rentals: Golf Carts

Members and guests only. Walking
permitted.

Fees:

Weekday: 18-hole: $7.50 Cart: $5.50
9-hole: (N/A) Cart: $2.75
Weekend: 18-hole: $7.50 Cart: $5.50
9-hole: (N/A) Cart: $2.75

Located on Hwy 72 southwest of Cuero.

Los Ebanos Golf Course   (3,607 yds) 956-765-8336

710 Lincoln St.
Zapata, TX 78076
Contact: Raul Vasquez
Description: A reasonably short
nine-hole public course that has flat and
hilly fairways, double tees, only two
water hazards, no traps, and small
greens. Food. **Par:** 35.
Rentals: Golf Carts, Pull Carts
Open to the public. Walking permitted.

Fees:

Weekday: 18-hole: $9 Cart: $8 9-hole:
$5 Cart: $4
Weekend: 18-hole: $9 Cart: $8 9-hole:
$5 Cart: $4

Located two blocks west of the
courthouse on Lincoln.

Scholarship Opportunities

The schools listed below offer either partial or full golf scholarships in the state of Texas. Call the individual school if interested in additional information. If you would like information on college golf scholarships in other areas, contact the National Golf Foundation in Jupiter, Florida.

Four-Year Schools

Abilene Christian University, Abilene, TX

Baylor University, Waco, TX

East Texas State University, Commerce, TX

Houston Baptist University, Houston, TX

Incarnate Word College, San Antonio, TX

Lamar University-Beaumont, Beaumont, TX

Prairie View A&M University, Prairie View, TX

Rice University, Houston, TX

St. Edwards University, Austin, TX

St. Mary's University of San Antonio, San Antonio, TX

Sam Houston State University, Huntsville, TX

Southern Methodist University, Dallas, TX

Southwest Texas State University, San Marcos, TX

Stephen F. Austin State University, Nacogdoches, TX

Texas A&M University, College Station, TX

Texas Christian University, Fort Worth, TX

Texas Lutheran College, Seguin, TX

Texas Southern University, Houston, TX

Texas Tech University, Lubbock, TX

Texas Wesleyan University, Fort Worth, TX

University of Texas Pan-Am, Edinburg, TX

University of Texas at San Antonio, San Antonio, TX

University of Texas at Austin, Austin, TX

University of Texas at Arlington, Arlington, TX

University of Houston, Houston, TX

University of Mary Hardin-Baylor, Belton, TX

University of North Texas, Denton, TX

University of Texas at El Paso, El Paso, TX

Two-Year Schools

Alvin Community College, Alvin, TX

Lon Morris College, Jacksonville, TX

Midland College, Midland, TX

Navarro College, Corsicana, TX

Odessa College, Odessa, TX

Paris Junior College, Paris, TX

San Jacinto College/North Campus, Houston, TX

Temple Junior College, Temple, TX

Western Texas College, Snyder, TX

Index